God's Elect and the Great Tribulation:
An Interpretation of
Matthew 24:1–31 and Daniel 9

God's Elect and the Great Tribulation

An Interpretation of Matthew 24:1–31 and Daniel 9

Charles Cooper

Strong Tower Publishing
Bellefonte, PA

Strong Tower Publishing

P. O. Box 973

Milesburg, PA 16853

www.strongtowerpublishing.com

ISBN-10: 0970433042

ISBN-13: 978-0-9704330-4-6

Library of Congress Control Number: 2008920036

Cover design by Beth Thomas

Table of Contents

Chart Index

Acknowledgements

Jesus warns His followers to count the cost before undertaking any significant task, lest one begins but is not able to finish resulting in shame and humiliation. To write this book was a significant task requiring the help of a number of individuals. My wife and daughter sacrificed time and attention for me to study and write; Sola Scriptura supported me financially; Robert and Serena Myers, Jon Schoenfield, Jim Root, Carnell Burlock, H. L. Nigro, and Dean Tisch either edited, gave constructive comments, encouraged, and/or helped me work out a particularly problematic text at one time or another; and Beth Thomas provided the artwork for the cover. All of these individuals were significant in the production of this book. I am thankful! It is our hope that God will honor it with favor.

Preface

Robert D. Van Kampen is one of my heroes. For those who knew him, he was a man of great strength, conviction, passion, and drive. In just over sixty years, he accomplished more than most people dare to dream, let alone accomplish. Yet, in the end, it was none of these things that won my admiration.

Bob is a hero to me because he challenged one of my core convictions and forced me to change. This is a feat that only two others have accomplished in my life so far. As a graduate of Dallas Theological Seminary and a teacher at Moody Bible Institute, I had a box within which were positions that could not change and still leave me in good favor with either of them. One such position, in their view, was the timing of the rapture—pretribulational.

In the typical style of "Perry Mason," "Murder, She Wrote," "Colombo," and "Matlock," Bob found one little clue—a clue that didn't fit. For everyone else, that clue seemed insignificant, but to the clever-minded investigator, it was the foundation for unrest. For Van Kampen, it was the cosmic darkening of the sun, moon, and stars that immediately precedes the coming of Jesus Christ. By lining up all of the prophetic events yet to occur (either before or after this sign, as the scriptures dictate), Van Kampen founded a position on the timing of the Lord's return to remove God's elect to heaven, now labeled *prewrath*.

In light of this sign, the clue that now demanded my reevaluation of the whole pretrib system was the suddenly clear and unambiguous fact that the pretrib system had an irreconcilable contradiction at its core. Built on the false premise that God does not and will not prophetically deal with either ethnic Israel or the church outside of each's respective dispensation, the pretrib system rejects any applicability for the church in Matthew 24:1–31. In the pretrib system, the fulfillment of Matthew 24:1–31 requires the resumption of the Jewish dispensation, which God halted by inserting the dispensation of the Gentiles (the church age). Thus, according to the traditional pretrib position, God cannot and will not resume any work with national ethnic Israel until He finishes His special work among the Gentiles.

One day, while working through Acts 2:17–21, it dawned on me that Peter used a Jewish prophetic text to explain the beginning of God's special work among the Gentiles. More significantly, the passage indicates that the ministry of the Holy Spirit (Acts 2:17–21) occurs *during* "the last days." Hebrews 1:1–2 also places the ministry of Jesus Christ during this same period. Thus, the period from the beginning of the Lord's ministry until He finishes taking for Himself a people from among the Gentiles (Acts 15:13), the Bible calls "the last days." In light of this fact, it is reasonable to conclude that the ministry of Jesus and the ministry of the Holy Spirit occur during the same period. Equally, I was quickly led to see that the prophecy of the destruction of Jerusalem, which found fulfillment in A.D. 70 during the church's dispensation, was prophesied by the Lord Jesus thirty-plus years earlier *during the Jewish dispensation*. These two contradictions made the pretrib position untenable for me.

These insights caused me to throw out all that I had learned about Matthew 24 and Daniel 9. This book is some of the fruit of my reeducation over the past fifteen years. In the following pages, I will not only help you better appreciate the meaning of Matthew 24:1–31 and Daniel 9, but I will demonstrate the incontrovertible fact that Matthew 24:1–31 applies to the church.

Introduction

Some years ago, the author had one of those unforgettable evenings that often serves as an illustration for a sermon or a speech. After accepting an invitation to attend a home Bible study, he found himself sitting in a circle with about thirty other people. The leader of the Bible study, seated to his left, began. He indicated the passage of scripture for consideration. He read it. He then instructed the group to begin to his left, and each person, moving clockwise, was to answer it: "What does this passage mean to me?" As a teacher of hermeneutics at a leading Bible college at the time, the author immediately knew he was in for a treat.

With paper and pen, he listened closely to each person as they attempted to answer the question. Sure enough, it was not long before one gave an interpretation of the passage that ran completely counter to that given by another four seats earlier. To the author's amazement, no one caught it. About an hour or so later, it was the author's turn. By the time the question was put to him, he had recorded at least seven different "meanings" of the text. Only on two occasions did people notice a contradiction between two or more answers.

From the perspective of one who has spent years studying and teaching hermeneutics, the problem arose because the original question itself was problematic—the leader had confused interpretation with application. Before attempting to explain the basic meaning of any text, one needs to first gain an appropriate interpretation of a passage. A passage may have multiple applications, but it can have only one meaning. This is true even for prophetic passages, which may establish a pattern that may occur more than once. As well, the meaning of a passage may involve several aspects or pieces that may, in turn, involve total or partial fulfillments. Yet, fundamentally, a passage still has but one meaning. At the beginning, the leader should have explained the basic meaning of the passage and then given each person the opportunity to explain how the passage might apply to him or herself.

Many commentaries written about Matthew 24:1–31 appear to make the same error. They confuse interpretation with application. Only after identifying the best possible understanding of what the text means should we attempt to explain how that meaning applies to the church or believers in general.

In 1989, David L. Turner wrote an article in which he surveyed the possible ways evangelicals interpret Matthew 24:1–31. He wrote,

> Evangelical studies of Matthew 24 tend to emphasize either the A.D. 70 destruction of Jerusalem (preterist view), the eschatological return of Christ (futurist view), or some combination of the two (preterist-futurist views).[i]

According to Turner, there are four basic views that capture most modern evangelicals on this passage. The first group, which Turner labels as futurist, "stresses the age-ending return of Christ and finds little if anything in these verses which addresses the destruction of Jerusalem in A.D. 70 or the current age."[ii] A great majority of futurists argue that Matthew 24:1–31 applies to Jewish believers immediately before the return of Christ. Most see no part of the bride of Christ involved in these events. A second view, the preterist view (which is completely opposite the first) locates the whole of Matthew 24:1–31 in the destruction of Jerusalem in A.D. 70. This position sees much of the description given in this passage as highly symbolical, thus not necessarily requiring a literal fulfillment. Turner classifies the two other views as "mediating positions between the first two."[iii]

Turner, himself, takes the position that Matthew 24:1–31 is best explained by taking "the traditional preterist-futurist view."[iv] Turner's interpretation of Matthew 24:1–31 is that

> [Matthew] 24:4–14 describes the course of the present age, during which "enduring to the end" and "preaching the gospel of the kingdom" are the Church's duties. In 24:15–28 the "Abomination of Desolation" is understood to refer both to the A.D. 70 destruction of Jerusalem and to the ultimate abomination against God's people committed by the eschatological antichrist. Christ's return to earth is described in 24:29–31. Finally, 24:32–41 underlines the certainty of the prophecy's fulfillment with the assertion that Jesus' contemporaries will not die before they see his prophecy fulfilled.[v]

With the exception of the futurist view, all views listed by Turner demand that Matthew 24:1–31 deal in one way or another with the destruction of Jerusalem in A.D. 70.

It is our conviction that both preterists of various shades and futurists such as pretribulationists have missed the significance of Matthew 24:1–31. Most dispensational futurist and covenantal preterists attempt application before proper interpretation. At a very basic level, the gospel of Matthew is a set of short stories that biographically tell of Jesus and what He did during His ministry on earth. On a higher level, we have Matthew's arrangement of the material to argue to a certain conclusion that is important to him about the kingship of Jesus. A final level concerns the Holy Spirit's design of the material to teach us a deeper significance concerning how God is Immanuel (God with us).

Most scholars recognize that the gospel of Matthew consists of five books, with a final section devoted to the Passion of Christ. Each book consists of a narrative section followed by a discourse section. Scholars are not in agreement concerning the significance of Matthew's unique structure.[vi] Perhaps it was an easy way for Matthew to arrange the material for his audience to read and remember. Regardless, it is immediately obvious at a higher level that Matthew intends for his readers to conclude by reading his book that Jesus is a true Davidite and that, as such, He can and does fulfill all the promises God gave concerning Abraham and David. Jesus is that long awaited King who fulfills all of God's promises to Israel.

At the third or highest level, the Holy Spirit designs Matthew's material to convey the extraordinary measures God undertook to accomplish His eternal plan to come to be among us as one of us—Immanuel. The route that God took is beyond human comprehension. For Jesus to be among us as one of us, He had to have a miraculous conception and birth and a life marked by suffering, rejection, death, resurrection, waiting, and eventual exaltation to reign upon the earth. It is important for any interpreter to keep these issues clear when offering insights into Matthew's text.

It is our belief that many commentators do not understand Matthew's use of the eschatological or the Olivet Discourse. The Lord's primary purpose for giving the discourse to Peter, James, John, and Andrew is not necessarily the same purpose employed by Matthew. In fact, Matthew uses the Olivet Discourse to answer an entirely different question from His disciples than the one the Lord originally answered. This matter we shall deal with in detail later.

Chapter One
A Preliminary Caution

Once we settle the matter of interpretation, another equally important issue arises—application. Many believers have been taught that Matthew 24:1–31 does not apply to the church, primarily because it deals with the great tribulation, which many futurists teach to be the wrath of God. This conclusion also has, for a support, the idea that Daniel's Seventieth Week is a return to the Jewish dispensation, which according to some Bible teachers requires God to remove the church before He resumes His work with Israel.

We believe that insisting on a sharp distinction between God's work in Israel and His work in the church is a false presupposition that directly contradicts scripture. Most dispensational futurists see this distinction as necessary to prevent the replacement of Israel with the church, which characterizes the understanding of most reformed theologians. However, while the intent of the futurists is correct, their argument is built on silence. One futurist scholar who wrote widely on the return of Christ argued,

> The tribulation is said to deal with the Jewish people primarily, to be an unprecedented time of trouble, and to be followed by their deliverance from their enemies, the Gentiles.[vii]

This writer based his conclusion on the absence of a direct statement of applicability to the church as being evidence of no applicability. This, taken with the fact that passages like Daniel 9:24 specifically speak of Daniel's final week as achieving Jewish outcomes, forms the basis of this claim.

However, such reasoning is faulty. Since neither the term "church" nor the entity it represents occurs in the Old Testament, are we to conclude that no passages in the Old Testament apply to the church? The answer is a resounding *no!* Determining applicability of certain passages in the Old Testament requires extra care, especially if one is going to base a theological system on it. To deny Old Testament applicability on the basis of the absence of a direct statement of applicability is easily shown to be in error.

If we follow the suggested method of Old Testament interpretation stated above, no one would apply Joel 2:28–32 to the church as the text stands:

> After all of this I will pour out my Spirit on all kinds of people. Your sons and daughters will prophesy. Your elderly will have revelatory dreams; your young men will see prophetic visions. Even on male and female servants I will pour out my Spirit in those days. I will produce portents both in the sky and on the earth—blood, fire, and columns of smoke. The sunlight will be turned to darkness and the moon to the color of blood, before the day of the LORD comes—that great and terrible day! It will so happen that everyone who calls on the name of the LORD will be delivered. For on Mount Zion and in Jerusalem there will be those who survive, just as the LORD

has promised; the remnant will be those whom the LORD will call. (Joel 2:28–32)[1]

However, Peter applied the passage directly to the church. In fact, it provided the basis for the beginning of God's special work among Gentiles "to take from among them a people for his name sake" (Acts 15:14). Upon the ascension of Jesus, the faithful followers of Christ were to witness and make disciples of all nations. This mission was to be inaugurated by the reception of the Holy Spirit. Ten days after Jesus' ascension, the Holy Spirit came in fulfillment of God's promise. Peter explains this on the basis of Joel 2:28–32. The specific formula used in Acts 2:16 suggests a literal fulfillment.[viii] It is not "like," "similar," or "typical," but rather, what Joel actually promised. Joel 2:28–32 is specifically quoted as the biblical explanation for the manifestation of the Holy Spirit in Jerusalem on the day of Pentecost.[ix] With the outpouring of the Spirit, we learn what happened to the Jewish remnant of righteousness. They became the Lord's Spirit-empowered witnesses to the world.

Peter's quotation of Joel 2:28–32 evidences several changes from its Old Testament counterpart, however. The most important change concerns the added phrase "in the last days." The original phrase "after all of this" is very broad and offers no clue as to when, from Joel's perspective, the event would occur. However, with the alternate phrase "in the last days," the timing becomes clear. The outpouring of the Holy Spirit occurs during the period called "the last days," the period preceding the day of the Lord.[x] "The gift of the Spirit is thus a token that the last days foretold by the prophets have arrived."[xi]

---

[1] Unless otherwise noted, all biblical quotations are taken from the New English Translation (NET) Bible, which is found at: http://www.bible.org/netbible.

Unlike the situation in previous generations, both male and female, young and old, slave and free, will reveal God's will. Secondly, heavenly wonders and earthly signs will mark the beginning of the eschatological day of the Lord (2:19–20). Thirdly, salvation is available to anyone requesting it (2:21). The book of Acts does contain prophecies, visions, and miraculous signs.[xii] However, there are no cosmic disturbances on a magnitude prophesied by Joel. Therefore, we understand the Pentecost experience to be a beginning of the fulfillment of Joel 2:28–32, but not the total fulfillment.[xiii] This confirms that a process of fulfillment has begun. The process began with the outpouring of the Spirit and will end with the day of the Lord. The time period between these two events is called "the last days," the church age, or the "dispensation of mystery."

Peter's use of Joel 2:28–32 ought to be enough to silence those who want to speak of limitations on the ability of the Old Testament to speak directly to events in the church age. Only God can limit Old Testament application to the New Testament age. This is one of a number of passages that prove this point. Lacking any explicit basis for application to the church age, we should grant Matthew 24 this same license. However, as we shall see, Matthew 24 has an explicit basis for application to the church.

A second false assumption that causes some to reject the applicability of Matthew 24 to the church is the appeal to a separation between God's work in the church age and God's work in the Jewish age. Some are quick to point out that Matthew 24 deals with Jewish-age issues related specifically to Israel, while the rapture is a church-age event. The fundamental notion is that God does not mix dispensations. While some hold this view, the significance of the Lord's prophetic announcement of the destruction of Jerusalem in Matthew 24 seems to escape their notice. This announcement was certainly given in the age of the Jews.

However, its fulfillment occurred during the church age. As for those who argue that God cannot and will not work with the Jews during the church age, and that He likewise will not work with the church in the Jewish age, Matthew 24:1–2 and its A.D. 70 fulfillment should silence them.

Another line of reasoning concerning Matthew 24's applicability has to do with ignorance on the part of the disciples. The following comments reflect this typical conclusion:

> To the pretribulationist it is obvious that the rapture is not in view in this passage. Up to this point the disciples had had no instruction on this subject.... Their questions indicated that they were first of all concerned about the destruction of Jerusalem which Christ had predicted in Matthew 24:2.... What they were talking about was Christ's coming to establish His kingdom and the end of the age preceding it, during which, from their viewpoint, they could still be living. Accordingly the nature of the question is such that the church is not in view, nor is the rapture introduced. In a word, the disciples wanted to know the signs leading up to the establishment of the millennial kingdom. [xiv]

Concerning this man's notion that the ignorance of the apostles determined how Christ would answer their questions, we strongly disagree. Even a casual reading of the New Testament will show that the apostles knew little of God's purposes until they were revealed by Christ and the Holy Spirit. Even on matters they most certainly should have understood, they were often ill-informed or did not understand the full intent of God regarding the matter. Their questions and the Lord's answers involve difficult issues to understand, but approaching the text without certain presuppositions will yield a better interpretation.

The writer quoted above was obviously biased at this point. His presuppositions made him unable to see clearly regarding Matthew 24. While it is certainly possible that the disciples were limited in their understanding as they asked questions, Jesus had no such constraint on His answers. The disciples did not understand that the coming of the kingdom would consist of two advents, with a significant gap between them. Only as the Lord revealed these details would they have a clue. A careful reading of the Gospels reveals limited knowledge on every single aspect of God's future plans. Yet, the Lord taught them, even when they were totally off base.

The idea that the disciples were ignorant of a planned evacuation of the saints to heaven simply does not square with John 14:1–3. Jesus delivered the Olivet Discourse on a Tuesday, and the words of John 14 He spoke on a Thursday night.[xv] Two days separated these events. What is of great interest to us is the fact that, to our knowledge, the disciples did not ask Him for clarification, although they certainly had other questions (see John 14:5, 8, 22; 16:17). We realize that this is an argument from silence; however, to say that the disciples did not know about a future evacuation is also an argument from silence.

Thus, we see a direct application of Matthew 24 to the church on the basis of three supporting facts: the use of the term "elect" in Matthew 24; Matthew's reformulation of the second question at Matthew 24:3; and the teaching of the church fathers regarding direct applicability. These three topics follow in the next three chapters.

The remainder of this book will build upon this foundation and attempt to accomplish the following: (1) to support the prewrath position in its conclusion that insisting on a sharp distinction between God's work in Israel and His work in the church is a false presupposition that directly contradicts scripture; (2) to support the prewrath position in its conclusion that Matthew 24:1–31 does apply to the church, the bride of Christ; (3) to set forth a clear biblical exposition of Matthew 24:1–31 and (4) to correct the false and misleading conclusions about both the timing and fulfillment of Daniel 9:24–27.

Chapter Two

The Elect: God's Children Throughout the Ages

The decision on the part of some to disavow the applicability of Matthew 24:1–31 is regrettable. In so doing, some believers have failed to appreciate the intent of Matthew recorded in the Olivet Discourse. The question of applicability is important. To support our claim, we must look closely at the details of this great work. A biblical support for the applicability of Matthew 24 to the church concerns the Lord's reference to "the elect" in Matthew 24:21–22. The Lord states,

> "For then there will be great suffering unlike anything that has happened from the beginning of the world until now, or ever will happen. And if those days had not been cut short, no one would be saved. But for the sake of the elect those days will be cut short. Then if anyone says to you, 'Look, here is the Christ!' or 'There he is!' do not believe him. For false messiahs and false prophets will appear and perform great signs and wonders to deceive, if possible, even the elect."

Who are the "elect" of Matthew 24?[xvi]

The English term "elect" translates the Greek *eklektos*. *Eklektos* belongs to a group of words in Greek that has the basic sense "to pick or choose," with the emphasis of *eklektos* being "that which has been chosen."[xvii] Of the twenty-two occurrences of *eklektos* in the Greek New Testament, the English Standard Version translates fourteen as "elect."[xviii] "Elect" derives from the Latin word *electus*. Its usage in the New Testament reflects the Latin Vulgate's influence on our English Bible versions.[xix]

The Bible describes three groups that can rightly be designated "elect" or "chosen": (1) the Messianic line, (2) national Israel, and (3) the saints. The "Messianic line" refers to Jews and Gentiles who ensured that Jesus would be born of man. "National Israel" refers exclusively to Jews who are of the physical seed of Abraham, Isaac, and Jacob. By the designation "saints," the Bible typically refers to both Jews and Gentiles who are the exclusive spiritual seed of Abraham.

God's Elect Throughout the Ages

Messianic Line (Physical Seed)
Chosen to Sire a Son

The gospel of Matthew begins with a genealogical defense that proves Jesus was a Davidite by adoption. As such, He was (and is) able to sit on the throne of David. This is the accomplishment of God's promise to David and Abraham. The gospel of Luke genealogically demonstrates that Jesus is *the* Adamic son.[xx] As such, He must fulfill God's promise to Adam and Eve because Jesus had no physical son. That an Adamic son/Davidite would sit upon the throne of David forever is affirmed in 2 Samuel 7:8–17, where we read:

> "So now, say this to my servant David: 'This is what the LORD of hosts says: I took you from the pasture and from your work as a shepherd to make you leader of my people Israel. I was with you wherever you went, and I defeated all your enemies before you. Now I will make you as famous as the great men of the earth. I will establish a place for my people Israel and settle them there; they will live there and not be disturbed any more. Violent men will not oppress them again, as they did in the beginning and during the time when I appointed judges to lead my people Israel. Instead, I will give you relief from all your enemies. The Lord declares to you that he himself will build a *dynastic house* for you. When the time comes for you to die, I will raise up your descendant, one of your own sons, to succeed you, and *I will establish his kingdom.* He will build a house for my name, and I will make his *dynasty permanent.* I will become his father and he will become my son…*Your house and your kingdom will stand before me permanently; your dynasty will be permanent.*'"
> [xxi] (italics added)

In response to David's desire to build God a house, God offers a plan to build David a royal house, a dynasty of kings. God promises David that his house and kingdom "shall endure before Me forever; your throne shall be established forever" (2 Sam. 7:16). God's gracious promise to David is fulfillment of a promise made a millennium earlier to Abraham. In Genesis 17:6, the Lord God informs Abraham, "I have made you exceedingly fruitful, and I will make nations of you, and kings will come forth from you." This promise is repeated twice (Gen. 17:16; 35:11).

However, prior to Abraham, God was working out a promise to Adam and Eve. An Adamic son would crush the head of the serpent (Satan). This Adamic son would end satanic opposition and interference in God's affairs once and for all. The great-grandson of Abraham who received the honor of fulfilling the royal lineage was Judah. Genesis 49:10 records the promise: "The scepter shall not depart from Judah, nor the ruler's staff from between his feet, until Shiloh comes, and to him shall be the obedience of the peoples."

Regarding the meaning of "scepter," one has written:

> The sceptre is the symbol of regal command, and in its earliest form it was a long staff, which the king held in his hand when speaking in public assemblies...and when he sat upon his throne he rested it between his feet, inclining towards himself...מְחֹקֵק [ruling staff] the determining person or thing, hence a commander, legislator, and a commander's or ruler's staff (Num. 21:18); here in the latter sense, as the parallels, "sceptre" and "from between his feet," require. Judah—this is the idea—was to rule, to have the chieftainship, till Shiloh came, i.e., forever.[xxii]

Much debate has gone on regarding the meaning of the term "*Shiloh.*" Is it a reference to a person or a city? Perhaps neither! Rather, the sense seems to be that once Judah receives it, he will never lose it.[xxiii]

The long journey from promise to fulfillment is the core of Old Testament history. From Adam to Abraham, to Judah to David, and finally to Jesus Christ required each generation to produce a son who would continue the lineage.

National Israel (Physical Seed of Abraham) Chosen for Service

To be the physical seed of Abraham ensures that one is chosen for service. National Israel is the only people group in the history of mankind to whom God gave the special designation "chosen for service." Deuteronomy 7:6–8 outlines their election to service. The text states,

> For you are *a people holy* to the Lord your God. He has *chosen* you to be his people, prized above all others on the face of the earth. It is not because you were more numerous than all the other peoples that the Lord *favored* and *chose* you—for in fact you were the least numerous of all peoples. Rather it is because of his *love* for you and his faithfulness to the promise he solemnly vowed to your ancestors that the Lord brought you out with great power, redeeming you from the place of slavery, from the power of Pharaoh king of Egypt. (italics added)

This passage makes it clear that God intends Israel to recognize that their election is first and foremost a privilege. Pride is an incorrect response to God's special dealings with Israel.

Deuteronomy 7 depicts the nation of Israel as God's holy people—holy in the sense of being set apart to serve as God's showpiece on earth. As "His people," Israel is "prized above all others on the face of the earth." Clearly, the emphasis here is on the national group. Individuals will reap the benefits of God's election of the nation, yet it is the *group* that receives the designation "a people holy to the Lord your God."

Exodus 19:5–6 states,

> "'And now, if you will diligently listen to me and keep my covenant, then you will be my special possession out of all the nations, for all the earth is mine, and you will be to me a *kingdom of priests* and a holy nation.' These are the words that you will speak to the Israelites." (italics added)

With respect to national Israel's election to service, the designation a "kingdom of priests" is very helpful to our understanding of God's purpose in Israel's election. Concerning this key designation, the NET Bible notes,

> The construction "a kingdom of priests" means that the kingdom is made up of priests.... This kingdom of God will be composed of a priestly people. All the Israelites would be living wholly in God's service and enjoying the right of access to him. And, as priests, they would have the duty of representing God to the nations, following what they perceived to be the duties of priests— proclaiming God's word, interceding for people, and making provision for people to find God through atonement.[xxiv]

(See also Deuteronomy 33:9–10.)

Every man, woman, boy, and girl born into national Israel is duty-bound to serve God in this capacity. Physical birth is the only criterion.

Saints (Spiritual Seed of Abraham)
Chosen for Salvation

The apostle Paul writes, "If you belong to Christ, then you are Abraham's seed" (Gal. 3:29). We agree that

> If Christ is Abraham's offspring, according to the promise (cf. v 16), then those who are Christ's, participating in him by faith, whether Gentiles or Jews, are likewise Abraham's offspring (cf. v 7).[xxv]

However, the apostle Paul clearly distinguishes between Jews elect to service and Jews elect to salvation. He writes in Romans 11:7, "What then? Israel failed to obtain what it was diligently seeking, but the elect obtained it. The rest were hardened." The difference between "the elect" and "the rest" who were hardened is God's election of the nation to service, but few to salvation.

Earlier the apostle Paul states,

> It is not as though the word of God had failed. For not all those who are descended from Israel are truly Israel, nor are all the children Abraham's true descendants; rather "through Isaac will your descendants be counted." This means it is not the children of the flesh who are the children of God; rather, the children of promise are counted as descendants. (Rom. 9:6–8)

Paul's point is obvious. Physical birth alone will not ensure a Jew inclusion in the family of God. It is faith in Jesus Christ as God's remedy for sin that ensures inclusion in God's family. Because inclusion is faith-based, salvation is also possible for Gentiles. However, just as with the Jews, inclusion in God's family ultimately requires God's election. Paul establishes this fact in Ephesians 1:4, where he writes, "For he chose us in Christ before the foundation of the world that we may be holy and unblemished in his sight in love." God's choice precedes the creation.

Therefore, national Israel is elect to service. Within national Israel are a number of Jews elect to salvation. Romans 9:6–8 makes this clear. Also among the elect to salvation is a Gentile host, which explains God's present work in creation. This reflects the sense of Acts 15:13–14, which states, "After they had stopped speaking, James answered, saying, 'Brethren, listen to me. Simeon has related how God first concerned Himself about taking from among the Gentiles a people for His name.'" The elect of God to salvation include both Jews and Gentiles.

The Question

Now we return to our original question. To which group of chosen ones is the promise of Matthew 24 applicable—those chosen to sire a son (Messianic line); those chosen for service (national Israel); or those chosen for salvation (Jewish and Gentile elect)? Most pretribbers have historically relegated Matthew 24 to "the Jewish waste-paper basket."[xxvi] However, it would appear that Matthew 24:24 removes national Israel from consideration. The passage states, "For false messiahs and false prophets will appear and perform great signs and wonders to deceive, if possible, even the elect." The Lord Jesus declares that the deceptive campaign of the false messiahs and prophets will be so successful that "if possible, even the elect" could be victims.

What does "if possible" mean? A comparison of several passages is helpful in drawing a conclusion:

"If Possible" Usage

Matthew 24:24	Matthew 26:39	Romans 12:18	Galatians 4:15
For false christs and false prophets will arise and will show great signs and wonders, so as to mislead, if possible, even the elect.	And He went a little beyond them, and fell on His face and prayed, saying, "My Father, if it is possible, let this cup pass from Me; yet not as I will, but as You will."	If possible, so far as it depends on you, be at peace with all men.	Where then is that sense of blessing you had? For I bear you witness that, if possible, you would have plucked out your eyes and given them to me.

In Galatians 4:15, "if [it were] possible" expresses a possibility that, in reality, is contrary to fact in the world of Paul and his audience.[xxvii] All the desire in the world will not change the fact that one human is not able to simply pluck out his eyes and give them to another.[xxviii] Thus, Paul is expressing a desire that is possible to conceive in the mind, but has no factual basis in first-century reality. Romans 12:18 similarly utilizes the phrase "if [it is] possible." However, unlike Galatians 4:5, this verse uses a first class condition. The Greek language in and of itself does not speak to the issue of reality in this case. Whether Paul's exhortation is or is not ultimately a real possibility we must gather from the context and the general tenor of scripture.

The apostle Paul is expressing a desire that is possible to conceive in the mind, but remains an impossibility for humans. Paul expresses an ideal that all believers should make every effort to attain. Yet, no human is capable of attaining perfection in his relationships with all others. Each of us might greatly reduce the number of relational problems he has after many years of working at it. However, during the many years of learning to be at peace, one will still have problems. It is not one's simple sphere of influence, but "all men" that is the object of our intent. Who among us can so control himself that no word, deed, attitude, or mishap unsettles him towards others? It is a desired goal, but few—if any—can attain it.

We next find this phrase on the lips of our Lord Jesus in Matthew 26:39. On the very night, within hours of our Lord's surrender to His enemies, He struggled to submit to death. In His prayer to the Father, Jesus asks for another possibility. The Greek language is rather straightforward here.[xxix] In essence, Jesus opens His prayer with a call for a hypothetical consideration. This hypothetical has no basis in reality, but serves to express the Lord's struggle to submit to death. That the Lord's call to consider a hypothetical alternative is not grounded in possibility has support from Matthew 26:42, which states, "My Father, if this cannot pass away unless I drink it, Your will be done." With a very similar Greek construction to that of verse 39, Jesus makes a statement that is directly contradictory to verse 39. In verse 42, He admits that "it is not possible" for Him to escape death.

We are now ready to look at Matthew 24:24, where "if [it is] possible" is an "idiomatic parenthetical insertion into a purpose clause."[xxx] Having expressed the goal or purpose of the rise of false christs and false prophets in the days of unparalleled persecution, Matthew adds a parenthetical comment: "if [it is] possible, even the chosen ones." For Matthew, the goal of the false ones is to mislead. The level and sophistication of the "signs and wonders" will place God's chosen ones in jeopardy of deception, "if [it is] possible."

The obvious question is: "Will the chosen ones suffer deception or not?" Is deception a possibility? The reader will notice that each time the key phrase "if possible" appears, the bracketed phrase [it is] is inserted. That's because the verb is missing in the Greek construction. It is common for New Testament authors to leave out verbs in certain sentences where the context makes the author's intent clear. This is much like the way our pop English expression, "What up?" leaves out the verb "is." Bible interpreters know which verb is to be inserted; however, there is debate about its tense.[xxxi]

It comes down to the question of whether a true believer can be misled by a false prophet and, more importantly, by a false christ. The NASB's "mislead" translates πλανάω (*planaō*). The basic meaning is "to cause someone to hold a wrong view and thus be mistaken—'to mislead, to deceive, deception, to cause to be mistaken.'"[xxxii] For the four Gospels, "πλανάω has above all the sense of eschatological deception"[xxxiii]—that is, a deception that is limited to the period immediately adjacent to the Lord's return. A detailed explanation of the persecution by Satan/Antichrist, of which deception will be a major part, follows in chapter four.

However, suffice it to say that the eschatological deception prophetically announced in Matthew 24 / Mark 13 /Luke 21 will be unparalleled in human history. The "great signs and wonders" that the false christs and false prophets will perpetrate are characteristically described in exactly the same terms as those used in describing the miracles of our Lord and the apostles. While the workers of the eschatological miracles are consistently labeled as *false* christs and *false* prophets, their works are never so labeled, with the exception of 2 Thessalonians 2:9.[2]

The Book of Revelation portrays the works of Antichrist and his false prophet as the real deal. Revelation 13:3 describes the beast from the sea (Antichrist) in exactly the same resurrection language as that applied to Jesus Christ. Revelation 13:13 describes the works of the second beast (the beast from the earth) as "great signs" and gives, as an example, his bringing fire down from heaven in the presence of men. Revelation 13:15 also adds that the second beast can give life to an inanimate object. Such works put the false christs and false prophets operating during this time in a unique class.

---

[2] By "false," perhaps Paul's point is that the signs and wonders are authentic, but their goal or purpose is false or evil.

It is by these works that Matthew underscores that God's chosen ones might be deceived "if [it is] possible." His point is not that the chosen will be deceived, but that the works will be so authentic that the chosen ones could fall victim to them. In other words, the works are the real deal. If the chosen ones could be deceived, these works would definitely do it. However, the chosen ones cannot and will not fall victim. Matthew's "if [it is] possible" is a hypothetical put forward to make the case for authentic miracles and not to expose the Achilles' heel of believers.[3]

The apostle John put forward a simple test to expose the true motives of any would-be messiah. He writes, "Who is the liar but the one who denies that Jesus is the Christ? This is the antichrist, the one who denies the Father and the Son" (1 John 2:22). Again John writes,

> By this you know the Spirit of God: every spirit that confesses that Jesus Christ has come in the flesh is from God; and every spirit that does not confess Jesus is not from God; this is the *spirit* of the antichrist, of which you have heard that it is coming, and now it is already in the world. (1 John 4:2–3)

Matthew 24:24 removes national Israel from consideration as the subject of the Lord's remarks because national Israel will fall victim to Satan and his Antichrist's deceptive campaign. Daniel 9:27 says that national Israel's

---

[3] Some might wonder why the Lord would give such a detailed report concerning all that will happen during the end times if true believers will not be deceived by false christs and false prophets. He tells us so we will know exactly what is happening and why. He warns us, not because He is afraid that true believers will abandon the faith, but because He knows that we will be afraid and may thus lose opportunities to be witnesses for God in a time of crisis.

leadership will enter into a covenant relationship with Satan and his Antichrist. In the context of the final consummation, the Lord Jesus indicates "many will come in my name, saying, 'I am the Christ,' and they will mislead many" (Matt. 24:5).[4]

Revelation 17 depicts national Israel's ultimate deception. John describes Jerusalem, and by definition her inhabitants (national Israel), as "the mother of harlots." Her spiritual adultery flows out of her commitment to promote the cause of Satan and his Antichrist rather than her true God and His Son Jesus Christ. John states, "I will show you the condemnation and punishment of the great prostitute who sits on many waters, with whom the kings of the earth committed sexual immorality and the earth's inhabitants got drunk with the wine of her immorality" (Rev. 17:1–2). In context, the great prostitute is working her influence to convince the kings of the earth to commit to Satan/Antichrist's agenda. In a sense, the great prostitute is the primary advocate for Satan and his Antichrist during the final period of Daniel's Seventieth Week.

That the mother of harlots is the city of Jerusalem, which by metonymy[5] refers to the inhabitants in the city, is an accurate though unpleasant conclusion that finds support in the book. The phrase "the great city" occurs seven times in the book of Revelation (11:8; 16:19; 17:18; 18:10, 16, 18, and 19). By close examination of each occurrence, we are able to establish the identity of the referent.[xxxiv]

---

[4] The "many" who will be misled (deceived) are those who do not know Jesus or His Word. In the context of Matthew 24:5, the difference between "you—the Lord's followers" and "many—those who do not know the Lord" is His Word about what to look for and what to avoid.

[5] "A figure of speech that consists of the use of the name of one object or concept for that of another to which it is related, or of which it is a part, as 'scepter' for 'sovereignty,' or 'the bottle' for 'strong drink,' or 'count heads (or noses)' for 'count people.'" (www.dictionary.com).

> And their dead bodies *will lie* in the street of
> the great city, which mystically is called
> Sodom and Egypt, where also their Lord was
> crucified. (Rev. 11:8)

After a successful ministry of three-and-a-half years,
God's two witnesses, who work on the earth during the time
of unparalleled distress, are finally murdered by
Satan/Antichrist. It is their dead bodies that will lie "in the
street of the great city." The author of the Revelation then
gives two statements to clarify the identity of this city.

The title "the great city" occurs in the Old
Testament.[xxxv] Jeremiah 22:8 makes reference to Jerusalem
as such. In context, Jerusalem has suffered the judgment of
God—a judgment that the nations recognize as God's
punishment because she "forsook the covenant of the Lord
their God and bowed down to other gods and served them."
We see Jerusalem connected with spiritual harlotry. This
point John will make both spiritually and geographically.

First, Jerusalem is "mystically called Sodom and
Egypt." For the term "mystically" (*pneumatikos*—
πνευματικος), we find various translations. The NIV has
"figuratively." The NET Bible has "symbolically." The New
King James Version translates the term literally—
"spiritually." Concerning the meaning, A. T. Robertson
writes, "This late adverb from πνευματικος [*pneumatikos*]
(spiritual) occurs in the New Testament only twice, in 1 Cor.
2:14 (13) for the help of the Holy Spirit in interpreting God's
message and here in a hidden or mystical (allegorical)
sense."[xxxvi] Because of this usage, some recognize two
possible options:

> The city is ungodly and is not to be located in any
> one geographical area but is any ungodly spiritual
> realm on earth. Of course, if the city is assumed to

be a literal Jerusalem, then πνευματικῶς must refer only to the spiritual character of that city.[xxxvii]

Assuming for the moment that the latter option is correct, what spiritual connection exists between the great city and Sodom and Egypt?

Sodom was an ancient city that suffered divine destruction by Almighty God for its wickedness. Genesis 19:13 reports the angels' instructions to Lot, "We are about to destroy this place, because their outcry has become so great before the Lord that the Lord has sent us to destroy it." Jude 7 reports two characteristics of Sodom: (1) indulging in gross immorality and (2) going after "strange flesh." Sodom and Gomorrah are accused of "casting themselves with abandonment to sexual immorality." The reference to "strange flesh" is literally "different flesh." This is a euphemistic way of referring to Sodom's sin when the men of the city sought to rape the angels sent by God. With this act, the sin of Sodom and Gomorrah reached its peak. Thus, the key idea is gross sexual immorality of the most perverse kind.

This description is similar to what we find in the Old Testament. David J. MacLeod writes,

> In Genesis 13:13 we are told the men of Sodom were *"wicked exceedingly and sinners."* Later, in Genesis 18:20–33, its citizens are called *"wicked,"* and the LORD says, *"their sin is exceedingly grave."* The prophet Ezekiel (16:46–50) says this, *"Sodom . . . and her daughters had arrogance, abundant food, and careless ease, but she did not help the poor and needy. Thus they were haughty and committed abominations before Me."*[xxxviii]

Ezekiel's complaint is primarily one of harlotry (Eze. 16:40). Sodom earned the title as one city known for gross immorality that brought one of the most severe divine judgment recorded in history.

Interestingly, Sodom is compared to only one other city in the Old Testament. Isaiah 1:9 reports, "Hear the word of the Lord, you rulers of Sodom; give ear to the instruction of our God, you people of Gomorrah." God reports that Jerusalem has guilt like that of Sodom. Ezekiel depicts a familial relationship between Sodom and Jerusalem. He states, "Behold, this was the guilt of your sister Sodom: [...] arrogance, abundant food and careless ease, but she did not help the poor and needy" (Eze. 16:49). Ultimately, her guilt was harlotry. This explains the reference in Revelation 11:8.

One of Jerusalem's sins is spiritual harlotry. She is the ultimate harlot because she has broken covenant relationship with the one true God only to join herself to Satan and his Antichrist. Revelation 17 will depict Jerusalem as the ultimate harlot because of gross sexual immorality, connecting her with the ancient city of Sodom.

The second identifying reference is Egypt. What characteristic of Egypt will Jerusalem depict in a spiritual way? Egypt is a nation mentioned in the Bible whose gods received personal attention from Almighty God. Isaiah 19:1–4 makes it clear that God's judgment against Egypt is because of her worship of idols and false gods. With reference to the great Exodus, Numbers 33:4 declares, "The Lord had also executed judgments on their gods."[xxxix] Egypt's reliance on her gods in the face of the overwhelming evidence that the God of the Hebrews alone reigns supreme is the spiritual connection to Jerusalem.

With the ministry of the two prophets for three-and-a-half years, Jerusalem's commitment to Satan and his Antichrist in the face of overwhelming evidence of God's supremacy will make her a spiritual parallel to Egypt in the worst way. Having established her spiritual identity, John turns to one final identifying characteristic. As God specifically punished and defeated the gods of Egypt, He will punish and defeat Jerusalem's false gods—Satan and his Antichrist. Once again with plagues and wonders, God will free His people from the slavery of "Egypt" by deposing a king and the supernatural forces behind him. This time, God will also free the earth.

One final identifying phrase occurs in Revelation 11:8. The great city is "where also their Lord was crucified." By this statement, not only are we able to conclusively identify the city of reference, but also the relationship intended by the reference to Sodom and Egypt. The first word, *where* (ὅπου) is critical to understanding the intent of this passage. The *Analytical Lexicon of the Greek New Testament* identifies ὅπου (where) as an adverb of place;

> used as a subordinating conjunction for relative clauses; literally, denoting place *where, to* or *in what* place (MT 6.21); as a conjunction for indefinite relative clauses...*wherever, to* or *in whatever place* (Mark 6.56); figuratively, as a correlative introducing the more immediate circumstances or presuppositions, as e.g. in the proverb "where there's a will, there's a way," *where* (HE 9.16); as imparting a causal sense *whereas, insofar as, since.*[xl]

The *Exegetical Dictionary of the New Testament* states, "When used literally, [ὅπου] occurs with the indicative and means *where*. It is frequently found after a reference to place."[xli] Thus, the choice between a literal versus figurative usage in Revelation 11:8 leans toward literal usage:

"Where" References

Reference	Phrase	Designation
Revelation 2:13	Where Satan's throne is	Pergamum (a city)
Revelation 2:13	Where Satan dwells	Pergamum (a city)
Revelation 11:8	Where also their Lord was crucified	The great city
Revelation 12:6	Where she had a place prepared by God	The wilderness
Revelation 12:14	Where she was nourished	The wilderness
Revelation 14:4	Wherever He goes	They follow the Lamb
Revelation 17:9	Where the woman sits	Seven mountains, seven kings
Revelation 20:10	Where the beast and the false prophet are	Lake of fire and brimstone

All but the most liberal scholars will acknowledge that the "lake of fire and brimstone" is a literal place. The eternally damned are consistently portrayed as being assigned to a place of suffering. Revelation 20:10 indicates that Satan will join the beast (Antichrist) and the false prophet in the lake of fire and brimstone. In the chronology of the book of Revelation, the beast and the false prophet will have been in the lake for one thousand years by the time Satan joins them. Revelation 12:6 and 14 are easily confirmed as also representing a real, physical place. Revelation 12 concerns the nation of Israel; consequently, "wilderness" can only refer to that geographical region south or southeast of Jerusalem.[xlii] Revelation 2:13 contains two occurrences of ὅπου ("where"). We offer little proof that a physical location is the referent here. As the verse is found in the letter to the church in Pergamum, a city historically known for cultic worship of various kinds, few need doubt the city's designation by the Lord.

In Revelation 14:4, the grammar establishes that not so much a specific literal place is in view as a general commitment with an unspecified destination.[xliii] Revelation 17:9, understood in light of Revelation 17:7, which states, "I will tell you the mystery of the woman and of the beast that carries her, which has seven heads and ten horns," makes it clear that the relationship between the woman and the beast is figurative and not literal.

Thus, an examination of usage alone will not permit us to draw a conclusion as to whether ὅπου ("where") is used literally or figuratively in Revelation 11:8. Ὅπου (*hōpou* = "where") can have two possible grammatical connections in this verse:

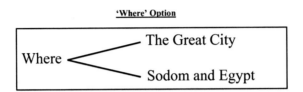

'Where' Option

One would normally expect the relative adverb clause to follow its antecedent closely, in which case "where also their Lord was crucified" would modify "Sodom and Egypt." If the verse is taken this way, we learn another spiritual attribute of the great city, but nothing about its literal identity. The other possibility is that "where also their Lord was crucified" modifies "the great city." If so, we would discover conclusively the identity of this city.

That a relative adverb clause may not immediately follow its antecedent is clear from John 20:12, where a phrase divides the clause and the antecedent, just as in Revelation 11:8. At least one-quarter of the occurrences of this particular relative adverb clause precede the antecedent. Thus, the position of the clause in the sentence is inconclusive. However, taking all the data together, we favor the literal city of Jerusalem. The Lord Himself states, "For it cannot be that a prophet would perish outside of Jerusalem. O Jerusalem, Jerusalem, the city that kills the prophets" (Luke 13:33–34). Given that the two witnesses are the last two great prophets to be killed for communicating God's will, Jerusalem is the logical place for their death.

"Their Lord" is a reference to the two witnesses. It is the two witnesses' Lord who was crucified. This can only refer to Jesus Christ and His death. There is no other individual referenced as "Lord" in the Bible to have suffered crucifixion but Jesus. With the exception of a few scholars who spiritualize the whole book of Revelation, most agree that Revelation 11:8 refers to Jerusalem.

> The great city was split into three parts, and the cities of the nations fell. Babylon the great was remembered before God, to give her the cup of the wine of His fierce wrath. (Rev. 16:19)

The next verse where the phrase "the great city" occurs is important. The seventh and final bowl judgment concerns the destruction of all the population centers of the world. The importance of this reference results from the fact that "the great city" is distinguished from "the cities of the nations." "The nations" (τῶν ἐθνῶν) as a plural noun occurs 130 times in the New Testament and refers to those who do not belong to the Jewish or Christian faith.[xliv] Spiros Zodhiates concurs when he writes, "In the Jewish sense, *tá éthnē*, the nations, means the Gentile nations or the Gentiles in general as spoken of all who are not Israelites...i.e., the heathen, pagan nations."[xlv] Eugene Pond has done an exhaustive study of *tá éthnē* ("the nations") in the New Testament and concludes that Revelation 16:19 refers "to nations or peoples of the world who oppose God or are without Him."[xlvi]

"The cities of the nations" are here distinguished from "the great city." That's because "the great city" is not among the Gentile cities, but is the Jewish city of Jerusalem. It will be "split into three parts." Where the Gentile cities suffer destruction, Jerusalem will suffer a three-fold division to be followed by the outpouring of God's severe wrath. This outpouring relates to Babylon the great. Because later in the book John will call "the great city" by the name "Babylon the Great," most scholars reason back that "the great city" refers to either the city of Rome[xlvii] or to a future rebuilt capital of Iraq. However, those who follow this reasoning fail to appreciate the grammatical and theological data that points to a different conclusion.

> "The woman whom you saw is the great city, which reigns [literally, has a kingdom] over the kings of the earth." (Rev. 17:18)

Revelation 17:18 specifically identifies the great city as "the woman," who is described in Revelation 17. An inductive study of Revelation 17 unmistakably identifies this woman to be the great city, which is the literal city of Jerusalem, which by metonymy refers to Jews living in Jerusalem.[xlviii]

Revelation 17:5 lists three names for the woman: (1) Babylon the Great; (2) The Mother of Harlots; and (3) The Mother of the Abominations of the Earth. Each name is a "mystery." The term "mystery" signals that the reader must look beyond the words for that which the language intends. "Mystery" signifies hiddenness, veiled under the symbol.

One writer states,

> A mystery does not denote an *unknowable* thing, but one which is withdrawn from knowledge or manifestation, and which cannot be known without special manifestation of it.[xlix]

The first occurrence of the term "mystery" in the book of Revelation can help us understand the correct method of interpretation. In Revelation 1:20, we learn that there is a one-to-one correspondence between the symbol and that which it represents in a particular vision. In this vision, (1) stars represent angels and (2) lampstands represent churches. This method of interpretation has a close affinity with the book of Daniel. Like the book of Revelation, the book of Daniel involves similar visions with angelic interpretation. In each case, what is revealed is identified as a "mystery."

Many scholars recognize a relationship between Daniel 2, 7, and 9–10 and the book of Revelation. Evidence of this is Revelation 1:13–15:

> And in the midst of the lampstands was one *like a son of man.* He was dressed in a robe extending down to his feet and he wore a wide golden belt around his chest. His head and hair were as white as wool, even as white as snow, and his eyes were like a fiery flame. His feet were like polished bronze refined in a furnace, and his voice was like the roar of many waters.

Notice the similarity to the words of John:

> I looked up and saw a man clothed in linen; around his waist was a belt made of gold from Upaz. His body resembled yellow jasper, and his face had an appearance like lightning. His eyes were like blazing torches; his arms and feet had the gleam of polished bronze. His voice thundered forth like the sound of a large crowd.

Revelation 1:13–15 joins ideas and concepts from Daniel 3:25; Daniel 7:13; and Daniel 10:3–5 for the identity of Jesus Christ. G. K. Beale, Ph.D., argues for an allusion on the part of John to Daniel 2:29, 45 in Revelation 1:19. He concludes that that allusion continues in Revelation 1:20. He writes,

The validity of the Dan. 2:29, 45 allusion in 1:19 is further confirmed by the following phrase, τò μυστήριον ("the mystery"), which also follows in Dan. 2:29 and 45."[l]

Beale's comments on the use of "the mystery" (τò μυστήριον) in the book of Revelation is insightful and helpful. He writes,

> John also brings in τò μυστήριον ("the mystery") from Daniel precisely at this point to emphasize the ironic nature of the fulfillment and its reversal of expectations. In Daniel 2 "mystery" has to do with the hidden meaning of a symbol whose interpretation has eschatological significance. "Mystery," on the surface, in Rev. 1:20 refers to the hidden meaning of the stars and lampstands, which are about to be interpreted. But "mystery" also carries the connotation of unexpected, end-time fulfillment included in the meaning of the stars and lampstands in the present context. Indeed, μυστήριον ("mystery") occurs elsewhere in Revelation, as elsewhere in the NT, to indicate fulfillment of prophecy in an unexpected manner.[li]

This is precisely the understanding one will need to fully appreciate Revelation 17–18. Revelation 17–18 describes prophetic fulfillment in a manner so unexpected that most New Testament scholars have totally missed the intent of the text. Nowhere is this more evident than concerning the identity of the woman.

Revelation 17:5 begins, "On her [the woman's] forehead was written a name, a mystery." Thus, the woman is a prophetic figure who will fulfill prophecy in an unexpected manner. The unexpectedness with regard to the woman is her identity. Notice that John states, "a name, a mystery." The NET Bible's translation reflects the translators' decision about the relationship between "name" and "mystery."[lii] In other words, the term "mystery" is not part of what is written on her forehead. Since the angel does not offer an explanation for the term, we understand it to function the same way here as it does in Revelation 1:20; 10:7; and 17:7. Thus, the mysterious name written is symbolic and in need of explanation. Just as in Daniel 2, 7, and 10 and Revelation 1 and 10, what is symbolically represented has a tangible, literal reality.

Revelation 17 presents four facts regarding the identity of the woman:

(1) The woman is called Babylon the Great.

A majority of scholars are divided concerning whether this woman is a real city and, if so, which one. The fact that she is called Babylon the Great makes some conclude that the literal city of ancient Babylon is intended. Others favor the ancient city of Rome. However, these scholars are blinded to the fact of genre and historical precedent.

The meaning of Revelation 17–18 is buried in apocalyptic language. Every aspect of John's vision requires explanation by the interpreting angel. Since we know that the term "Babylon" is not literal in Revelation 17:5, we must look for the literal referent.

The term "Babylon" occurs in 1 Peter 5:13 and provides precedent and support for our conclusion here. It states, "She who is in Babylon, chosen together with you, sends you greetings, and so does my son Mark." This is an important precedent. As with Revelation 17–18, scholars are divided as to whether the literal city of Babylon, another city in the Roman Empire, or Rome itself is in view here. This text provides a strong case for our conclusion that Babylon can symbolically represent another city.

We suggest that Peter is writing from Jerusalem because there is absolutely no basis for seeing Peter in Babylon of Mesopotamia and writing to the Jews who had been scattered as he himself had been. Had Peter, in fact, been writing from Babylon, we would expect him to list himself among "those who reside as aliens scattered throughout" (1 Peter 1:1). He would be a fellow alien with them.[liii] Some have the opinion that Peter was in a Roman garrison town in Egypt that bore this name—Babylon. As Peter was an apostle of prominence, this would be highly doubtful. An overwhelming number of scholars take the term "Babylon" as a cryptograph for "Rome." An early church father also took this position.[liv] This is largely based on their interpretation of Revelation 17–18, which is interesting particularly given that Revelation 17–18 is highly debated as to its meaning. This is an excellent example of circular reasoning.

We understand Jerusalem as the crypt behind the New Testament use of "Babylon." Peter's cryptic message was necessary to prevent more persecution for those who lived there. The primary point of 1 Peter 5:13 is this: Babylon can and does serve as a cryptic reference for a city.

If Babylon in Revelation 17:5 is a cryptic reference to Jerusalem, we must press on to discover what quality or attribute of Babylon the future Jerusalem will acquire. Babylon has the designation μεγάλη ("great"), a term used in the book of Revelation eighty times. Since no name given the woman is positive but reflects a negative disposition towards the woman by the author, it makes more sense to take μεγάλη ("great") in a similarly negative sense—to a great degree, intense, terrible.[lv] She is great, but for all the wrong reasons.

There is agreement among many scholars that

[t]he historic city and empire of Babylon were always depicted by the prophets as the ungodly power *par excellence*. Thus even after the fall of Babylon, Babel, as they saw it, represented for later Jewish readers of Scripture, and also for early Christians…the very epitome and type of an ungodly and domineering city.[lvi]

However, scholars are once again reading into the Revelation preconceived ideas without a textual basis. That is, they have not paid close enough attention of John's references to the Old Testament.

To fully appreciate Revelation 17–18's connection with Jerusalem, we must turn our attention to Isaiah 21. In this great chapter, we first find the words, "Fallen, fallen is Babylon." At God's behest, the prophet Isaiah reports to Judah that their dependence on Babylon to break the strong grip of Assyria so soon after the fall of Israel (the ten northern tribes) was futile. Isaiah is not dealing with the Babylon of Judah's seventy-year captivity. Rather, Isaiah deals with a situation that occurred 175-plus years earlier. In 722 B.C., Merodach-Baladan[lvii] captured and took Babylon from the Assyrians. Finally, in 702 B.C., the Assyrians defeated Merodach-Baladan and his coalition of the willing. After some success against the Assyrians, the Judeans thought Merodach-Baladan would defeat the Assyrians. However, several years earlier, Isaiah had informed Judah that God would not allow Merodach-Baladan to defeat or break the yoke of Assyria. It is Isaiah's prophecy of this fact that appears in Isaiah 21.

King Hezekiah of Judah made an alliance with Merodach-Baladan and his coalition in the hope that he would break the Assyrian domination of the region. However, Isaiah reports the bad news: "fallen, fallen is Babylon." Trusting in Babylon's king proved disappointing. John echoes language from Isaiah's account to announce parallel consequences[lviii] that Jerusalem will suffer for her foray into world politics. The city of Babylon under Merodach-Baladan tried to influence world events by breaking the grip of Assyria, only to suffer complete defeat. Babylon the Great (Jerusalem) will do the same. She will attempt to convince the world that Antichrist will succeed against Jesus Christ, only to suffer defeat as ancient Babylon did.

John's allusion to Isaiah 21 and Judah's prior dealings with Babylon are perfectly reflected in John's depiction of Jerusalem as Babylon the Great. By trusting in the beast empire to deliver her from the conquest of Jesus Christ, Jerusalem will prove to be Babylon *par excellence.*

(2) The woman is called the Mother of Harlots.

To qualify for the designation "mother of harlots," the candidate must be an idolater *par excellence.* That is, she is the queen of idolatry. Because the woman is not a literal human, she clearly is a figurative representation of an entity guilty of spiritual harlotry. Both Judah and Jerusalem are repeatedly accused of harlotry (Hos. 1:2; Jer. 7:9). Spiritual adultery refers "to the faithlessness of the nation rather than to rampant sex among the people."[lix] With regard to Judah and Israel,

This figurative use was based on the marriage-like relationship of the Lord and the nation of Israel (Jer 3:20). When the people gave their allegiance to idols rather than God he charged that they "went a whoring after" other gods (KJV) or "played the harlot after" other gods (Jgs 8:33).[lx]

Isaiah (1:21) labels Jerusalem a harlot, as does Jeremiah (13:27). Ancient Babylon had the same reputation (Eze. 23:17). Isaiah also ascribes this title to Tyre and Nineveh, the ancient capitals of Lebanon and Assyria. Of the four cities, which one deserves the title "mother of harlots"? That city which has done more to promote false commitments to foreign gods than any other, while at the same time under covenant agreement with the one true God. Only one city on earth has the rights to that title: Jerusalem. She alone had the great privilege of having the manifested presence of God. She alone had unparalleled blessings from God. She alone has had the benefits of unparalleled acts of supernatural deliverance. Jerusalem has been the epicenter of God's works on the earth for millennia. Yet, in the eschatological future, she will turn to a false God and champion that the whole world join her. This makes her the mother of harlots.

(3) She is called the Mother of the Abominations of the Earth.

The third designation of the woman in Revelation 17:5 is Mother of the Abominations of the Earth. In a superlative sense, the woman is the mother of abominations. She is the guiltiest of producing depravity on the earth. Of some interest is the fact that βδέλυγμα ("abomination") appears in the New Testament six times (Mark 13:14 /Matt. 24:15; Luke 16:15; Revelation 17:4, 5; 21:27). The

Exegetical Dictionary of the New Testament states that βδελύγμα ("abomination") "designates generally the *object of loathing* and has...a religious-ethical connotation. Thus it means essentially what is *an abomination before God.*"[lxi]

The Old Testament defines at great length those sins deserving of this title, the greatest of which is idol worship.[lxii] In Luke 16:15, the Lord Jesus' summary is "that which is highly esteemed among men is an abomination before the sight of God." The woman will ultimately esteem that which is the most abominable of all. She will worship Antichrist and Satan and lead the cheers for the world to do the same. This makes her the mother of abominations.

(4) The woman murdered the saints and the witnesses of Jesus.

A fourth identifying trait of the woman is *murder*. She is guilty of the murder of both saints and the witnesses of Jesus. John declares, "And I saw the woman drunk with the blood of the saints and with the blood of the witnesses of Jesus." The verb "drunk" is a figure of speech. To be "drunk with blood" means to have murdered profusely. The woman is guilty of murder. The objects of her actions are saints and witnesses.

We think that the text indicates two separate groups at this point: "Saints" are not identical with "witnesses." The repetition of the phrase "with the blood of" suggests the possibility of two separate groups. Similar expressions in Revelation 17–18 also suggest two separate groups. Revelation 18:20 has the combination "saints, apostles, and prophets." Two verses in the Revelation are conceptually close to Revelation 17:6: (1) Revelation 18:24 combines "the blood of prophets, and of saints and of all who have been slain on the earth." Here, John did not include the phrase "the blood" with the two final groups. This we understand to indicate that "the blood" goes with each group. (2)

Revelation 16:6: John combines "the blood of saints and prophets." The terms themselves make clear that two groups are meant. This strongly supports our conclusion that 17:5 has two different groups in view.

The association of the woman with Satan/Antichrist, who is directly responsible for the murder of the two witnesses in Revelation 11, and her specific identification with the murder of the Lord's witnesses in light of the murder of the two witnesses occurring in her streets, would seem to make a strong case for her identity, in our opinion. This provides a linkage between the two witnesses, the great city, and Babylon the Great. Jesus specifically identified Jerusalem as the murderer of prophets and divine messengers (Matt. 23:37, Luke 13:37). He also placed the guilt of all murders from "Abel [Gen. 4:10] to Zechariah the Son of Barachiah [2 Chron. 24:22]" on that Jewish mindset characterized in the generation of Jews directly responsible for His death.

It is at once clear that no Jew alive at the time Jesus made that statement had participated in the physical act of killing Zechariah. Yet, the Lord will hold those who manifest the same attitude guilty. In Matthew 23:36, He states, "Truly I say to you, all these things will come upon this generation." We understand "generation" to refer to the mindset of the people and not the particular individuals living at the time of Christ. We do so because at the time of our Lord's public ministry, many Jews trusted in Him. Thus, not every member of that generation was guilty. This comports well with our identification of the woman of Revelation 17 as Jerusalem. Our Lord places the blame for all murders of the saints and prophets on that Jewish mindset that manifests itself in killing God's messengers. This very fact appears in Revelation 18:24, which states, "And in her [the woman = Jerusalem] was found the blood of prophets and of saints and of all who have been slain on the earth."

Revelation 19:2 states, "He has avenged the blood of His bond-servants on her [the great city = the woman = Jerusalem]." This stands in fulfillment of Matthew 23:35. Since God is fair and just, we understand that His vengeance will affect only the guilty. Thus, His vengeance on the woman is the result of her guilt. Since she is guilty of the death of all saints, apostles, and prophets, the woman can only be Jerusalem.

(5) The woman is clothed with priestly garments.

When we examine Revelation 17–18, one striking feature of the image of the harlot that is emphasized is her clothing. She is arrayed in "purple and scarlet, and adorned with gold and precious stones and pearls" (17:4; 18:16). This combination of words in the Greek is identical to the description of the high priest's garments found in the Greek translation of the Old Testament. This certainly accords with the role Jerusalem will play in the eschatological future when she champions the cause of Satan and his Antichrist before the world.

There other reasons that support our conclusion that the woman = the great city = Babylon the Great = the great harlot = Jerusalem. However, the point is well made for those who look to scripture only. Israel will not be found faithful to the Lord, but instead will form a spiritual connection with Satan/Antichrist, which will result in her destruction. Therefore, national Israel is not the elect mentioned in Matthew 24:21. God's decision to limit the duration of Satan/Antichrist's campaign of terror is not because of national Israel. Neither is it because of the Messianic line that ultimately came to be connected with the tribe of Judah.

The Messianic Line of Judah

The support for ruling out the Messianic line within Judah causes us to turn our attention once again to the Revelation. Revelation 12:1–6 records:

> Then a great sign appeared in heaven: a woman clothed with the sun, and with the moon under her feet, and on her head was a crown of twelve stars. She was pregnant and was screaming in labor pains, struggling to give birth. Then another sign appeared in heaven: a huge red dragon that had seven heads and ten horns, and on its heads were seven diadem crowns. Now the dragon's tail swept away a third of the stars in heaven and hurled them to the earth. Then the dragon stood before the woman who was about to give birth, so that he might devour her child as soon as it was born. So the woman gave birth to a son, a male child, who is going *to rule over all the nations with an iron rod.* Her child was suddenly caught up to God and to his throne, and she fled into the wilderness where a place had been prepared for her by God, so she could be taken care of for 1,260 days.

Who is this woman? She is the Messianic line that runs down through human history, from Adam to the tribe of Judah—initially, that remnant of men and women who have ensured that God's promise and program of fulfillment has never failed. Two clues help us identify the woman: (1) her adornment and (2) the Son she bore.

The description, "a woman clothed with the sun, and with the moon under her feet, and on her head was a crown of twelve stars" is reminiscent of Joseph's dream detailed in Genesis 37:9–10. The text relates,

Now he had still another dream, and related it to his brothers, and said, "Lo, I have had still another dream; and behold, the sun and the moon and eleven stars were bowing down to me." And he related it to his father and to his brothers; and his father rebuked him and said to him, "What is this dream that you have had? Shall I and your mother and your brothers actually come to bow ourselves down before you to the ground?"

Joseph's dream predicted the eventual outcome of Joseph and his family. He ruled over them and they served him in Egypt.

There are significant differences between the Genesis 37 account as it relates to Joseph and the account of the woman in Revelation 12, however. In the Genesis account, the sun, moon, and eleven stars, respectively, are Jacob, Rachel, and Joseph's brothers. However, in Revelation 12, the woman is not the sun, moon, and stars. Rather, she is wearing the sun, standing on the moon, with a crown of twelve stars. Thus, the elements adorn the woman. The significance of the Genesis account for Revelation 12 is that it teaches us how to correctly interpret Revelation 12.

The reality depicted in Revelation 12:1 is the ultimate typological fulfillment of the Jacob scenario. Jacob and Rachel produced a son all others serve. The son of the woman will rule the nations. Other connections between Genesis 37 and Revelation 12:1 are these: both sons spent time away before they ruled; both sons ruled over more than just their own families; both sons received and ruled under another; and both sons will save their people from seven years of trouble.

The other identifying mark for the woman occurs in Revelation 12:5. She "gave birth to a son, a male child, who is going to rule over all the nations with an iron rod. Her child was suddenly caught up to God and to his throne." Such designation befits no one but Jesus Christ. Earlier, Revelation 2:26–27 states, "And he who overcomes, and he who keeps My deeds until the end, to him I will give authority over the nations; and he shall rule them with a rod of iron, as the vessels of the potter are broken to pieces, as I also have received authority from My Father." Jesus Christ can only give "authority over the nations" if He himself has such authority—authority He receives from God the Father.

The context emphasizes the sovereign kingship of the male child. He rules the nations with an iron rod, or absolute authority. This is the purpose of his birth. Since sovereign kingship is a birthright of the male child, he can only be a Davidite. As a Davidite, the male child is both of the tribe of Judah and a descendant of King David who traces his heritage back to Adam.

The only historical entity capable of producing this Davidite is the Messianic line of Judah. Mary and Joseph, earthly parents of Jesus, were both of the tribe of Judah and descendants of King David (Luke 1:27).[lxiii] It is clear that Mary's stature as both a devotee of God and her Davidic linage are critical to her choice by God. The woman of Revelation 12 certainly must meet this standard. Just as with Mary, not all the tribes of Israel are included in the parental designation of the "man-child."

It is not for the sake of the Messianic line within Judah (the remnant) that God limits the rule of Satan and his Antichrist during the second half of Daniel's Seventieth Week; the woman (the Messianic line of Judah) is put in protective custody for 1,260 days (forty-two months or three-and-a-half years),[lxiv] so there is no need to limit the rule of Satan and his Antichrist for the woman's sake. Therefore, we are safe to conclude that neither national Israel nor the remnant of Jews in Judah make up "the elect" mentioned in

Matthew 24. National Israel will be deceived and the Messianic line of Judah will be in protective custody. Accordingly, the only possible option is the saints earlier identified as the saved. Revelation 12:17 states, "So the dragon became enraged at the woman and went away to make war on the rest of her children, those who keep God's commandments and hold to the testimony about Jesus." Who are "the rest of her children?"

Revelation 12:5 informs us that the woman gave birth to a Man-Child. Without details, John informs us that the woman had other offspring. John employs the Greek term *spermatos* ("seed," used idiomatically for "offspring," "children," or "descendant"). This is unusual. *Spermatos* (from which we get our English word "sperm") is customarily associated with the male progenitor and not the female. However, there is one rather interesting occurrence of *spermatos* in connection with a woman that is instructive.[lxv] Genesis 3:15 states, "And I will put hostility between you and the woman and between your offspring and her offspring; her offspring will attack your head, and you will attack her offspring's heel." God informs the serpent of the consequences of misleading Eve in the Garden. Hostility will exist between the serpent and Eve and their offspring.

In the Septuagint,[lxvi] Genesis 3:15 utilizes the term *spermatos* in reference to Eve. *Spermatos* allows for either a group (collective seed) or individual (singular seed). Some argue that "[t]he 'offspring' of the woman was Cain, then all humanity at large, and then Christ and those collectively in Him."[lxvii] Interestingly, the Septuagint uses "he." It translates the Hebrew *zera* ("seed") with the Greek *sperma*, a neuter noun. The expected antecedent pronoun is "it [*auto*] will crush your head," but the Greek has "he" (*autos*), which suggests that the translators interpreted "seed" as a male individual.[lxviii] Similarly, the apostle Paul in Galatians 3:16 speaks of "seed" in the singular. He identified Christ as the single "seed" intended in the promissory blessing to Abraham.

For our purposes, the woman (Eve) is connected with *spermatos*. Both Eve and her "offspring" are critical to the righteous fulfillment of God's program to crush Satan and his plan. Similarly, the woman (remnant of Judah) and Man-Child (Jesus) of Revelation 12 are critical to the fulfillment of God's program to crush the dragon and his plan. In context, we expect that "the rest of her children" are of the same nature[lxix] as the Man-Child, since they share the same mother and must overcome the dragon's destructive program. Two descriptive clauses help in the identification of the woman's children. John declares that "the rest of her children" *keep God's commandments* and *hold to the testimony about Jesus.*

On five other occasions in the book of Revelation, John utilizes similar defining traits to identify a group of individuals. Notice the chart below:

Saints Description in Revelation

Revelation 1:9 Apostle John	Revelation 6:9 Martyrs	Revelation 14:12 The Saints	Revelation 19:10 Brothers of John	Revelation 20:4 Beheaded Martyrs
Word of God	Word of God	Commandments of God	Testimony of Jesus	Testimony of Jesus
Testimony of Jesus	Testimony which they had maintained	Their faith of Jesus		Word of God

The slight differences between the clauses as they appear in each of these verses above do not undermine their signal that true believers in Jesus Christ are depicted. These are members of God's elect before the foundation of the world. The woman's offspring are true believers in Jesus Christ. Therefore, by a process of elimination, we conclude that the elect of Matthew 24 represent a generation of Jewish and Gentile members of Christ's bride. In light of Matthew 24:22, we understand the Lord to mean that God's desire to ensure that some of His elect will live to see the Son of Man coming on the clouds will be fulfilled.

Chapter Three

'Parousia': The Royal Return of Our King

A second and more critical biblical support for the applicability of Matthew 24 to the church is Matthew's use of the term *parousia*. It occurs in Matthew 24:3 and verses 27, 37, and 39. This unique term occurs in Matthew 24, but is absent from the parallel passages in Mark 13 and Luke 21. Obviously, the question is *why*? To answer this question, we first must answer the following questions: (1) Did Jesus actually use the term? (2) Or did Matthew use the term simply to clarify the disciples' question and the Lord's answer? (3) Does the term help argue Matthew's purpose for writing his gospel? These questions speak to the composition and purpose of the gospel of Matthew.

The term παρουσία (*parousia*) occurs in the New Testament twenty-four times. It occurs fourteen times in the writings of the apostle Paul, six times in non-Pauline epistles, and four times in the gospel of Matthew. W. Radl argues,

> The basic meaning of the word is to be derived from the verb πάρειμι, "be present." Thus παρουσία originally meant *presence*. Since, however, πάρειμι can take on the sense of "come, approach"... παρουσία frequently means "*arrival* as the onset of presence."[lxx]

He also states,

> In regard to the meaning *arrival* one can further distinguish between the general concept and the specific use of the word. Only 2 Cor 7:6, 7 (Phil 1:26) speaks of a common arrival. In 2 Thess 2:9 and 2 Pet 3:12, where the Antichrist and the Day of the Lord respectively are the subjects of the coming, the use of παρουσία approaches the more specific usage. In the remaining 16 occurrences παρουσία is a technical term for Christ's coming at the end of time.[lxxi]

The term *parousia* is variously translated. Dr. W. Harold Mare writes, "A brief look at Parousia in Liddell-Scott'[s] *A Greek-English Lexicon* shows that this word was used from the Homeric period down through that of the NT, with meanings ranging from the *presence* of persons to their *arrival* or *advent*."[lxxii] Dr. John F. Walvoord argues that *parousia* "has come to mean not simply *presence* but the act by which the presence is brought about, i.e., by the *coming* of the individual."[lxxiii] Hogg and Vine take the opposite view.

> The usual translation is misleading, because 'coming' is more appropriate to other words...the difference being that whereas these words fix the attention on the journey to, and the arrival at, a place, *parousia* fixes it on the stay which follows on the arrival there. It would be preferable, therefore, to transliterate the word rather than translate it, that is to use 'parousia,' rather than 'coming,' wherever the reference is to the Lord Jesus.[lxxiv]

With regard to the Lord's return and the meaning of *parousia*, there are two questions. First: Is the emphasis on the act of coming or the resultant state of His coming? Second: Is the word *parousia* used to refer to different arrivals of Christ for different purposes or does it refer to a single, multi-phased arrival that is initiated by the rapture of the church and ends with the battle of Armageddon? It is our conviction that both nuances occur. There is simply too much connected with our Lord's return to limit the term to one or the other.

It is our conviction that the technical term *parousia* represents a multi-faceted event each time it occurs and that each passage must be evaluated in light of this conclusion. Hogg and Vine's suggestion that *parousia* be transliterated (merely changing the Greek letters into English letters rather than translating it into "coming") instead of translated is a good one. This allows readers to evaluate each passage in light of the context for themselves. Hogg and Vine offer one other suggestion that is worthy of our attention. They indicate, "The Parousia of the Lord Jesus is thus a period with a *beginning*, a *course*, and a *conclusion*" (italics added).[lxxv] We are in agreement with this point. However, we do not agree with their division of this period with regard to the timing of the events that will occur.[lxxvi]

The following diagram depicts our understanding of the eschatological *parousia* of the Lord Jesus Christ:

The 'Parousia' of Christ

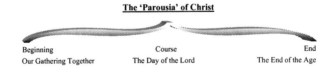

Beginning	Course	End
Our Gathering Together	The Day of the Lord	The End of the Age

Again, the term *parousia* is used twenty-four times in the New Testament.[lxxvii] Of these, seventeen refer to the coming of Jesus in the future.[lxxviii] If *parousia* in the seventeen future-oriented verses can be shown to refer to a multi-faceted event, just with different emphases, then sufficient grounds will be established to warrant designating *parousia* as the most precise term to refer to the future return of Jesus Christ. Let's examine each occurrence in each writer outside Matthew 24 first.

Use of 'Parousia' by James

Let's take in chronological order the thirteen occurrences of *parousia* in the New Testament outside Matthew's gospel that refer to the future ministry of Jesus Christ. We begin with a double reference in the book of James.[lxxix] James 5:7–8 states,

> Be patient, therefore, brethren, until the coming [*parousia*] of the Lord. Behold, the farmer waits for the precious produce of the soil, being patient about it, until it gets the early and late rains. You too be patient; strengthen your hearts, for the coming [*parousia*] of the Lord is at hand.

The book of James is specifically addressed "to the twelve tribes which are scattered abroad." These Jewish Christians (the righteous remnant of Israel) are urged to exercise patience until the *parousia* of Christ.[lxxx] In light of the nearness of this event, James comforts the suffering Jewish Christians with the knowledge that Jesus, "the Judge is standing at the door" (James 5:9). However, the fullest benefit of the Lord will come in connection with His *parousia*.

James' focus is the beginning of Christ's *parousia* as that time when the suffering that James' audience is presently experiencing falls away. James uses the Greek preposition *heōs*, translated "until." Louw and Nida give the sense of this word as "the continuous extent of time up to a point."[lxxxi] Dr. R. P. Martin, in agreement with Dr. Douglas Moo, states that "ἕως ("until") contains the idea both of purpose (goal) and time."[lxxxii] That is, the goal of our suffering and the time when it will be removed is at the initiation of the Lord's *parousia.*[lxxxiii] This supports our belief that the very beginning of Christ's *parousia* will spell relief for God's people.

It is inconceivable that James would encourage Christians to be excited about the Lord's coming at Armageddon without reference to the future evacuation (rapture), when all saints to date will experience eternal deliverance. Deliverance from suffering for God's elect comes at the beginning of the *parousia* of Christ.

Use of 'Parousia' by Paul

Paul picks up James' theme about Christ's coming to bring relief to His people. He writes of the Thessalonians, "For they [the Macedonians] themselves declare...how you [the Thessalonians] turned to God from idols to serve the living and true God and to wait for His Son from heaven." It is clear that the Thessalonians are waiting for the *parousia,* which will remove them from this earth to heaven. Interestingly, the first and each subsequent chapter in Paul's first letter to the Thessalonians ends with a reference to the Lord's return—1 Thessalonians 2:19, 3:13, 4:15, and 5:23.

1 Thessalonians 2:19

The first occurrence of the term *parousia* in the writings of Paul is in 1 Thessalonians 2:19, which states, "For who is our hope or joy or crown of exultation? Is it not even you, in the presence of our Lord Jesus at His coming [*parousia*]?" The church at Thessalonica was composed mostly of Gentiles, but also included some Jews.[lxxxiv] Paul informs the Thessalonians that they are his hope and joy in the presence of Christ at His *parousia*.

The phrase ἐν τῇ αὐτοῦ παρουσίᾳ (at His *parousia*) begins with the Greek preposition ἐν (*en*), which with the dative case here expresses time. Concerning this passage, the Greek lexicon states that the usage denotes "the point of time when something occurs."[lxxxv] Dr. Daniel B. Wallace indicates that the dative of time "largely has the force of point."[lxxxvi] It is at the initiation of the Lord's *parousia* that Paul plans to present the Thessalonians as his hope, joy, or crown of exultation.

1 Thessalonians 3:13

Here, Paul adds a prayer that Jesus will cause love to grow among the Thessalonians, "so that He may establish your hearts blameless in holiness before our God and Father at the coming [*parousia*] of our Lord Jesus with all His saints." This is the second occurrence of *parousia* in Paul's writings. As in 1 Thessalonians 2:19, here Paul is emphasizing the beginning of Christ's *parousia*. Again, Paul uses the Greek prepositional phrase, ἐν τῇ παρουσίᾳ. *Ev* is Paul's favorite preposition to introduce the Lord's *parousia*.

Pretribulationists understand this passage to refer to the Lord's return at Armageddon. John F. Walvoord adds this passage to his "second *parousia*" column. A great influence on Walvoord and others is Paul's inclusion of the concluding phrase "with all His saints." Scholars debate the focus of the term *saints* in 1 Thessalonians 3:13. *Tōn hagiōn* (*Τῶν ἁγίων* = "the saints") can refer to either angels or believers. We support the position that Paul intended angels by the term translated "saints" in 1 Thessalonians 3:13. We offer the following reasons as justification.

First, there is no explicit biblical statement that saints—i.e., believers—will return with Christ at Armageddon unless this passage can be proven to refer to it. Second, scripture does support angelic accompaniment of the Lord at His *parousia*. The book of Jude quotes Enoch: "Look! The Lord is coming with thousands and thousands of his holy ones." By this verse, Jude indicates that thirty-five hundred years before Christ's incarnation, Enoch prophesied the glorious coming of Christ to earth with thousands of His angels (Jude 14). In 2 Thessalonians 1:6–8, Paul includes "His mighty angels" as an accompaniment in connection with the revelation of Jesus Christ from heaven to take vengeance on those who persecute the Thessalonians. Notice 2 Thessalonians 1:6–8:

> For after all it is only just for God to repay with affliction those who afflict you, and to give relief to you who are afflicted and to us as well when the Lord Jesus shall be revealed from heaven with His mighty angels in flaming fire, dealing out retribution to those who do not know God and to those who do not obey the gospel of our Lord Jesus.

Paul informs the Thessalonians that they can fully expect to get relief *anesis* (ἄνεσις = "relief, rest, relaxation") from their persecution (θλῖψις) at the revelation of the Lord Jesus from heaven. Paul, himself, expects to get relief at the Lord's revelation. The only way this passage could refer to

Armageddon specifically would be if Paul and the Thessalonians had already missed the rapture. The reader should not miss the clear fact that Paul includes himself among those who will find relief at the Lord's revelation.

Paul adds a note in 2 Thessalonians 1:9–10 concerning the timing of the revelation of Christ when both he and the Thessalonians will receive their long awaited relief. He writes, "And these will pay the penalty of eternal destruction...when He comes to be glorified in His saints on that day and to be marveled at among all who have believed" (2 Thess. 1:9–10). Naturally, pretribbers assign this passage to Christ's coming at Armageddon.

But a closer look will reveal the impossibility of this conclusion. At the revelation of Jesus Christ from heaven with His mighty angels in flaming fire, the tables will turn. The persecutors will become the persecuted and the persecuted will become the ones in relaxation. It is at this time that two things will happen. Verse 10 contains two purpose clauses. Having explained what the revelation of Jesus Christ will mean for the wicked, Paul turns his attention to God's people. There are two purposes connected with the Lord's coming: (1) to be glorified in His holy ones and (2) to be marveled at by all those who believe.

The first purpose clause ("to be glorified in His holy ones") is better understood to refer to angels. His mighty angels who accompany Him from heaven will do as they have always done (see Rev. 5:11–12). With respect to the first clause, Charles A. Wanamaker writes,

> The first clause was almost certainly constructed from the LXX version of Ps. 88:6 (89:7), which speaks of God ἐνδοξαζόμενος ἐν βουλῇ ἁγίων ("being glorified in the council of the saints"). [lxxxvii]

Concerning this verse, the notes to the NET Bible say, "a God who is honored in the great angelic assembly." This reflects the belief of the translators that *the saints* in Psalm 89:7 refers to angels.[lxxxviii] Given that Paul offers no clarification, his readers would have identified *the saints* as angels, as well. This is particularly the case in light of what follows in the second purpose clause.

The second purpose clause ("to be marveled at by all those who believe"), which is parallel to the first, clearly refers to believers. Paul further defines this second group by the phrase "and you [Thessalonians] did in fact believe our testimony." It seems that the group described as "all who have believed" first have the opportunity to marvel at the person of Christ on that "day." This "day" is the day in which we all shall see Him for the first time—Paul, the Thessalonians, you, and me. That Paul includes the Thessalonians in this event demands that it include the rapture. This is what the Thessalonians were waiting for (1 Thess. 1:9–10).

A second support for angelic accompaniment at the initiation of Christ's *parousia* is found in Matthew 13:36–43. Specifically, in this passage Christ instructs His disciples that the angels will be the reapers at the end of the age, when believers will be safely gathered and the wicked will be punished: "The Son of Man will send forth His angels, and they will gather out of His kingdom all stumbling blocks, and those who commit lawlessness" (v. 41). The Lord also stated in Matthew 16:27, "For the Son of Man is going to come in the glory of His Father with His angels; and will then recompense every man according to his deeds." This is consistent with His description in Matthew 24:31: "And He will send His angels with a great sound of a trumpet, and they will gather together His elect" and beautifully explains His earlier comments.

The third reason we believe *saints* in 1 Thessalonians 3:13 refers to angels is that there is no explicit biblical statement about Christ's return at Armageddon in 1 Thessalonians. While we understand that this is an argument from silence, Paul does innumerate those events that precede the Lord's return and specifically warns of the destruction to follow it. That destruction is clearly a part of the Armageddon campaign. The other specific events that compose the Armageddon event listed in Revelation 19:11–21 are not discussed in 1 Thessalonians. The great supper of God, Antichrist's destiny in the lake of fire, the bride's return to earth, the gathering of the nations at Armageddon, and the mark of the beast are not even mentioned in this letter.[lxxxix]

Notice also that it is the *parousia* that is the cutoff point for this passage. After the *parousia* occurs, this prayer either will have been answered or it won't. First Thessalonians 3:13 is a promise associated with God's intent to evacuate His people.

1 Thessalonians 4:15

The third occurrence of the term *parousia* in Paul's writings is 1 Thessalonians 4:15: "For we tell you this by the word of the Lord, that we who are alive, who are left until the coming of the Lord, will surely not go ahead of those who have fallen asleep." Paul instructs the Thessalonians that those who survive until the time of Christ's *parousia* will be taken to be with the Lord when He comes from heaven. This is an event certainly connected with the beginning of Christ's *parousia* when believers are removed and the wrath of God is poured out on those who remain.

Few rapturists debate the meaning and intent of this passage. Since we all believe that the elect must be removed from the earth before the wrath of God falls, this text must intend action associated with the initiation of the Lord's *parousia.*[6]

1 Thessalonians 5:23

The fourth instance occurs in 1 Thessalonians 5:23: "Now may the God of peace himself make you completely holy and may your spirit and soul and body be kept entirely blameless at the coming of our Lord Jesus Christ." Here, Paul prays that the Lord will preserve the Thessalonians blameless until the *parousia* of Christ. Echoing 1 Thessalonians 3:13, Paul again uses the same Greek expression. "In both places the construction is compendious; the writers' prayer is that their converts may be preserved entirely without fault *until* the Parousia and be so found *at* the Parousia, when they will be perfected in holiness."[xc] Paul emphasizes an action connected with the beginning of Christ's *parousia*. No indication is given that the Thessalonians need perseverance through Christ's *parousia*, but only up until or at the start of it, when believers will be transformed from mortal to immortality. At this point, perseverance will no longer be an issue for God's people.

---

[6] At this point, historical posttribbers will cry foul. We understand that there are those who would consider themselves "rapturists" who believe that the elect will be protected on the earth *through* the time when the wrath of God falls, just as the Israelites were protected during the plagues on Egypt and were not removed until after the plagues were over. However, the idea that God will lift believers up into the air, only to immediately bring them back to earth strains credulity. Such a view is a feeble attempt to make an allowance for Paul's teaching that believers will be taken up in the air. So, we are not convinced that true posttribbers are technically rapturists.

2 Thessalonians 2:1

The first instance of *parousia* in 2 Thessalonians occurs at 2 Thessalonians 2:1 and it reads, "Now brethren, concerning the coming [*parousia*] of our Lord Jesus Christ and our gathering together to Him, we ask you..." What Paul describes in 1 Thessalonians 4:15–17 in detail, he summarizes here. Paul places himself in the same category as the Thessalonians. They will be gathered together at the *parousia* of Christ. Most rapturists see this verse as referring to the rapture. Consistent with Paul's references in 1 Thessalonians, the emphasis is on the beginning of our Lord's *parousia*.

2 Thessalonians 2:8

The second occurrence of the term *parousia* in 2 Thessalonians can be found in 2 Thessalonians 2:8: "And then the lawless one will be revealed, whom the Lord will destroy by the breath of his mouth and wipe out by the manifestation of his arrival" (NET Bible, First Edition). Here, Paul acknowledges that Jesus will slay the lawless one "with the breath of His mouth" and "wipe [him] out by the manifestation of his arrival [*parousia*]." Pretribulationists debate this verse because of its obvious connection with the lawless one—Antichrist. They assign this verse to a second *parousia,* which they believe happens at Armageddon when Christ comes with His saints.

However, there is no *explicit* biblical statement that the church (the bride of Christ) accompanies Him at Armageddon.[7] There is no textually explicit indication that

---

[7] Most understand Revelation 19:14, which states, "The armies that are in heaven, dressed in white, clean, fine linen, were following him on white

there are two *parousia* events presented in the New Testament. There is a simple and more logical explanation. One other fact argues against the pretribulational interpretation of 2 Thessalonians 2:8: After Antichrist recovers from his wound, he is not physically killed again. Revelation 19:20 indicates that, at Armageddon, he will be "cast alive into the lake of fire burning with brimstone."

A closer examination of 2 Thessalonians 2:8 reveals that the verb "slay" does not have its usual literal meaning. Rather, "[T]he verb [which] is frequently used to designate murder; [here is metaphorical, suggesting that] the end of the lawless one will be as decisive as that of a man who is murdered."[xci] The translation "bring to an end" better explains Paul's intent. Leon Morris captures the essence of the verse when he writes, "In the present passage the verb refers to the robbing of the Man of Lawlessness of all significance, rather than to his destruction."[xcii]

Paul's intended meaning in 2 Thessalonians 2:8 is this: "And then that lawless one will be revealed whom the Lord will overthrow with the breath of His mouth and render insignificant by the appearance of His coming." Therefore, Paul is not indicating that Antichrist will be physically killed at a second *parousia* of the Lord, as pretribbers commonly teach. Rather, the Lord will diminish the significance of Antichrist. First, He will cut short the persecution by Antichrist by taking away the object of his persecution, as He predicted in Matthew 24:22. The church will be snatched away to heaven, which will embarrass Satan and Antichrist before the world. Then the trumpet and bowl judgments will make Satan and Antichrist's reign on earth a living hell. Revelation 16:13–14 indicates that Satan, the Antichrist, and the False Prophet will use demonic deception to convince the

---

horses," to be a reference to the church. However, this is an assumption based on silence and not an explicit statement in scripture.

---

world to come and fight at Armageddon. These facts signal a greatly diminished world leader.

Notice that Paul understands that the man of lawless will suffer at "the manifestation of His [the Lord's] coming." The emphasis is clearly on the beginning of the Lord's *parousia*.

1 Corinthians 15:23

The final place in the writings of Paul where the term *parousia* occurs is 1 Corinthians 15:23, which states, "But each one in his own order: Christ the first fruits, afterward those who are Christ's at His coming [*parousia*]." Paul informs the Corinthians, who were predominately Gentiles, that the next phase of the first resurrection will occur at Christ's *parousia*. The timing of the resurrection for the Corinthians is at the *parousia* of Jesus Christ.

Few would dispute that Paul emphasizes an action that is connected with the beginning of Christ's *parousia* here. It is important to recognize that, in all six verses where he uses the word *parousia,* Paul places the emphasis on the beginning of Christ's one and only *parousia*. However, what is abundantly clear is that events will follow the beginning of the Lord's *parousia* that relate to the wicked on this earth.

Use of 'Parousia' by Peter

2 Peter 1:16

The apostle Peter also makes a contribution to our discussion. He says, "For we did not follow cunningly devised fables when we made known to you the power and coming [*parousia*] of our Lord Jesus Christ, but were eyewitnesses of His majesty." Some have concluded that Peter is here discussing the first coming of Christ. However, Lenski argues, "The double terms have but one article: 'the power of our Lord Jesus Christ and Parousia,' so that 'power and Parousia' constitute one idea, 'power' bringing out the thought of the omnipotent might involved in the Lord's second coming."[xciii]

If so, it would appear that Peter is speaking of the beginning event connected with the Lord's *parousia*. If those who receive Peter's letter obey his instructions, they can have full assurance of their outcome. He writes in 2 Peter 1:11, "For thus an entrance into the eternal kingdom of our Lord and Savior, Jesus Christ, will be richly provided for you." It is this promise that Peter rehearses in 2 Peter 1:16–21.

2 Peter 3:3–4

Peter's second reference to Christ's *parousia* occurs in 2 Peter 3:3–4. Here, Peter informs his readers that "scoffers will come in the last days ... saying, 'Where is the promise of His coming [*parousia*]?'" Few would argue that this is not a reference to the beginning of the Lord's future ministry on earth—i.e., the rapture—given that once the church is removed from the earth, "all things" certainly will not continue as they were from the beginning of creation.

2 Peter 3:12

Peter's final reference occurs in 2 Peter 3:12. In this verse, it is "the day of God" that is coming (*parousia*). [xciv] Notice:

Since all these things are to melt away in this manner, what sort of people must we be, conducting our lives in holiness and godliness, while waiting for and hastening *the coming of the day of God*? Because of this day, the heavens will be burned up and dissolve and the celestial bodies will melt away in a blaze! But, according to his promise, we are waiting for new heavens and a new earth, in which righteousness truly resides. (2 Peter 3:11–13, italics added)

This question is important because, on its surface, there seems to be a contradiction between the apostles Peter and John. Both Peter and John indicate that the heavens (and elements) and the earth will, at some point in the future, cease to exist. If the two phrases are synonymous, then Peter seems to describe destruction before the temporal kingdom starts while John seems to describe destruction after the temporal kingdom ends.

Revelation 16:14 identifies "the great day of God" with the battle of Armageddon, which concludes the bowl judgments. This places "the great day of God" within or at the conclusion of the day of the Lord. Revelation 6:17 states, "the great day of their wrath" will come. God the Son will execute the wrath of God the Father following the seals of Revelation 6. Therefore, the wrath of God and the wrath of Christ occur during the same period. In light of this, we conclude that "the day of God" and "the day of the Lord" are synonymous. However, this still leaves the issue of the apparent contradiction between Peter and John.

We know that the extent of the destruction of the universe prior to the beginning of the temporal kingdom is great. The trumpet and bowl judgments outline significant cosmic destruction, which if taken literally, will require at least a substantial renovation of the earth at the beginning of the temporal kingdom. Just how extensive that renovation will be is the question. Will the present heavens and elements cease to exist prior to the beginning of the temporal kingdom as they will at its end (as suggested in Revelation 21:1), just prior to the beginning of the eternal kingdom?

We reconcile Peter and John by understanding Peter's description of what happens at the beginning of the day of the Lord. Revelation 6:12–17 explains that the day of the Lord begins with cosmic disturbances in the sun, moon, and stars, with the result that the universe is dark and the sky splits apart, exposing the earth to the brilliant light of heaven. This event Peter describes with metaphorical language of destruction and dissolution. The day of God, on the other hand, gives way for the temporal kingdom, which will require a "new" earth. Peter's term "new" (*kainos*) can refer to something new in time, new in a class, or previously unknown. Often the idea of "new in quality" predominates. The new heavens and earth are new in the sense that righteousness fills them rather than wickedness.

Here we find a reference to events that will transpire during the course of our Lord's *parousia*. The divine wrath that will destroy the created order begins after the removal of the church, which occurs at the beginning of Christ's *parousia*.

Use of 'Parousia' in John

The letters of John contain only one occurrence of the term *parousia*. "And now, little children, abide in Him, that if He appears, we may have confidence and not be ashamed before Him at His coming [*parousia*]" (1 John 2:28). John's use of that little word "if" introduces a third class condition, which indicates that something may or may not happen. What is conditional here is not the event itself (Christ will return), but the uncertainty of its timing.

The fact that John adds an element of uncertainty requires that we understand this passage as a reference to Christ's future ministry of removing the church before the wrath of God begins. There is uncertainty about the timing of the beginning of the Lord's *parousia,* but there is no uncertainty about the period following the conclusion of Daniel's Seventieth Week. Armageddon, as to timing and context, is fully detailed in the scriptures.[xcv]

Use of 'Parousia' in Matthew

The final four instances of *parousia* in the New Testament, with reference to the future ministry of Christ, occur in Matthew 24:3, 27, 37, and 39. Matthew 24:27, 37, and 39 use the term *parousia* in the fixed formula: "the coming of the Son of Man." These are the most unusual occurrences of the term *parousia* in the New Testament. Pretribbers attempt to make them a reference to the battle of Armageddon only rather than a reference to the overall event of Christ's coming, beginning with the rapture of the church. Otherwise, Matthew 24 applies to the church and seriously undermines pretribulationism.

As discussed earlier, Matthew's use of the term *parousia* fosters several questions. To answer those questions, we will have to consider several issues: (1) the date of Matthew's gospel; (2) the purpose of Matthew's gospel; (3) the construction of Matthew's gospel; and finally, (4) the significance of the term in Matthew 24.

The Date of Matthew's Gospel

The question of the date of Matthew's gospel is important because it will establish whether the term *parousia* had developed a technical significance in the Christian community. If James, Paul, Peter, and John (first epistle) wrote their works before Matthew, we are better able to understand the historical context from which Matthew developed his understanding of the term and what possible nuances were available when he wrote his gospel.

There is considerable debate among scholars concerning the dates of the writings that comprise the New Testament. The destruction of Jerusalem by the Romans in A.D. 70 is the breakpoint. Many would argue for a date significantly after or significantly before the destruction of Jerusalem, primarily because no author makes reference to the destruction of Jerusalem outside the predictions in Matthew 24, Mark 13, and Luke 21. The assumption of most is that, once fulfilled, an event specifically prophesied by Jesus and so significant in the history of the Jews could not and would not be skipped over by a New Testament author. Given that Matthew devotes two chapters to the Lord's comments about the destruction of Jerusalem (as most scholars teach), it is absolutely inconceivable that he could have known about the destruction of Jerusalem, which would have proven the Lord's prophetic words true, and not have mentioned it. For us, this is a decisive issue given Matthew's heavy emphasis on fulfillment.

Therefore, many scholars agree that Matthew's gospel was written before the destruction of the second temple in Jerusalem. The final destruction of Jerusalem occurred after the war that led to the ultimate destruction of Jerusalem began three-plus years earlier. In light of these factors, we date the composition of Matthew's gospel between five and ten years prior to the city's final destruction.[xcvi]

It is our thinking that Matthew wrote his gospel after James, Paul, Peter, and John wrote their epistles containing the term *parousia*, and that if his use of the term were different from theirs, he would certainly have offered some corrective insight. Matthew, on occasion, explains to his audience information that clarifies something he wrote. He explained Hebrew and Aramaic words so that his readers would better understand his points. He quotes Old Testament passages to explain New Testament events. In light of this pattern, we conclude that Matthew means the technical sense of the term *parousia* as Paul, Peter, James, and John did.

The Purpose of Matthew's Gospel

Unlike John in his gospel, Matthew does not offer his readers an explicit statement concerning his purpose. This has led some to conclude that "[a]ttempts to delineate a single narrow purpose are therefore doomed to failure."[xcvii] Perhaps the real issue is one of consensus. The purpose we may discover, but agreement is highly unlikely.

Concerning the purpose of Matthew's gospel, Dr. Daniel B. Wallace is helpful. He writes,

> The *purposes* of this gospel are certainly manifold.... Nevertheless, there do seem to be three main objectives. First, this gospel was written to demonstrate that Jesus was the Messiah.... Second, the book was written to give an answer to the question, "If Jesus is the Messiah, why did he fail to establish his kingdom".... Third, the gospel was written to confirm the legitimacy of the Gentile mission.... (emphasis in original)[xcviii]

Wallace illustrates what one must do absent an explicit purpose statement: examine what is written and extrapolate back to a general purpose. Recently, scholars have begun to look at New Testament writings through the lens of narrative criticism.[8] Of particular interest is the matter of *plot*. Simply put, plot is the "why" for the things that happen in a story.

Mark A. Powell argues convincingly that the primary plot of Matthew's gospel is "God's plan and Satan's challenge."[xcix] In essence, Matthew's plot "concerns the divine plan by which God's people will be saved from their sins."[c] God intends to save His people through Jesus. Who, why, when, where, and how undergird the gospel of Matthew. At the same time, the resistance God's plan encounters hold these together. Satan and his surrogates attempt to prevent the divine plan from unfolding.

Satan's attempts to thwart God's plan are multi-phased. Two of these Powell recognizes as subplots involving the religious leaders and the disciples. Ultimately, Jesus overcomes all resistance and God's plan goes forth to capture all He intends to save. While the reader receives sufficient information regarding how Satan intends to thwart God's plan, few details are given concerning who Satan is, why he is the leader of the resistance, where he came from, or when the resistance started. This is not the case with Jesus. Matthew devotes significant material to developing our knowledge of Jesus.

It is this detail that provides an explanation for Matthew's use of the term *parousia* in his reporting of the Olivet Discourse. Matthew develops the primary aspect of the identity of Jesus: His kingship, which directly threatens Satan and non-elect mankind, more so than any other.

---

[8] Narrative criticism is a relatively recent approach in literary interpretation. As a technical term, it is particularly used in biblical exegesis. Based on the recognition that many biblical texts are stories, including the four canonical gospels and major parts of the Hebrew Bible, narrative criticism uses models and questions derived from modern literary theory to interpret them. See http://en.wikipedia.org/wiki/Narrative_criticism.

Matthew repeatedly establishes Jesus' kingship throughout the book. Each chapter contains at least one reference to it. Notice the following chart:

Kingship References in Matthew

	Reference	Meaning	Significance
Matt. 1:1	Son of David	The Davidite	Royal Lineage
Matt. 2:2	King of the Jews	King by Birth	Divine Appointment
Matt. 3:17	My Beloved Son	Coronation Formula	Divine Confirmation
Matt. 4:17	Kingdom of Heaven	Reign of God	Kingly Realm
Matt. 5:3	Kingdom of Heaven	Reign of God	Kingly Realm
Matt. 6:9	Your Kingdom Come	Reign of God	Kingly Authority
Matt. 7:29	Authority	Dominion	Messianic
Matt. 8:29	Son of God	Descent	Divine
Matt. 9:27	Son of David	The Davidite	Royal Lineage
Matt. 10:23	Son of Man	Descent	Human
Matt. 11:19	Son of Man	Descent	Human
Matt. 12:8	Kingdom of God	Reign of God	Kingly Realm
Matt. 13:41	His Kingdom	Reign of God	Kingly Realm
Matt. 14:33	God's Son	Descent	Divine
Matt. 15:22	Son of David	The Davidite	Royal Lineage
Matt. 16:13	Son of Man	Descent	Human
Matt. 17:22	Son of Man	Descent	Human
Matt. 18:1	Kingdom of Heaven	Reign of God	Kingly Realm
Matt. 19:28	His Glorious Throne	Reign of God	Kingly Realm
Matt. 20:21	Your Kingdom	Reign of God	Kingly Realm
Matt. 21:5	Behold Your King	Coronation	Confirmation
Matt. 22:44	Lord	Master	Allegiance
Matt. 23:39	Lord	Master	Allegiance
Matt. 24:3, 27	Parousia	Regal	Kingly Return
Matt. 25:34	The King	Dominion	Messianic
Matt. 26:7	Anointing	Coronation	Confirmation
Matt. 27:11	King of the Jews	Dominion	Messianic
Matt. 28	All Authority	Dominion	Messianic

An explicit statement that Jesus is Israel's king occurs in Matthew 21. This chapter begins with Matthew's account of the event that is often referred to as the Lord's "triumphal entry" into Jerusalem, which begins His final week on earth prior to His crucifixion, death, burial, and resurrection. Matthew 21:1–10 (NIV) states,

As they approached Jerusalem and came to Bethphage on the Mount of Olives, Jesus sent two disciples, saying to them, "Go to the village ahead of you, and at once you will find a donkey tied there, with her colt by her. Untie them and bring them to me. If anyone says anything to you, tell him that the Lord needs them, and he will send them right away." This took place to fulfill what was spoken through the prophet: "Say to the Daughter of Zion, 'See, your king comes to you, gentle and riding on a donkey, on a colt, the foal of a donkey.'" The disciples went and did as Jesus had instructed them. They brought the donkey and the colt, placed their cloaks on them, and Jesus sat on them. A very large crowd spread their cloaks on the road, while others cut branches from the trees and spread them on the road. The crowds that went ahead of Him and those that followed shouted, "Hosanna to the Son of David!" "Blessed is He who comes in the name of the Lord!" "Hosanna in the Highest!" When Jesus entered Jerusalem, the whole city was stirred and asked, "Who is this?"

Matthew answers their question. It is Jesus, your King. Interestingly, Jesus comes as a sovereign king, but in peace. This is in contrast to His coming described in the Olivet Discourse, where He comes in judgment. In peace, He rides on a donkey, but in judgment, He rides on the clouds as the divine cloud rider, who rescues the righteous and punishes the wicked.

Dr. Allen Ross comments,

Matthew…records the verses from the prophet Zechariah to say that this event was the fulfillment of that oracle…. The introductory words of the prophecy come from Isaiah 62:11 but the main part of it from Zechariah 9:9.... If we look at Zechariah more closely, the first "burden" begins in chapter 9 and continues through chapter 11. It concerns the anointed King who would be rejected. The second burden, beginning in chapter 12 and going through 14, concerns the rejected King who would be enthroned. This is clearly, then, the part of the prophecy leading up to the rejection and death of messiah. The core of the oracle is that the King would enter the holy city with humility and peace, riding on a donkey, on a colt, the foal of a donkey.... By this entry Jesus was compelling the people to recognize Him, at least for the moment, as the coming King predicted in Zechariah. They would have to consider this event in the light of that prediction.[ci]

In light of Matthew's explicit statements concerning the Lord's kingship both prior to and after chapter twenty-four, his insertion of the term *parousia* makes perfect sense. The term was another way for Matthew to make an explicit statement concerning the kingship of Jesus Christ. It powerfully portrays His return in language befitting the eternal king. It is simply another avenue to build his case that Jesus is the King of the Jews. That Matthew inserted the technical term for the Lord's return signals his intent to influence his readers' understanding of his use of the Olivet Discourse. The question regarding why Matthew inserted this term relates to the composition of Matthew's gospel.[cii]

The Construction of Matthew's Gospel

There are those who concern themselves with how the writers of the gospels composed their writings. The prevailing opinion is that Matthew used three sources: (1) the gospel of Mark; (2) an oral tradition designated Q;[9] and (3) other oral materials designated M.[10] Since so much of the material in Matthew's gospel is verbatim from Mark's gospel, most see Matthew's gospel as an expansion of Mark. Matthew also uses material that is common to Luke's gospel, but not in Mark.

Of particular importance to our discussion is the relationship between the Olivet Discourse in Matthew and the Discourse in Mark and Luke. It is thought that the discourses in Matthew and Mark are significantly similar. Luke's discourse appears to be different both in terms of content and emphasis. However, how does this explain Matthew's use of the term *parousia* four times and Mark and Luke's lack of usage?

A comparison of the disciples' questions in Matthew, Mark, and Luke is helpful:

A Comparison of the Disciples' Question

Matthew 24:3	Mark 13:4	Luke 21:7
When will these things be?	When will these things be?	When will these things happen?
What will be the sign of Your coming and of the end of the age?	What will be the sign when all these things are going to be fulfilled?	What will be the sign when these things are about to take place?

Matthew's alteration of the second question of Peter, James, John, and Andrew[ciii] is very informative. Douglas Hare writes, "The key to Matthew's understanding of the entire discourse is provided by the critical changes he makes in the

---

[9] Q represents the German word *Quelle*, which means "source." Many scholars believe that Matthew and Luke used a second source to compile their gospel accounts. This special source is designated as Q.

[10] The Letter M represents that material that is unique to Matthew's gospel.

material taken over from Mark at Mt. 24:3."[civ] Therefore, Matthew is no longer addressing the historical destruction of Jerusalem. Rather, with the addition of "Your *parousia*" and "the end of the age," he focuses his readers to the Lord's return only—a return that Matthew couches in regal language to once again emphasize the kingship of Jesus.

The Significance of the Term in Matthew 24

By Matthew's insertion of the term *parousia* into his discussion of the Olivet Discourse, he accomplishes two things: (1) he establishes direct applicability for the church; and (2) he forms a commentary on the exposition of James, Paul, Peter, and John's understanding of the Lord's eschatological return. We are able to dispel the pretribulational notion that the New Testament speaks of two *parousia*s of the Lord Jesus. Rather, there is only one *parousia*, and it has multiple phases.

Chapter Four
The Church Fathers Taught Direct Applicability

One final support for the applicability of Matthew 24 to the church concerns the interpretation of those who immediately followed the generation of the apostles—the church fathers. Until A.D. 325, the fathers consistently taught the applicability of Matthew 24 to the church. However, this fact alone does not automatically mean that we should adopt their position. The church fathers were mere interpreters of history and scripture as we are. They provide a historical reference point for us, since we are two millennia removed from the original writers of New Testament scripture. Therefore, we do not follow them blindly; nor do we reject their conclusions out of hand. Rather, we compare their conclusions with the scriptures. If their conclusions comport with scripture, we see no reason to abandon their convictions regarding the matter of our Lord's return.

Dr. Larry V. Crutchfield (who holds a pretribulational rapture position), professor of Early Christian History and Culture at Columbia Theological Seminary, has read and written on the post-apostolic fathers. His research has led him to label the end-time views of the earliest fathers "imminent intratribulationism."[cv] Crutchfield states, "It [imminent intratribulationism] is perhaps more descriptive of the tribulational views of the millenarian fathers."[cvi]

He argues:

> The reason for this peculiar hybrid is that...
> Scripture clearly teaches that Christ's coming could
> occur at any moment.... On the other hand, until
> Constantine's Edict of Milan... persecution of
> every sort [was] a present reality for believers in
> the Roman Empire. For many, this coupled with
> the belief that Christians must be tested and
> purified by fire...led to something like the
> Thessalonian error.... The church, it was thought
> was already in the Tribulation and could therefore
> expect the any-moment return of the Lord.D[cvii]

We take issue with Crutchfield regarding his
assessment that the fathers were "led to something like the
Thessalonian error."[cviii]. Crutchfield's compelling statement
and its implication raise several critical questions. First, why
would the church fathers understand the Lord's return as
imminent only in the context of persecution? Second, where
did they get the notion that purification of the church would
precede the Lord's return? Third, where did the church
fathers get the notion that the church would experience the
persecution of Satan and his Antichrist? There are two
passages that could form the basis of this belief—
Matthew 24:4–31 and 2 Thessalonians 2:1–12. Let's turn our
attention to the writings of the fathers to separate truth from
falsehood regarding what they actually wrote.

The Didache

No document is of greater interest to our discussions
concerning the early church's view of the timing of the
Lord's return than the Didache (pronounced DID-uh-kay) or
The Teachings of the Twelve Apostles. Joseph Verheyden

concludes, "It is here that one finds the closest parallels to the eschatological discourse of Matthew."[cix]

Concerning the issue of dating the Didache, Dr. Bruce M. Metzger writes, "[M]ost [scholars] prefer a date in the first half of the second century."[cx] However, this date refers to the final edited composition and not necessarily to the independent collections that make up the final document.

Kurt Niederwimmer comments, "This document, which is approximately the length of Paul's letter to the Galatians, consists of four clearly separate sections."[cxi] J.A. Kleist adds, "The Didache purports to be an instruction based on the sayings of the Lord and given by the Twelve Apostles to pagans who wished to become Christians."[cxii] By definition, this requires an editor who collected the "sayings" and crafted them into a unified whole.

The fourth and final section of the Didache, Didache 16, is at the heart of our discussion. It is eschatological in nature. It consists of a short eschatological exhortation to holiness (16:1–2) and a brief description of the sequencing of the Lord's return (16:3–8). Given that the gospel of Mark, which many scholars assign priority, indicates that Jesus spoke an extended eschatological discourse (the Olivet Discourse) prior to His crucifixion and that Matthew and Luke record a similar version (although with significant differences from the gospel of Mark), it seems that either an oral or written copy of the Lord's pronouncement was widely known.[cxiii]

There is no explicit historical evidence that connects any of the original twelve disciples with the actual writing of the Didache. It does not claim direct apostolic authorship. However, this document enjoyed a very favorable position among believers in the second, third, and fourth centuries.

The decision to exclude the Didache from the New Testament canon took a number of years. During the early years before the canon received finalization, the Didache enjoyed a favorable status. Some scholars have insisted that it was thus counted by some as part of the New Testament canon. Eusebius' inclusion of the Didache in his canonical list is the basis of this conclusion.

Eusebius (A.D. 260–340) is known as "The Father of Church History."[cxiv] In Eusebius' book, *Ecclesiastical History*, written in A.D. 325, one finds materials covering the first three hundred years of church history. It is in this great work of Eusebius that we find one of the earliest lists of the books of the New Testament canon. He classifies the writings into four categories: (1) recognized, (2) disputed, (3) spurious, and (4) heretical. In the "recognized" category, Eusebius places the four gospels, the Book of Acts, the Epistles of Paul, 1 John, and 1 Peter. The final book of this category is the Apocalypse of John.

In the "disputed" category, Eusebius lists the epistles of James and Jude, the second epistle of Peter, and the second and third epistles of John. Among the "spurious" books, Eusebius' third category, we find the Acts of Paul, the Shepherd, the Apocalypse of Peter, the epistle of Barnabas, the Didache, the Apocalypse of John, and the gospel of Hebrews. In Eusebius' final category, designated "heretical," he lists the gospels of Peter, Thomas, and Matthias, and the Acts of Andrew, John, and other apostles.

While the term *spurious* in modern speech has a negative connotation, it did not have negative connotations during Eusebius' time. Rather, *spurious* described books not included in the New Testament as scripture but having value for the church.[cxv] Notice that Eusebius places the Apocalypse (Revelation) of John in both the recognized and spurious categories. It is clear that Eusebius was struggling to make sense of the material available to him at that time. We can easily criticize him. However, our point is simply that he accepted some books and rejected others on the basis of their content and authorship.

The heretical books were never acceptable. Eusebius makes a very interesting comment concerning the heretical category. He writes:

> [T]he thought and purport of their contents are completely out of harmony with true orthodoxy and clearly show themselves that they are the forgeries of heretics. For this reason they ought not to be reckoned among the spurious books, but are to be cast aside as altogether absurd and impious.[cxvi]

The heretical books have no value whatsoever as it relates to God's communications to His church. Eusebius offers compelling support that the Didache was well known and well favored by the early church fathers. In a document written forty years after Eusebius' book, Athanasius of Alexandria writes:

> After listing the canonical writings of the Old and New Testaments...[Eusebius] mentions..."other books not recognized as canonical, but recommended by our ancestors for reading by those who have recently entered and wish to learn the word of faith"—that is, books that, although not included in the canon, nevertheless enjoy a certain regard as...books approved by the church and, accordingly, appropriate reading for baptismal candidates.[cxvii]

Athanasius not only accepts the Didache, but also encourages its use for training new believers in the fundamentals of the faith. That is compelling! The early fathers saw nothing wrong with the teachings contained in this document. The decision to reject the Didache as non-canonical did not negate its usefulness to the church. Therefore, we can take Didache 16, which deals with the return of Christ, as consistent with the beliefs of early church fathers. There is not one recorded criticism of the eschatology contained in the Didache by the early church fathers.

Chapter sixteen follows below.[cxviii]

> Be watchful for your life; let your lamps not be quenched and your loins not ungirdled, but be ready; for you know not the hour in which our Lord comes. And you shall gather yourselves together frequently, seeking what is fitting for your souls; for the whole time of your faith shall not profit you, if you be not perfected at the last season. For in the last days the false prophets and corrupters shall be multiplied, and the sheep shall be turned into wolves, and love shall be turned into hate. For as lawlessness increases, they shall hate one another and shall persecute and betray. And then the world-deceiver shall appear as a son of God; and shall work signs and wonders, and the earth shall be delivered into his hands; and he shall do unholy things, which have never been since the world began. Then all created mankind shall come to the fire of testing, and many shall be offended and perish; but they that endure in their faith shall be saved by the Curse Himself. And then shall the signs of the truth appear; first a sign of a rift in the heaven, then a sign of a voice of a trumpet, and thirdly a resurrection of the dead; Yet, not of all, but as it was said The Lord shall come and all His saints with Him.[cxix] Then shall the world see the Lord coming upon the clouds of heaven.

The knowledgeable reader will detect a very strong relationship between Matthew 24 and Didache 16.[cxx]

Reference	Didache	Matthew 24
Watch	v. 1	v. 42
The hour	v. 1	v. 42; 44
False prophets	v. 3	v. 11
Love to hate	v. 3	v. 12
Lawlessness increase	v. 4	v. 12
Hate one another	v. 4	v. 10
Betray	v. 4	v. 10
Signs/wonders	v. 4	v. 24
Unparalleled season	v. 4	v. 21
Many offended	v. 5	v. 10
Endure in faith	v. 5	v. 13
Sign appears	v. 6	v. 30
Sign in the heaven	v. 6	v. 30
Trumpet	v. 6	v. 31
The Lord coming upon the clouds of heaven	v. 8	v. 30

Less certain is the nature of the relationship between the Didache and Matthew 24. That is, does Matthew depend on the Didache or vice versa? Or is there a source common to both?

Joseph Verheyden states, "Matthew is the source for the Didache."[cxxi] Verheyden offers the charge, "So here is a final warning and exhortation: when reading the Didache, watch Matthew!"[cxxii] Until recently, this was the majority view regarding the relationship between Matthew and the Didache.

However, in a recent work, *The Gospel of Matthew's Dependence on the Didache*, by Alan J. P. Garrow, a different view emerges. He argues that "it is most likely that Matthew knew the Didache's apocalypse in its present context, rather than as an independently existing tradition."[cxxiii] Garrow ably demonstrates that at each and every place where Matthew 24 and Didache 16 demonstrate the presence of material held in common, Didache 16 has a non-Markan eccentricity.[cxxiv] In other words, the only material Matthew 24 and Didache 16 have in common is that material in Matthew 24 that is not common to the gospel of Mark. Garrow concludes,

> [I]n view of the numerous other points of contact between the rest of the Didache and Matthew's Gospel[14] it is more likely that Matthew knew *Did.* 16.3–6, 8–9 as the conclusion of 'The Teaching of the Lord, by the Twelve Apostles, to the Gentiles', and thus used it to supplement Mark's words of Jesus with regard to the events of the End.

The point that Garrow is making is this: The best possible explanation for the similarities and differences between Matthew 24 and Didache 16 is that the material of Didache 16 predates Matthew 24.[cxxv] This is a critical point for our discussion. If Garrow is correct and Matthew and Mark were influenced by the end-time materials of Didache 16, then this adds weight to our conclusion. The eschatology of Didache 16 was not objectionable to the New Testament writers, but formed one of the bases of their writings.

There certainly is room for debate about the relationship between the Didache and the Gospels regarding the matter of sources. Garrow's conclusions are not widely accepted. However, there is no debate about the overall content of the sixteenth chapter of the Didache. In any event, what is most important to our discussion concerns the eschatological position reflected in the two books. The ambiguity of Matthew 24:31 regarding whether or not the resurrection is in focus is explicit in Didache 16:6. Both the authors of the Didache and the early church fathers applied the words of Jesus that we now have in Matthew 24 to the church. Both the authors of the Didache and the early church fathers applied Matthew 24 to the church.

Justin Martyr

Prior to A.D. 325, several church fathers could demonstrate a conviction concerning the applicability of Matthew 24 to the church. For our purposes, we shall consider but one—Justin Martyr, primarily because he was the first church apologist.[11] Writing in response to the attacks against Christianity from both Judaism and Roman paganism, Justin Martyr and others wrote to confront the lies and distortions espoused against Christ and His Beloved. Justin Martyr reports his response to God's drawing:

> ...straightway a flame was kindled in my soul; and a love of the prophets, and of those men who are friends of Christ, possessed me; and whilst revolving his words in my mind, I found this philosophy alone to be safe and profitable. Thus, and for this reason, I am a philosopher.[cxxvi]

Even though Justin was a prolific writer, only three of his works have survived: two separate *Apologies*, which were composed at Rome, and the *Dialogue* with a Jew named Trypho, which holds importance for our discussion.

---

[11] With regard to the designation "apologist," *The New International Dictionary of the Christian Church* says that it was "given to a number of early Christian writers (c.120–220) who belonged to a period in history when the growing Christian Church was meeting with ever-increasing hostility in every department of public life.... They worked on the frontier of the Church, seeking to defend the Faith from misrepresentation and attack, commending it to the inquirer and demonstrating the falsity of both Judaism and Polytheism" (J. D. Douglas, ed., *The New International Dictionary of the Christian Church* [Grand Rapids: Zondervan Publishing House, 1974], p. 57). Therefore, we shall place a greater weight on the writings of these men because of the gravity of the circumstance under with which they composed and wrote their arguments.

That Justin Martyr taught the return of Christ in the context of tribulation is undeniable and without debate. He taught that Jesus Christ came "as suffering, inglorious, dishonoured, and crucified,"[cxxvii] with regard to His first advent. However, in connection with His return, "He shall come from heaven with glory, accompanied by His angelic host...."[cxxviii]

Justin Martyr clearly believed that the Lord's return would be directly connected to the reign of Antichrist. He writes,

> He [Jesus Christ] shall come from heaven with glory, when the man of apostasy, who speaks strange things against the Most High, shall venture to do unlawful deeds on the earth against us the Christians.[cxxix]

Similarly, he connects the future persecution at the hands of the man of apostasy with Daniel's Seventieth Week. He writes,

> [A]nd he whom Daniel foretells would have dominion for a time, and times, and an half, is even already at the door, about to speak blasphemous and daring things against the Most High. But you, being ignorant of how long he will have dominion, hold another opinion. For you interpret the 'time' as being a hundred years. But if this is so, the man of sin must, at the shortest, reign three hundred and fifty years, in order that we may compute that which is said by the holy Daniel—'and times'—to be *two* times only. All this I have said to you in digression, in order that you at length may be persuaded of what has been declared against you by God, that you are foolish sons.[cxxx]

In summarizing the beliefs of Justin Martyr, Larry Crutchfield states,

> What emerges from all of this is that Justin expected the Antichrist to appear soon, speak blasphemous things against God, and continue the persecution of the saints begun by the Roman state. While the details of the commencement and duration of Antichrist's reign with relation to his appearing are not made clear by Justin, he certainly believed that it was in the context of ongoing persecution that Christ would come to rescue those who trust in Him…. The essentials of Justin's outline of end-time events have already been given above. So here we present only a summary outline without commentary: 1) Appearance of the man of apostasy; 2) Second Advent of Christ; 3) Battle of Armageddon; 4) First resurrection; 5) Millennium; 6) Second resurrection; 7) General judgment of all; and 8) The eternal state, proceeded by conflagration, then renewal.[cxxxi]

Assuming Crutchfield is correct, and knowing Justin Martyr's conviction to found his beliefs on scripture, we hasten to ask, "What is the scriptural basis for Martyr's claim?"[12] To answer this question, we must turn to the writings of Irenaeus.

---

[12] Of course, pretribbers or others who want to discredit Justin Martyr might point to areas where his positions were badly at odds with scripture. For example, there are things he wrote that (as far as we can tell) really look as though he believed in baptismal regeneration. However, such reasoning begs the question. Whether Justin Martyr is right or wrong in his eschatology must be determined from scripture and by not a comparison of how many things we agree and disagree with him about.

Irenaeus

To gain a better appreciation of the biblical basis of the early fathers' eschatology, we turn to the writings of Irenaeus, a third-generation Christian and disciple of a disciple of the Apostle John.[cxxxii] Philip Schaff, a student of the early fathers, characterizes Irenaeus as "neither very original nor brilliant, but eminently sound and judicious."[cxxxiii] Of the important works written by Irenaeus, only two survive. *Against Heresies* has proven to be of invaluable help to us in understanding the basis of the early fathers' theology as it relates to their view of scripture. The second surviving work of Irenaeus is helpful in that it provides information concerning the core beliefs of the early church after the Apostles.

Crutchfield concludes that "The centerpiece of Irenaeus' teaching on the time of the tribulation and the relationship of the church to it seems to be the prophecies of Daniel 7:7–8, 23–25…and Revelation 17:12."[cxxxiv] However, Irenaeus explicitly states that the church will experience the persecution of Antichrist,[cxxxv] and we fail to understand how a dispensational-leaning Irenaeus could draw such a conclusion on the basis of the book of Daniel—particularly given that the term *church* or the entity as such does not appear in the Old Testament or in Revelation 4–19 by explicit reference.

It would appear that Crutchfield failed to appreciate Irenaeus' inclusion of Matthew 24 and 2 Thessalonians 2 in that centerpiece.

In Book V, Chapter XXV, Irenaeus writes,

[A]s the Lord also declares: "But when you shall see the abomination of desolation, which has been spoken of by Daniel the prophet, standing in the holy place (let him that reads understand), then let those who are in Judea flee into the mountains; and he who is upon the house-top, let him not come down to take anything out of his house: for there shall then be great hardship, such as has not been from the beginning of the world until now, nor ever shall be."[cxxxvi]

Later in the same chapter, he again states,

From all these passages are revealed to us, not merely the particulars of the apostasy, and [the doings] of him who concentrates in himself every satanic error, but also, that there is one and the same God the Father, who was declared by the prophets, but made manifest by Christ. For if what Daniel prophesied concerning the end has been confirmed by the Lord, when He said, "When you shall see the abomination of desolation, which has been spoken of by Daniel the prophet"....[cxxxvii]

Finally, in Book V, Chapter XIX, Irenaeus states,

And therefore, when in the end the Church shall be suddenly caught up from this, it is said, "There shall be tribulation such as has not been since the beginning, neither shall be." For this is the last contest of the righteous, in which, when they overcome they are crowned with incorruption.[cxxxviii]

Irenaeus also utilized the second chapter of 2 Thessalonians. He writes,

And again, in the Second to the Thessalonians, speaking of Antichrist, he says, "And then shall that wicked be revealed, whom the Lord Jesus Christ shall slay with the Spirit of His mouth, and shall destroy him with the presence of his coming; [even him] whose coming is after the working of Satan, with all power, and signs, and lying wonders." Now in these [sentences] the order of the words is this: "And then shall be revealed that wicked, whose coming is after the working of Satan, with all power, and signs, and lying wonders, whom the Lord Jesus shall slay with the Spirit of His mouth, and shall destroy with the presence of His coming." For he does not mean that the coming of the Lord is after the working of Satan; but the coming of the wicked one, whom we also call Antichrist. If, then, one does not attend to the [proper] reading [of the passage], and if he do not exhibit the intervals of breathing as they occur, there shall be not only incongruities, but also, when reading, he will utter blasphemy, as if the advent of the Lord could take place according to the working of Satan. So therefore, in such passages, the hyperbaton must be exhibited by the reading, and the apostle's meaning following on, preserved; and thus we do not read in that passage, "the god of this world," but, "God," whom we do truly call God; and we hear [it declared of] the unbelieving and the blinded of this world, that they shall not inherit the world of life which is to come.[cxxxix]

He also states,

This he does, in order that they who do [now] worship the devil by means of many abominations, may serve himself by this one idol, of whom the apostle thus speaks in the second

Epistle to the Thessalonians: "Unless there shall come a falling away first, and the man of sin shall be revealed, the son of perdition, who opposes and exalts himself above all that is called God, or that is worshipped; so that he sits in the temple of God, showing himself as if he were God." The apostle therefore clearly points out his apostasy, and that he is lifted up above all that is called God, or that is worshipped—that is, above every idol—for these are indeed so called by men, but are not [really] gods; and that he will endeavour in a tyrannical manner to set himself forth as God.[cxl]

Thus, at least two explicit New Testament scriptural bases for the Irenaeus' position regarding the church's relationship to Daniel's Seventieth Week are found in Matthew 24 and 2 Thessalonians, chapter two.

Hippolytus

With Hippolytus, we move into the third century after the Lord's ministry on earth. The second century had proved to be an intense time of eschatological concern for those who followed Christ. Evidently, the coming of Christ had received some attention by heretical teachers of a sect known as the Montanists.

The man from whom this sect took its name claimed ordination by Christ as a prophet, speaking under the authority of the Holy Spirit. One particular element of his message was an expectation of the impending Second Advent of Christ and the establishment of His millennial rule on earth. To bring clarity to the confusion caused by the teachings of Montanus and his followers and other influences of the period, Hippolytus sought to set the record straight.

For Hippolytus, D. G. Dunbar concludes:

Scripture is the touchstone of truth. Failure to give close attention to scripture leads to self-deception and false teaching.... It is not sufficient, however, simply to counter heretical teachings with those of scripture, for even the heretics use the Bible and corrupt it to their own ends. Thus, there is need to oppose not only esoteric traditions but also individualistic misunderstanding of Scripture.... Hippolytus finds the solution to the problem in the doctrine of apostolic succession. It is the apostolic tradition, transmitted faithfully and, therefore, guaranteed by the succession of the bishops, which insures the proper interpretation of Scripture....

Given such an understanding of the interplay between Scripture and tradition, we would expect to find in Hippolytus not only a strong appeal to the Bible but also a pronounced reliance on the earlier eschatological exegesis of the church. Such reliance is what we do find—especially a reliance on Irenaeus. Thus, Irenaeus is the source not only for specific points of Hippolytean exegesis...but also for the overall eschatological approach....

There is, therefore, not a great deal of new material in Hippolytus. He does develop a few original themes; but by and large he is not an innovator but a preserver and collector of what has gone before. This suggests that in Hippolytus we find a kind of "main-line" eschatology, which may have been quite widespread during the closing decades of the second century.D[cxli]

Hippolytus explicitly states that the church will experience the persecution of Satan and his Antichrist. He said, "Now, concerning the tribulation of the persecution which is to fall upon the Church from the adversary...."[cxlii] Similarly, he states, "That refers to the one thousand two hundred and threescore days (the half of the week) during which the tyrant is to reign and persecute the Church...."[cxliii]

Below, in a rather extended section, we present Hippolytus' discussion of this topic. One of the problems of assessing the position of the church fathers is the often case of their words being taken out of context. Therefore, we quote in full length and without comment the words of this great man so that you, the reader, might draw your own conclusion regarding the meaning:

> Now, concerning the tribulation of the persecution which is to fall upon the Church from the adversary, John also speaks thus: "And I saw a great and wondrous sign in heaven; a woman clothed with the sun, and the moon under her feet, and upon her head a crown of twelve stars. And she, being with child, cries, travailing in birth, and pained to be delivered. And the dragon stood before the woman which was ready to be delivered, for to devour her child as soon as it was born. And she brought forth a man-child, who is to rule all the nations: and the child was caught up unto God and to His throne. And the woman fled into the wilderness, where she hath the place prepared of God, that they should feed her there a thousand two hundred and threescore days. And then when the dragon saw it, he persecuted the woman which brought forth the man-child. And to the woman were given two wings of the great eagle, that she might fly into the wilderness, where she is nourished for a time, and times, and half a time, from the face of the serpent. And the serpent cast (out of his mouth water as a flood after the woman, that he might cause her to be carried away of the flood. And the earth helped

the woman, and opened her mouth, and swallowed up the flood which the dragon cast) out of his mouth. And the dragon was wroth with the woman, and went to make war with the saints of her seed, which keep the commandments of God, and have the testimony of Jesus" [Revelation 12:1–6, 13–17].

By the woman, then clothed with the sun, "he meant most manifestly the Church, endued with the Father's word, whose brightness is above the sun." And by the "moon under her feet" he referred to her being adorned, like the moon, with heavenly glory. And the words, "upon her head a crown of twelve stars," refer to the twelve apostles by whom the Church was founded. And those, "she, being with child, cries, travailing in birth, and pained to be delivered," mean that the Church will not cease to bear from her heart the Word that is persecuted by the unbelieving in the world. "And she brought forth," he says, "a man-child, who is to rule all the nations;" by which is meant that the Church, always bringing forth Christ, the perfect man-child of God, who is declared to be God and man, becomes the instructor of all the nations. And the words, "her child was caught up unto God and to His throne," signify that he who is always born of her is a heavenly king, and not an earthly; even as David also declared of old when he said, "The Lord said unto my Lord, Sit Thou at my right hand, until I make Thine enemies Thy footstool." "And the dragon," he says, "saw and persecuted the woman which brought forth the man-child. And to the woman were given two wings of the great eagle, that she might fly into the wilderness, where she is nourished for a time, and times, and half a time, from the face of the serpent." That refers to the one thousand two hundred and threescore days (the half of the week) during which the tyrant is to reign and persecute the Church, which flees from city to city, and seeks concealment in the wilderness among the mountains, possessed of no other defense than the two wings of the great eagle, that is to say, the faith of Jesus Christ, who, in stretching forth His holy hands on the holy tree, unfolded two wings, the right and the left, and called to Him all who believed upon Him, and covered them as a hen her chickens. For by the mouth of Malachi also He speaks thus: "And unto you that fear my name shall the Sun of righteousness arise with healing in His wings."

The Lord also says, "When ye shall see the abomination of desolation stand in the holy place (whoso readeth, let him understand), then let them which be in Judea flee into the mountains, and let him which is on the housetop not come down to take his clothes; neither let him which is in the field return back to take anything out of his house. And woe unto them that are with child, and to them that give suck, in those days! for then shall be great tribulation, such as was not since the beginning of the world. And except those days should be shortened, there should no flesh be saved [Matthew 24:15–22]." And Daniel says, "And they shall place the abomination of desolation a thousand two hundred and ninety days. Blessed is he that waiteth, and cometh to the thousand two hundred and ninety-five days [Daniel 12:11–12]."

And the blessed Apostle Paul, writing to the Thessalonians, says: "Now we beseech you, brethren, concerning the coming of our Lord Jesus Christ, and our gathering together at it, that ye be not soon shaken in mind, or be troubled, neither by spirit, nor by word, nor by letters as from us, as that the day of the Lord is at hand. Let no man deceive you by any means; for (that day shall not come) except there come the falling away first, and that man of sin be revealed, the son of perdition, who opposeth and exalteth himself above all that is called God, or that is worshipped: so that he sitteth in the temple of God, showing himself that he is God. Remember ye not, that when I was yet with you, I told you these things? And now ye know what withholdeth, that he might be revealed in his time. For the mystery of iniquity doth already work; only he who now letteth (will let), until he be taken out of the way. And then shall that wicked be revealed, whom the Lord Jesus shall consume with the Spirit of His mouth, and shall destroy with the brightness of His coming: (even him) whose coming is after the working of Satan, with all power, and signs, and lying wonders, and with all deceivableness of unrighteousness in them that perish; because they received not the love of the truth. And for this cause God shall send them strong delusion, that they should believe a lie: that they all might be damned who believed not the truth, but had pleasure in unrighteousness [II Thess 2:1–12]." And Esaias says, "Let the wicked be cut off, that he behold not the glory of the Lord."

These things, then, being to come to pass, beloved, and the one week being divided into two parts, and the abomination of desolation being manifested then, and the two prophets and forerunners of the Lord having finished their course, and the whole world finally approaching the consummation, what remains but the coming of our Lord and Saviour Jesus Christ from heaven, for whom we have looked in hope? who shall bring the conflagration and just judgment upon all who have refused to believe on Him.

For the Lord says, "And when these things begin to come to pass, then look up, and lift up your heads; for your redemption draweth nigh [Luke 21:28]." "And there shall not a hair of your head perish." "For as the lightning cometh out of the east, and shineth even unto the west, so shall also the coming of the Son of man be. For wheresoever the carcase is, there will the eagles be gathered together [Matthew 24:27–28]." Now the fall took place in paradise; for Adam fell there. And He says again, "Then shall the Son of man send His angels, and they shall gather together His elect from the four winds of heaven [Matthew 28:31]." And David also, in announcing prophetically the judgment and coming of the Lord, says, "His going forth is from the end of the heaven, and His circuit unto the end of the heaven: and there is no one hid from the heat thereof." By the heat he means the conflagration. And Esaias speaks thus: "Come, my people, enter thou into thy chamber, (and) shut thy door: hide thyself as it were for a little moment, until the indignation of the Lord be overpast." And Paul in like manner: "For the wrath of God is revealed from heaven against all ungodliness and unrighteousness of men, who hold the truth of God in unrighteousness."

Moreover, concerning the resurrection and the kingdom of the saints, Daniel says, "And many of them that sleep in the dust of the earth shall arise, some to everlasting life, (and some to shame and everlasting contempt)." Esaias says, "The dead men shall arise, and they that are in their tombs shall awake; for the dew from thee is healing to them." The Lord says, "Many in that day shall hear the voice of the Son of God, and they that hear shall live." And the prophet says, "Awake, thou that sleepest, and arise from the dead, and Christ shall give thee light." And John says, "Blessed and holy is he that hath part in the first resurrection: on such the second death hath no power." For the second death is the lake of fire that burneth. And again the Lord says, "Then shall the righteous shine forth as the sun shineth in his glory." And to the saints He will say, "Come, ye blessed of my Father, inherit the kingdom prepared for you from the foundation of the world [Matthew 25:34]." But what saith He to the wicked? "Depart from me, ye cursed, into everlasting fire, prepared for the devil and his angels, which my Father hath prepared [Matthew 25:41]." And John says, "Without are dogs, and sorcerers, and whoremongers, and murderers, and idolaters, and whosoever maketh and loveth a lie; for your part is in the hell of fire." And in like manner also Esaias: "And they shall go forth and look upon the carcases of the men that have transgressed against me. And their worm shall not die, neither shall their fire be quenched; and they shall be for a spectacle to all flesh."

Concerning the resurrection of the righteous, Paul also speaks thus in writing to the Thessalonians: "We would not have you to be ignorant concerning them which are asleep, that ye sorrow not even as others which have no hope. For if we believe that Jesus died and rose again, even so them also which sleep in Jesus will God bring with Him. For this we say unto you by the word of the Lord, that we which are alive (and) remain unto the coming of the Lord, shall not prevent them which are asleep. For the Lord Himself shall descend from heaven with a shout, with the voice and trump of God, and the dead in Christ shall rise first. Then we which are alive (and) remain shall be caught up together with them in the clouds to meet the Lord in the air; and so shall we ever be with the Lord [I Thess 4:13–17]."

These things, then, I have set shortly before thee, O Theophilus, drawing them from scripture itself, in order that, maintaining in faith what is written, and anticipating the things that are to be, thou mayest keep thyself void of offence both toward God and toward men, "looking for that blessed hope and appearing of our God and Saviour," when, having raised the saints among us, He will rejoice with them, glorifying the Father. To Him be the glory unto the endless ages of the ages. Amen. [cxliv]

We trust you, the reader, to form your own opinions. Is it reasonable to conclude on the basis of what you just read that Hippolytus saw Matthew 24 as applicable to the church?

Conclusion

That the early church applied our Lord's remarks in Matthew 24 to their own context does not prove that their interpretation was correct. We are not to follow their writings blindly. However, there is nothing that compels us to turn away from their conclusions, for their conclusions do not contradict scripture—just the opposite is true. The applicability of Matthew 24 to the church cannot be denied simply because of its Jewish audience. Such arguments serve only to blind students of scripture to these important teachings.

Chapter Five
The Composition of Matthew 24:1–31

The Olivet Discourse (or, as scholars are apt to call it, "the eschatological discourse") is a series of pronouncements by the Lord Jesus concerning His physical return. In varying percentages, Matthew, Mark, and Luke contain this important discourse. Matthew dedicates chapters 24–25 to this one topic. Matthew 26:1–2 informs us, "When Jesus had finished all these words [of the Olivet Discourse] He said to His disciples, 'You know that after two days the Passover is coming, and the Son of Man is to be handed over for crucifixion.'" To read about what happened between those two days, we consult John 13:31–17:26, where we read among other things that our Lord promised the disciples that He would go to prepare a special place for them in His Father's mansion, after which He would come and take them to it. Thus, *two nights* before our Lord died, He discussed His return and its close proximity to the end of the age. On the *night* before He died, He told the disciples that when He returned He would take them to specially prepared living quarters (John 14:1–3). What is the relationship between the Lord's return detailed in Matthew 24–25 and His return promised in John 14:1–3?

Sadly, pretribulationists and preterists have so confused many believers that they see little or no application for modern saints in these passages. It is unfortunate that many believers do not understand Matthew 24 and thus miss the blessing of having a clear view of the *parousia* of the Lord Jesus. Having demonstrated the applicability of Matthew 24 to the church, let's examine the unique composition of Matthew 24:1–31.

The Context

Matthew 24–25 is a lengthy section that reveals the sequence of events connected with our Lord's return and ultimate reign upon the earth. Matthew 24 begins with a prophetic announcement by Jesus that the then-standing temple in Jerusalem would soon suffer destruction. Matthew 24:1–2 reports:

> Now as Jesus was going out of the temple courts and walking away, his disciples came to show him the temple buildings. And he said to them, "Do you see all these things? I tell you the truth, not one stone will be left on another. All will be torn down!"

After the Lord's prophetic announcement that Jerusalem and her inhabitants would suffer destruction due to their behavior in connection with His ministry (cf. 23:37–38), Matthew resumes the Lord's comments. However, at this point, Jesus is no longer in the temple court. As He is leaving the temple, on His way to Bethany by way of the Mount of Olives, He is stopped by the disciples to discuss the beauty of the temple complex.

Perhaps in response to the Lord's announcement that Jerusalem would be left desolate, the disciples call for Jesus to marvel at the temple complex. To this, Jesus responds with an explicit pronouncement that the temple would be completely destroyed. Such a drastic pronouncement would naturally engender more questions.

Matthew's Questions

> Having reached the Mount of Olives, as the Lord sat, his disciples came to him privately and said, "Tell us, when will these things happen? And what will be the sign of your coming and of the end of the age?"

Matthew's resumption of the disciples' education on the Mount of Olives is instructive. The disciples' original questions clearly focused on the timing of the destruction of the temple. According to Mark and Luke's account, the Lord responded to their questions with detailed information sufficient to recognize the fulfillment. However, it is at this point that the purpose of Matthew's gospel diverges from that of Mark and Luke. A comparison of the questions in the three gospel accounts exposes this change. *This is the most critical factor in understanding what Matthew wrote and what he intended his readers to understand with respect to chapters 24–25. This point is so critical that to miss it guarantees the interpreter shall error in his or her interpretation of what Matthew wrote.*[13]

Notice the three gospels' portrayal of the questions of the Lord's followers:

---

[13] The importance of this point explains the false notions of the preterists and pretribulationists because they totally misunderstand Matthew because they read into this gospel what they found in Mark and Luke, a point we shall demonstrate shortly.

Matthew 24:3	Mark 13:4	Luke 21:7
When will these things be?	When will these things be?	When will these things happen?
What will be the sign of Your coming and of the end of the age?	What will be the sign when all these things are going to be fulfilled?	What will be the sign when these things are about to take place?

It is quickly evident that Matthew's questions are distinct from those recorded by Mark and Luke. The key to a correct interpretation of Matthew 24–25 is the recognition that Matthew signals a change in focus and purpose by how he alters the second question of the disciples. Mark 13:3 limits the actual number of disciples who questioned Jesus to Peter, James, John, and Andrew. It is therefore patently clear that Matthew must have received the Olivet Discourse from someone other than Jesus. It is probable that Matthew, Mark, and Luke received the discourse from either or a combination of (1) Peter, James, John, and/or Andrew; (2) oral tradition; or (3) written sources. Since it is a known fact that John was alive within a few years of the destruction of Jerusalem by the Romans, it is possible that Matthew received it directly from him.[14]

Luke informs us in his gospel that "the things accomplished among us...were handed down to us by those who from the beginning were eyewitnesses and servants of the word" (Luke 1:1–2). Scholars do not agree about exactly what Luke means by "handed down." It could refer to either oral or written communications. To us, it is unimaginable that Luke would not have gone out of his way to find any living eyewitnesses to the events surrounding our Lord's ministry for eyewitness testimony. This seems at least

---

[14] We date the gospel of Matthew before the destruction of Jerusalem in A.D. 70.

reasonable in light of his statement that he had "investigated everything carefully from the beginning." While we cannot say dogmatically that every writer in the New Testament followed Luke's methodology when writing about the personal ministry of our Lord, we can at least say they put forward some effort guided by the Holy Spirit to communicate to us the essence of what He said or did.

Consequently, the source does not undermine the authenticity of what is written. The Holy Spirit ultimately ensured the writings to be authentic. It is therefore incumbent upon us to understand how the writers communicated our Lord's teachings. It is this author's view that we have in the Gospels a combination of the essence or the exact words of our Lord. Thus, each author was free to paraphrase, restate, or simplify the Lord's sayings as long as what he wrote reflects the essence of what He said. If one makes the following statement: "The author will see Jim first thing tomorrow," there are several ways to report what was said. The author said, "Jim would be his first appointment today." Or he might say, "Jim gets first dibs tomorrow." Or perhaps, "He indicated that Jim would be first." As one can see, there are multiple ways to express the essence of what was said without communicating it word for word.[15] Although each statement differs, neither is a contradiction of the original.

This very issue is important in considering Matthew 24:3. Douglas R. A. Hare writes,

> The key to Matthew's understanding of the entire discourse is provided by the critical changes he makes in the material taken over from Mark at Mt.

---

[15] We all understand the difference between reporting exactly what was said and stating in essence what was said. This distinction is important when studying the Gospels because three writers can report the same incident, but with great variations in wording, length, scope, and focus.

24:3....In the succeeding discourse the destruction of Jerusalem is forgotten; attention is focused rather on Jesus' Parousia, the events or signs leading up to it, and the necessity of preparing oneself spiritually and ethically.[cxlv]

By altering the original questions the disciples asked, Matthew is able to alter the focus and emphasis of the material. Where Mark and Luke have interest in the destruction of the temple, Matthew does not. While Matthew's first question is consistent with both Mark and Luke, he alters the second question significantly. As we discussed earlier, by leaving out the phrase "all these things,"[16] he separates the destruction of the temple and the Lord's return and the consummation of the age. This is a critical point and the implications cannot be overstated.

If our understanding of the consequences of Matthew's changes is correct, we must answer two questions: (1) why does Matthew not answer the first question? and (2) what textual clues signal this change? With respect to our first question, we understand Matthew's plot to be an explanation of how God plans to save mankind and Satan's challenge to it. The destruction of Jerusalem does not signal God's defeat of Satan, but appears as a failure on God's part to accomplish His plan for Israel. Jesus came to seek and save, but in the destruction of Jerusalem, it appears that the opposite is achieved. Perhaps, this is why Matthew does not answer the first question at all.

It is also possible that the reason Matthew does not answer the first question is because, in the original material

---

[16] Mark 13:4 repeats "these things" in both questions to the Lord in which case "these things" refers to the destruction of the temple. By leaving "these things" out of the second question, Matthew effectively changes the focus of his second question. The destruction of the temple is no longer at the heart of his question.

Jesus gave, he sees an opportunity to drive home the point that Jesus is the King of the Jews by the way He will return to rule upon the earth. Matthew also finds in the eschatological discourse the opportunity to present his final case for how Immanuel (God is with us) will occur.[17]

Regardless, by inserting the term *parousia*, which does not occur in any other gospel, and by adding a question about the end of the age, Matthew surgically removes Jerusalem's destruction as an emphasis of the Olivet Discourse and replaces it with a discussion of the Lord's *parousia* and the end of the age.[18] With the addition of

---

[17] We recognize three levels to the book of Matthew. Level one is the presentation of the facts concerning what the Lord said and did. Level two concerns Matthew's use of the material to argue that Jesus is the final and ultimate Davidite who will rule upon the earth in fulfillment of Davidic kingship. Level three is the tapestry of the Holy Spirit that explains how Immanuel (God is with us) occurs.

[18] The failure to see Matthew's disconnect has led to gross misinterpretations of Matthew 24—none more sad than the whole preterist doctrine, which forces Matthew 24 to depict the A.D. 70 destruction of Jerusalem by the Romans. Matthew's reformulation of the second question is not subtle. The notion that history will repeat itself, as it has so often done with respect to Jerusalem and the Jews, is lost on those who must have a one-time fulfillment. Both full and partial preterist views force Matthew 24 to answer questions he does not intend. Matthew 24:36 states emphatically that Jesus did not know the day or hour of His return. Yet, the preterists say that Matthew 24:34 demands the Lord's return before the end of the generation who heard the Lord's pronouncements.

This argument is difficult to reconcile with the fulfillment of Daniel 9:24–27. Daniel prophetically limited the duration of the second temple's existence to 483 years. Given that Jesus knew the time limit on Daniel's prophecy, He would have known that His return could not have occurred before the time limit of Daniel's prophecy found fulfillment. If He returned before the fulfillment of Daniel's prophecy and His return was accompanied by the destruction of Jerusalem, then Jesus could not have returned before the 483-year time limit was completed. This contradicts Matthew 24:34, where Jesus states that He did not know the day or hour of His return. He certainly knew it could not occur before the fulfillment of Daniel's prophecy.

chapter twenty-five, which is totally unique to Matthew's gospel, he clearly wants his readers to understand their need to be ready for the Lord's return, which will include judgment of all the nations of the world. Therefore, let's turn our attention to Matthew's reformulated question.

The Question

Matthew's reformulated question, "What will be the sign of Your coming, and the end of the age?" fosters more questions. Are there two separate events, i.e., (1) Your coming and (2) the end of the age? Or is there one event? Is there one sign for each or will one sign function for both? The nuance of a particular Greek construction used in Matthew 24:3 gives rise to these possibilities. The Greek literally says, "And what the sign of the your *parousia* and end of the age (καὶ τί τὸ σημεῖον τῆς σῆς παρουσίας καὶ συντελείας τοῦ αἰῶνος).[cxlvi] The reader notices an unusual awkwardness when the verse is translated literally. There is a rule in Greek grammar that when one noun is connected to another noun by "and" (καὶ) and the first noun (in this case, *parousia*) has the article "the" (τῆς) but the second noun (in this case, *end*) does not, then the two or more nouns can be the same, different, or subsets of one another. Thus, the Lord's *parousia* and the end of the age are either (1) the same event; (2) different events; (3) *parousia* is a subset of the end of the age; or (4) the end of the age is a subset of the Lord's *parousia*.

Unfortunately for us, the grammar only exposes the possibilities. To arrive at a correct answer, we must turn to an expert on this usage. Dr. Daniel Wallace wrote his doctoral dissertation on this specific issue. He argues that barring exceptional circumstances, option one should be passed over with regard to Matthew 24:3 due to the absence of an example of this specific nuance in any other portion of the New Testament.[cxlvii] We also reject the second option because Matthew indicates the possibility that only one sign signals the two events. Thus, the two events are not synonymous, but neither are they totally separate and distinct events. That leaves option three and four. If usage alone proved meaning, then option four wins. The term *parousia* occurs eighteen times with reference to the Lord's return in the New Testament, while the phrase "the end of the age" occurs a total of five times in the gospel of Matthew only.

Defining 'The End of the Age'

The phrase *sunteleias tou aiōnos* (συντελείας τοῦ αἰῶνος = "end" or "consummation of the age") first appears in Matthew 13. The Lord three times makes reference to the consummation of the age in connection with the great separation. Earlier in Matthew 13, the Lord puts forth a parable:

> "The kingdom of heaven is like a person who sowed good seed in his field. But while everyone was sleeping, an enemy came and sowed weeds among the wheat and went away. When the plants sprouted and bore grain, then the weeds also appeared. So the slaves of the owner came and said to him, 'Sir, didn't you sow good seed in your field? Then where did the weeds come from?' He said, 'An enemy has done this.' So the slaves replied, 'Do you want us to go and gather them?' But he said, 'No, since in gathering the weeds you may uproot the wheat with them. Let both grow together until the harvest. At harvest time I will tell the reapers, "First collect the weeds and tie them in bundles to be burned, but then gather the wheat into my barn."[cxlviii]

Later, the disciples approach Jesus about the meaning of this parable. Jesus then explains:

> "The one who sowed the good seed is the Son of Man. The field is the world and the good seed are the people of the kingdom. The weeds are the people of the evil one, and the enemy who sows them is the devil. The harvest is the end of the age, and the reapers are angels. As the weeds are collected and burned with fire, so it will be at the end of the age. The Son of Man will send his angels, and they will gather from his kingdom everything that causes sin as well as all lawbreakers. They will *throw them into the fiery furnace,* where there will be weeping and gnashing of teeth. Then *the righteous will shine like the sun in the kingdom of their Father.* The one who has ears had better listen!" (Matt. 13:37–43, italics added)[cxlix]

The parable teaches that our Lord's ministry involved raising up sons of the kingdom on the earth. At the same time, Satan raises up evil ones. Until the great separation, the sons of the kingdom and the sons of Satan will exist in close company. However, at the great separation, the angels will separate the sons of the kingdom from the sons of Satan.[19]

---

[19] It is a tacit assumption by many that the separation spoken of here refers to the sheep and goat judgment that follows Armageddon. However, that is reading into this text knowledge taken from another text. All we are told at this point is that the harvest, which is the end of the age, will occur. The angels will gather the wicked and cast them into the fire. What that process will look like or how long it will take or how the angels will separate the two groups is not detailed. The gathering and separating will not take place instantaneously. The wicked will not be cast into the fire without a trial, as it were. The removal of the wicked depicted in Matthew 13 must be harmonized with Revelation 8–10 and 16–19.

The great separation is *the end of the age*. We would expect the Lord to have said, "The harvest is *at* the end of the age." Yet, he said, "The harvest *is* the end of the age." What is the significance of this? Matthew 13:40 repeats verse 39, but states, "As the weeds are collected and burned with fire, so it will be *at* (ἐν = in or during) the end of the age."

To maintain consistency with Matthew 13:39, Matthew 13:40 is better translated, "so shall it be *during* the end of the age" to reflect the significance of the preposition ἐν.[cl] The great separation occurs *in the context of* the end of the age. Stated this way, it prevents the notion that the great separation takes place outside the end of the age.

The final occurrence of this key phrase is in Matthew 28:20, where, after His resurrection, our Lord commissions His disciples to make disciples of the Gentile nations. He concludes the commission with this promise: "And remember, I am with you always, to the end of the age."

One can correctly conclude that the mission of the disciple-making appointees stops with the end of the age. However, what is the specific point at which the mission ends? The Greek literally says, "And behold I with you all I am all the days until the end of the age (καὶ ἰδοὺ ἐγὼ μεθ' ὑμῶν εἰμι πάσας τὰς ἡμέρας ἕως τῆς συντελείας τοῦ αἰῶνος).[cli] With the explicit reference "all the days," (NASB = "always"), our Lord's primary emphasis is His continual presence in time. Thus, *until* (ἕως = *heōs*), focuses on "the *temporal*...aspect in which the beginning (ἀπό) and end (ἕως) of a period of time are signified."[clii] Thus, "The basic meaning seems to refer to a period of time up to a designated point."[cliii] Therefore, we conclude that the disciple-making mission does not extend into the end of the age, but culminates with its beginning.

Matthew 28:20 focuses on the end of a period of time. The disciples have the full assurance of our Lord's presence until the end of the age. Thus, we can say that the mission terminates *at* the end of the age because *during* the end of the age, the great separation will occur. Therefore, based on the parables of Matthew 13 and the Lord's promise of Matthew 28, we can say that the mission to make disciples of the nations will end prior to the beginning of the end of the age. After the end of the age begins—and during it—there will be a great separation. This informs our understanding of Matthew 24:3. The Lord's *parousia* must stand outside the end or consummation of the age. Otherwise, His disciples have no assurance of His presence during the time they would be exposed to the events connected with the end of the age, which is the harvest—the great separation of the righteous from the wicked.

Therefore, option four is grammatically possible and theologically consistent with other scripture. The end or consummation of the age is a part of the *parousia* of our Lord, with an emphasis on its end. We demonstrated in chapter two that the Lord's royal and regal return is a multi-phased event, having a beginning, running over a course of time, and having a conclusion.[20]

What Matthew has done for us is taken the Lord's teaching regarding the destruction of Jerusalem and His return and crafted a detailed explanation of the events that will immediately precede and follow the Lord's royal and regal return for His own.

That All-Important Sign

In Matthew's thinking, the end or consummation of the age is a subset of the Lord's *parousia*. Since no man knows the day or hour of the Lord's return (including the Lord Himself), Matthew can only trace those events that are

---

[20] For a discussion of the meaning of *parousia,* see chapter two.

a preamble to the end of the age. Since the end of the age is not signless, Matthew realized that he is able to detail that event which will at least make the Lord's *parousia* a less unanticipated event. Since Matthew had the benefit of having both the original questions and the Lord's answer before he wrote his gospel, it is critical that we understand that his reformulation of the second question is purposeful. He knows the answer to the question already. Therefore, that Matthew requests the sign of the end or consummation of the age means he believes the Lord's original answers reveals that sign. In other words, for Matthew to reformulate the question, but use the answer the Lord originally gave, would make little sense unless Matthew believes the Lord's original pronouncement answers his reformulated question. Therefore, there is one sign that signals both the Lord's *parousia* and the end of the age. What is that sign?

Unlike Mark and Luke, Matthew 24 contains a narrative section followed by parabolic sayings that underscore the need for faithful followers of Jesus to be prepared for an unexpected return, which will include judgment and reward for His followers. The narrative section of Matthew 24:4–31 has a clear agenda: to reveal the sign of the *parousia* of the Lord and the end of the age. The sign of the Lord's *parousia* and the end of the age is *the splitting apart of the heavens by the light of God's glory, which makes possible the eschatological evacuation of God's elect.*

The Building Blocks of Matthew 24:4–31

Since Matthew and Mark use much of the same material from the Lord's eschatological discourse, but with different agendas, we must conclude that the Lord's original material allows for more than one emphasis. Matthew emphasizes the Lord's regal return and the consummation of human history as we know it. To accomplish this, he uses two literary structuring devices. The first involves the final phases of birthing a baby, which gives way to new life, and the second involves a pattern which all major eschatological passages follow in presenting the scenario of the consummation of human history as we know it.

The Beginning Birth Pangs

The first literary device Matthew uses is the birthing analogy. Whether the unique way Matthew utilizes the birthing analogy was the Lord's or a product of Matthew's literary design is not clear. While certain features are found in both the end-time discourses of Mark and Luke, Matthew alone crafts his account to take maximum advantage of this literary device. Matthew 24:8 states, "All these things are the beginning of birth pains (ὠδίνων = ōdinōn)." The Greek term ōdin (ὠδίν) refers to the first pains associated with a woman about to give birth—literally, the birth pangs signal that nine months of pregnancy are about to come to an end.[cliv]

Metaphorically, Matthew uses the analogy to describe the events that will signal the imminent splitting of the womb of earth by the light of God's glory. Matthew 24:8 begins with the phrase, "these things," which refers to the beginning birth pangs. "All these things" refers specifically to the things mentioned in Matthew 24:5–7, i.e., false Christs, wars, rumors of wars, national conflicts, famines and earthquakes. These things are said to be "beginning birth pangs." "Beginning birth pangs" only refers to events connected with the soon birth of a baby. No woman experiences birth pangs for nine months. Thus, Matthew's emphasis is neither the beginning nor the duration of a pregnancy, but those events connected with the end.

Hard Labor Pangs

Matthew 24:9 confirms that the birth analogy is controlling Matthew's literary design. It states, "Then they will deliver you up to tribulation." The Greek noun *thlipsis* ("tribulation") "is always used in the figurative sense in the NT.... It is used of *persecution, affliction* or the experience of *oppression,* (extreme) *affliction, need,* or (inner) *tribulation.*"[clv] Louw and Nida suggest, "trouble involving direct suffering— 'trouble and suffering, suffering, persecution.'"[clvi] Interestingly, this same term describes an aspect of the process a woman goes through just prior to giving birth. In John 16:21, Jesus indicates that a woman experiences suffering in the final phase of the birthing process. He states, "When a woman gives birth, she has distress because her time has come, but when her child is born, she no longer remembers the suffering (*thlipsis*) because of her joy that a human being has been born into the world."

In both John 16:21 and Matthew 24:9, the same term describes the second aspect of birthing a baby. Metaphorically speaking, the elements of hard labor pangs that will characterize the days just prior to the splitting of the heavens by the light of the glory of God include: (1) death; (2) external hatred; (3) a falling away; (4) internal hatred; (5) false prophets; and (6) loveless society.

When we combine the fact that our Lord refers to the abomination of desolation in Matthew 24:15 (which is an explicit reference to Daniel 12:11) to an unparalleled time of distress (*thlipsis* = Daniel 12:1), it is hard to imagine that Matthew did not see a connection. We draw this conclusion in light of the prophetic pronouncements in the Old Testament that the world would experience tribulation (*thlipsis*).

Prophetic Tribulations

Isaiah 24–27 is typically identified as the "Little Apocalypse." Scholars recognize its prophetic nature. However, there is little agreement concerning what time period it indicates. *The Bible Knowledge Commentary* states:

> Known as "Isaiah's apocalypse," chapters 24–27 describe the earth's devastation and people's intense suffering during the coming Tribulation and the blessings to follow in the millennial kingdom.[clvii]

By *Tribulation* with a capital "T," Walvoord takes a futurist position and ties it to the fulfillment of Daniel's Seventieth Week. *The Commentary on the Old Testament* states,

> The cycle of prophecies which commences here has no other parallel in the Old Testament than perhaps Zech. 9–14. Both sections are thoroughly eschatological and apocryphal in their character.[clviii]

In contrast, *The New Bible Commentary* takes a historical/futurist view. It states:

> These four chapters, often loosely known as the 'Isaiah Apocalypse', show the downfall of supernatural as well as earthly enemies (24:21–22; 27:1), and of death itself (25:8). They contain (26:19) one of the two clear promises in the OT of bodily resurrection. But this wider scene is still viewed from Isaiah's own vantage-point of

Jerusalem, with Judah, Moab (25:10–12) and the great powers of Egypt and Assyria (27:12–13) in the near and middle distance. Overwhelming as the judgments are, the dominant note is of joy, welling up in the songs which frequently break into the prophecy.[clix]

Yet, the themes prevalent in Isaiah 24–27 are universal judgment, kingdom, feast prepared by the Lord, resurrection of the dead, and restoration of Israel.[clx] Such themes seem only appropriate in relation to Israel and Judah's eschatological future. Of interest to our discussion are the allusions and thematic similarities between Isaiah 24–27 and Matthew 24:4–31. Isaiah 26:16–18 states,

O Lord, they sought You in distress [*thlipsis*]; they could only whisper a prayer, your chastening was upon them. As the pregnant woman approaches the time to give birth, she writhes [*ōdin*] and cries out in her labor pains [*ōdin*], thus were we before You, O Lord. We were pregnant, we writhed [*ōdinō*] in labor, we gave birth, as it seems, only to wind. We could not accomplish deliverance for the earth, nor were inhabitants of the world born. (NASB)

A typical Jew who had knowledge of the era would see the precursors to the messianic woes in this passage. By messianic woes, we mean those calamities and trials such as famine, war, earthquakes, disease, apostasy, and family betrayal that are often quoted as occurring just prior to the Messiah's advent. In the Isaiah 26 passage above, the connection between tribulation (*thlipsis*), birth pangs (*ōdin*), and giving birth is evident. This, taken with Deuteronomy 4:29–31, certainly makes tribulation (*thlipsis*), birth, and (re)birth a part of the messianic woes. Deuteronomy 4:29–31 states,

But if you seek the Lord your God from there, you will find him, if, indeed, you seek him with all your heart and soul. In your distress [*thlipsis*] when all these things happen to you in the latter days, if you return to the Lord your God and obey him (for he is a merciful God), he will not let you down or destroy you, for he cannot forget the covenant with your ancestors that he confirmed by oath to them.[clxi]

Zephaniah the prophet adds that the eschatological day of the Lord will be a day of tribulation (*thlipsis*) for the people (Zeph. 1:15).[clxii] Our point here is that Matthew's audience would have found parallels from the Old Testament to understand this message. For God's people, the new age is born out of tribulation—i.e., messianic woes.

The Delivery

The final element of Matthew's birth analogy concerns the actual delivery. Just as the baby comes after hard labor, so the Lord promises deliverance for those who survive the intense persecution. Matthew 24:13 states, "But the one who endures to the end, it is he who shall be saved." According to Louw and Nida, *sōzō* ("to save") has three basic nuances: (1) *rescue* from danger (Matt. 14:30); (2) *save*, deliver in to divine salvation (1 Cor. 1:2) and (3) *heal*, to make healthy from an illness (Mark 6:56).[clxiii] Contextually, the best sense here is option one. Since salvation is the promised outcome for those who survive, it seems clear that Jesus is emphasizing physical deliverance.[21] The deliverance of God's elect out of the messianic woes

---

[21] Salvation from sin is of grace and not of works. Therefore, any reference to working to bring about one's deliverance must speak to physical deliverance and not spiritual salvation from the penalty of sin.

graphically matches the new life of a baby coming through the labor process.

Matthew 24:22 promises that the period of hard labor will not run its complete course, but will be cut short. Immediately after this "cutting short," cosmic darkness will envelop the universe. Matthew 24:29 states, "The sun will be darkened, and the moon will not give light, and the stars will fall from the sky, and the powers of the heavens will be shaken." This metaphorical language from the Old Testament describes the state of the universe just prior to the delivery—darkness.[22] Just as a baby comes from a world of darkness into light, so will the new age characterized as deliverance and reward.

Cosmic darkness is the Old Testament sign of God's eschatological day of the Lord—that period of time when God pours out His wrath against all wickedness in the heavens and on the earth.[23] This last and worst day of the Lord will involve deliverance and destruction. Just as the Lord's first coming literally fulfilled prophecy, so will His return. What is often depicted in the Old Testament in

---

[22] The cumulative effect of the sun, moon, and stars experiencing difficulty is that all light sources are extinguished.

[23] Preterists and others who force Matthew 24:29–31 to refer to the A.D.70 destruction of Jerusalem cannot afford to allow the text to speak naturally. Therefore, they must rob the language of literal fulfillment and make it mere metaphorical descriptions of "a powerful manifestation of God's power and reign within history." (See Jeffrey A. Gibbs, *Jerusalem and Parousia: Jesus' Eschatological Discourse in Matthew's Gospel* (St. Louis: Concordia Academic Press, 2000), pp. 188–189). In other words, the language is highly symbolic; some would even suggest "parabolic"— that the language is extravagant. Jeffery A. Gibbs (*Jerusalem and Parousia*, p. 190) states, "[T]he descriptions of distress within the realm of nature or of the larger cosmos figuratively communicate a theological truth without intending a literal referent or fulfillment of the language that describes such upheaval and catastrophe." Thus, Matthew 24:29 is purely figurative. No literal fulfillment was ever intended with regards to the cosmic depictions.

metaphorical language will find a literal "face value" fulfillment at our Lord's return. The cumulative effect (the sun darkened, the moon darkened, and the stars darkened) is cosmic darkness. The universe is completely devoid of light. It is through this womb of darkness that God's elect will pass to deliverance—eternal life with God in His kingdom. This is a necessary precondition for the sign of the *parousia* and the end of the age to appear.

The Sign

Having alluded to the deliverance that God's elect will experience out from tribulation (*thlipsis*) at Matthew 24:13, Matthew resumes his description with the sign of the *parousia* and the end of the age. When cosmic darkness is split by the light of the glory of God, the elect of God shall be delivered. Other than in the question of verse 3, Matthew 24:30 contains the only other occurrence of the term "sign" in Matthew 24. The whole point of reformulating the second question was to show the answer through the prophetic pronouncements of the Lord Jesus. Thus, there is a clear relationship between Matthew 24:3 and verse 30. However, that is the easy part. The hard part is demonstrating what that relationship is.

Matthew 24:30 states, "And then the sign of the Son of Man will appear in the sky." Much debate has gone into the identity of "the sign of the Son of Man." A comparison of the Olivet Discourse in Mark and Luke reveals the absence of the phrase "coming [*parousia*] of the Son of Man." The phrase is peculiar to Matthew. The title "Son of Man" also occurs more often in Matthew than any other gospel. Of the occurrences in Matthew, eight deal with the Lord's earthly ministry (8:20; 9:6; 11:19; 12:8; and 20:28); five His death and resurrection (17:9, 12, 22); and eleven His future coming (16:27, 28; 24:30, 44; and 25:31).

Only those who doubt the supernatural power of God fail to see a connection between Daniel 7:13 and our Lord's use of this title for Himself. Having come from heaven with plans to return, the Lord calls Himself the "Son of Man." He clearly intends for His audience to get the message: I will be back to reign over you in fulfillment of Daniel 7:13–14. How He will return is the only detail given in Daniel 7:13 concerning the "one like a Son of Man": He comes *with the clouds of heaven*. Of all the things that could have been said about this unique event, why make reference to "the clouds of heaven"?

The Prerogatives of the Divine Cloud Rider

The idea of a divine cloud rider is a rich tradition in the Old Testament and is a title exclusive to God the Father. In the Old Testament, God is regularly depicted riding on a cloud, riding in favor of His people and against their enemies. The divine cloud rider, often depicted in war, rides to save by destroying the wicked. Psalm 18:9–15 is helpful here. It reads,

> He made the sky sink as he descended; a thick cloud was under his feet. He mounted a winged angel and flew; he glided on the wings of the wind. He shrouded himself in darkness, in thick rain clouds. From the brightness in front of him came hail and fiery coals. The Lord thundered in the sky; the sovereign One shouted. He shot his arrows and scattered them, many lightning bolts and routed them. The depths of the sea were exposed; the inner regions of the world were uncovered by your battle cry, Lord, by the powerful breath from your nose.

In verse 6, the psalmist describes himself as being in the pains of childbirth. It is from his distress [*ōdino* = "birth pangs"] that he calls God for help. He depicts God riding on a storm cloud, coming from heaven to rescue His people. Salvation and judgment are the two halves of His mission.[clxiv] Psalm 104:3 explicitly states, "He [God] makes the clouds his chariot," as does Psalm 68:4 and Psalm 33, which convey the positive side—salvation. Several Old Testament passages depict the cloud rider in judgment: (1) In Isaiah 19:1, He rides against Egypt on a cloud; (2) In Nahum 1:3, He rides against Nineveh on a cloud. However, the passage of most importance for our discussion is (3) Daniel 7:13. There we read: "And with the clouds of the sky one like a son of man was approaching." Through this passage, we are able to explicitly identify Jesus as a divine cloud rider.[clxv] The Lord refers to Daniel 7:13 in Matthew 24:30 and Matthew 26:64. Both passages confirm that the Lord intended by the referent to ascribe deity to Himself.

Matthew 26:64 is most insightful regarding this conclusion. During the trials our Lord experienced the night prior to His crucifixion, He came before the chief priests and the whole Sanhedrin. During this trial, the high priest demand, "I charge you under oath by the living God, tell us if you are the Christ, the Son of God," Matthew records that our Lord replied, "You have said it yourself. But I tell you, from now on you will see the Son of Man *sitting at the right hand* of the Power and *coming on the clouds of heaven*." The priest's response to the Lord's answer is insightful: "Then the high priest tore his clothes and declared, 'He has blasphemed! Why do we still need witnesses? Now you have heard the blasphemy!'"

What is it that Jesus said that is considered blasphemous? Jesus recalls two Old Testament passages in His answer to the high priest. The first is Psalm 110:1, which says, "Here is the Lord's proclamation to my lord: Sit down at my right hand until I make your enemies your footstool!"

An examination of the New Testament will confirm Barry C. Davis' conclusion: Psalm 110 is the most frequently quoted or referenced psalm in the New Testament.[clxvi] Regarding Psalm 110, Herbert W. Bateman, IV states, "Old Testament scholars generally agree with form critics that Psalm 110 is a royal psalm because of its king motif."[clxvii] Regarding the purpose of this Psalm, Bateman states,

> Thus it seems reasonable to suggest that Psalm 110 is a typological-prophetic oracle of the Lord from the preexilic time period. David prophetically spoke the psalm to his "lord," Solomon, when Solomon ascended to the Davidic throne in 971 B.C. Psalm 110 was then applied in the New Testament to Jesus Christ as the ultimate and unique Davidic King and Lord.[clxviii]

Joseph A. Alexander's conclusion regarding Psalm 110 is worth stating here, as well. He said,

> The repeated, explicit, and emphatic application of this psalm, in the New Testament, to Jesus Christ, is so far from being arbitrary or at variance with the obvious import of the psalm itself, that any other application is ridiculous.[clxix]

It would appear that the meaning of Psalm 110:1, as the Lord used it, is this: God addresses the psalmist's Lord and instructs him to take a seat of honor at his right hand until God has defeated the king's foes and placed them under his feet.[clxx]

That the religious leaders of Jesus' day understood Psalm 110:1 to directly apply to the Messiah finds confirmation in light of an earlier exchange between Jesus and the leaders. Matthew 22:41–46 states,

While the Pharisees were assembled, Jesus asked them a question: "What do you think about the Christ? Whose son is he?" They said, "The son of David." He said to them, "How then does David by the Spirit call him 'Lord,' saying, 'The Lord said to my lord, "Sit at my right hand, until I put your enemies under your feet"'? If David then calls him 'Lord,' how can he be his son?" No one was able to answer him a word, and from that day on no one dared to question him any longer.

By this exchange, both Jesus and the Pharisees understood Psalm 110:1 to apply to Israel's Messiah. This explains one part of the high priest's anger at Jesus. By quoting this psalm in response to the priest's question, Jesus made explicit His claim.

The second reference in the Lord's answer to the high priest comes from Daniel 7:13. In essence, the Lord says, "From now on, you will see the Son of Man coming on the clouds of heaven." What did the high priest understand these words to mean? What is blasphemous about these words if applied to a man?

Many scholars have concluded that the title Son of Man emphasizes our Lord's humanity in contrast to His deity. But did He? Steven H. Sanchez asks, "If the title refers to his humanity, how is it that the Sanhedrin condemned him for applying it to himself?" Rather, Sanchez concludes, "This title expresses Christ's deity, authority, power, and judgment in association with his humanity."[clxxi] This would explain the reaction of the religious leaders. What is it about this title that does this?

Daniel 7:13–14 follows twelve verses that describe surreal beasts whose work it is to rule over mankind. However, at verse 13, a new figure enters the scene. Unlike the horrific and ferocious beasts, this new figure looks like a son of man—he is human. However, it is quickly evident that the figure is more than mere man because he is riding on the clouds of heaven, approaching the throne of the Ancient of Days. The cloud rider receives eternal kingdom rights over humanity with appropriate glory and dominion.

However, it is not the reception of dominion, glory, and a kingdom that the Lord emphasizes in Matthew 26:64. Neither is the central problem His application of the title "Son of Man" to Himself. No witnesses come forward to convict the Lord of utilizing this title, which Matthew demonstrates that He used repeatedly. In fact, there is not one attempt by the religious leaders to quell His use of the title.

Significantly, in both Daniel 7:13 and Matthew 26:64 is the phrase *coming on the clouds of heaven.*[clxxii] Again, we say that of all the critical details about the one like a son of man that Daniel chose to highlight, the cloud phenomenon must be more important than is normally understood. The significance of God and His relationship to the clouds begins back in the book of Genesis. The relationship between God and a cloud was manifest for thirty-eight years during the wilderness wanderings. The cloud was the evidence of God's presence with the people. Therefore, when Jesus claimed to be a divine cloud rider, He encroached on a prerogative of God alone. To come to earth riding on a cloud signaled both judgment and deliverance, which the Pharisees understood God Himself would do. For Jesus to claim to be a cloud rider meant that He was claiming deity, as well.

The most powerful connection between God and a cloud occurred with Moses during the exodus from Egypt. Exodus 33:7–9 states,

> Moses took the tent and pitched it outside the camp, at a good distance from the camp, and he called it the tent of meeting. Anyone seeking the

Lord would go out to the tent of meeting that was outside the camp. And when Moses went out to the tent, all the people would get up and stand at the entrance to their tents and watch Moses until he entered the tent. And whenever Moses entered the tent, *the pillar of cloud would descend and stand at the entrance of the tent, and the Lord would speak with Moses.* (italics added)

Of interest here is the insistence that "the pillar of cloud" is God. Unfortunately, the NET Bible agrees with most translations of the Hebrew text at verse 9. Translations insert "the Lord" here, when the Hebrew text does not. There is only one subject of verse 9. Correctly translated, Exodus 33:9 says:

The pillar of cloud would descend and the pillar of cloud would stand at the entrance of the tent and the pillar of cloud would speak with Moses.

Regarding this matter, Dr. Ronald Allen concludes, "The cloud is Yahweh."[clxxiii]

The high priest understood clearly that Jesus claimed to be the divine cloud rider who would come to earth to fulfill all the promises in the Old Testament that relate to the (re)birth of the nation (Jews) and to the judgment of the nations (Gentiles). It is this that they saw as blasphemous.

While the chief priests and the whole Sanhedrin rejected the Lord's claim, Matthew 24:30 reports a different outcome on the part of the nations when the Lord returns. With the appearance of the sign of the Son of Man in the sky, "then all the tribes of the earth will mourn." This important phrase begins with the Greek correlative adverb *tote* ("then"), which occurs twice in this verse in the sense of "thereafter" and introduces that which (immediately) follows temporally.[clxxiv] Thus, the sign appears. Then the tribes mourn and they see the Son of Man coming. One would think that the tribes would mourn after they see Son of Man coming, but this occurs after the sign appears, according to Matthew's account. This is very important. The sign of the Son of Man produces the mourning. Neither Mark nor Luke includes this particular aspect of the Lord's return in their accounts. However, Matthew does because it continues his analogy that the divine cloud rider's descent means both deliverance and destruction.

Matthew first addresses the fate of the wicked with a generalization about *all the tribes of the earth* (πᾶσαι αἱ φυλαὶ τῆς γῆς). This unique phrase has roots all the way back to Genesis. In both Genesis 12:3 and 28:14, Abraham will be an avenue of blessing or cursing to all the tribes (families) of the earth.[24] The negative side of this promise finds expression here in Matthew's statement—the tribes mourn (κόπτω = *koptō*), which means "to beat (one's breast), to mourn greatly." This word implies the strongest and most violent manifestations of grief one can have to death or tragedy. This is a rather strong response to the mere appearance of a sign. The obvious question is why?

The Sign Explained

Obviously, the sign will immediately spell bad news for the tribes of the earth. It is a similar passage to Matthew 24:29–31 that helps us identify the exact nature of the sign of the Lord's *parousia* and the consummation of the age. The Bible portrays only one future event that will accomplish this feat. Revelation 6:12–17 teaches,

---

[24] Whether the tribes of Matthew 24:30 includes Jews is debatable. However, a comparison of its usage in the Revelation will confirm that it does.

Then I looked when the Lamb opened the sixth seal, and a huge earthquake took place; the sun became as black as sackcloth made of hair, and the full moon became blood red; and the stars in the sky fell to the earth like a fig tree dropping its unripe figs when shaken by a fierce wind. The sky was split apart like a scroll being rolled up, and every mountain and island was moved from its place. Then the kings of the earth, the very important people, the generals, the rich, the powerful, and everyone, slave and free, hid themselves in the caves and among the rocks of the mountains. They said to the mountains and to the rocks, "Fall on us and hide us from the face of the one who is seated on the throne and from the wrath of the Lamb, because the great day of their wrath has come, and who is able to withstand it?"

This passage depicts cosmic and earthly disturbances exactly as Matthew 24:29 does, and in both instances, the same outcome is achieved. In Matthew's account, "all the peoples of the earth mourn." In John's, after the people hid themselves in caves and among the rocks of the mountain, they lament to the mountains and the rocks, "Fall on us and hide us from the face of the one who is seated on the throne and from the wrath of the Lamb."[25] However, John does not identify any of the cosmic or earthly disturbances as "the sign of the Son of Man" that Matthew indicates produces the emotional response of the tribes. Yet, in Revelation 6, the

---

[25] The call to the hills and mountains to "fall on us" and "hide us" echoes Hosea 10:8, which is quoted by our Lord as He goes to death (Luke 23:30). In Luke, the Lord prophetically announces that Jerusalem's residents will experience such intense suffering that they will desire death rather than life. Both Revelation 6:16 and Luke 23:30 reflect judgment on the people. Hosea 10:8 refers to the ten Northern tribes' response to God's judgment about to be delivered by Assyria. The point of this motif is death is better than facing the judgment.

effect of Matthew's sign is felt when God the Father and the Lamb manifest their presence. Thus, in John's account, either the sign does not occur. Either this or it *does* occur, but John simply does not identify it as such.

It is our contention that the sign does appear and that the context of Matthew 24:30 and Revelation 6:16 provide a basis for identifying it to be the splitting of the darkened sky with the light of the glory of God. Revelation 6:16 indicates that the people run from "the face of Him who sits on the throne." The book of Revelation is careful to establish that the throne sitter in the Revelation is God the Father. The fact that the people of the earth are aware of the Father can only be because His glory is manifested before them.

The assumption has been that Christ would return for the church with angelic accompaniment only. However, it is our belief that the sign of the Son of Man is the manifestation of the glory of God the Father that lights the sky and serves as a backdrop for the descent of the divine cloud rider—Jesus Christ. The term "presence" in Revelation 6:16 (NASB) is literally "face" (προσώπου). Since God the Father does not have a physical face, metaphorically, John is referring to the manifestation of God's presence. The wicked are so acutely aware of God's presence that they request death and burial rather than face Almighty God.

Matthew does not spell out the details at this point about what will happen to the tribes. Instead, he moves quickly to the positive outcome of God's promise to Abraham. Matthew 29:30 concludes, "they will see the Son of Man coming on the clouds of the sky with power and great glory." The term "they" refers to the tribes (families) of the earth. This confirms that our Lord's return will not be a secret. The divine cloud rider fulfills His promise to return riding on the clouds of the sky. Unlike His ascent, however, His descent has power and great glory as accompaniments. The text does not explain the exact nature of His power and glory. Yet, we are confident that it will involve expressions and manifestations appropriate for the King of kings and Lord of lords at His inaugural appearance before all mankind.

The Eschatological Evacuation

According to Matthew, the first order of business of the divine cloud rider after His manifestation is the collection of the elect. Matthew 24:31 affirms, "He will send forth His angels with a great trumpet." That angels suddenly are involved is a bit surprising, given that no reference is made to their descent with the Lord. The apostle Paul, however, confirms angelic accompaniment at this event in 2 Thessalonians 1:6–8. The angels go forth with a great trumpet. The Greek grammar limits the number of trumpets to only one. Yet, all the elect will hear it, which indicates supernatural assistance.

The purpose of the trumpet is not explicitly indicated. However, since the work of the angels is one of gathering the elect, it would appear that gaining the attention of the elect or signaling the angels to begin their work is its purpose. The purpose of sending forth is that "they will gather together His elect." The verb *episynagō* ("gather, assemble") occurs only in the gospels of Matthew, Mark, and Luke. However, the noun *episynagōgā*[clxxv] occurs in 2 Thessalonians 2:1. That Paul would use this unusual word only once and in the same context as the *parousia* of the Lord Jesus is significant. Is it mere coincidence or is Paul echoing the Lord's words? Was Paul aware of the Olivet Discourse and did it inform his view of eschatology? An examination of 1 and 2 Thessalonians reveals a significant number of parallels.

Notice the chart below:

Points of Contact between
Matthew 24 and 1 & 2 Thessalonians[i]

Characteristic	Matthew 24–25	1 & 2 Thessalonians
Parousia	24:3, 27, 37, 39	1 Thess. 2:19; 3:13; 4:15; 5:23; 2 Thess. 2:1, 8
The Lord's Descent	24:30	1 Thess. 4:16 2 Thess. 1:7
Descent from Heaven	24:30	1 Thess. 4:16 2 Thess. 1:7
Angelic Accompaniment	24:31	1 Thess. 3:13; 4:16 2 Thess. 1:7
Trumpet	24:31	1 Thess. 4:16
Survivors	24:13	1 Thess. 4:15, 17
Clouds	24:30	1 Thess. 4:17
To Meet the Lord	24:6	1 Thess. 4:17
No One Knows	24:36	1 Thess. 5:1–2
Thief in the Night	24:43	1 Thess. 5:2
Sudden Destruction	24:39	1 Thess. 5:3
Birth Pangs	24:8	1 Thess. 5:3
Watchers	24:42	1 Thess. 5:6
Drunkenness	24:45–49	1 Thess. 5:5–6
Salvation	24:13	1 Thess. 5:8
Power and Glory	24:30	2 Thess. 1:7–10
Gathering Together	24:31	2 Thess. 2:1
The Apostasy	24:10–11	2 Thess. 2:3
Antichrist	24:15, 24	2 Thess. 2:9–10

---

[i] We have not defined the precise way in which Matthew 24 and Paul's eschatology influence one other. For that, please see G. Henry Waterman, "The Sources of Paul's Teaching on the Second Coming of Christ in I and II Thessalonians," *JETS* 18 (Spring 1975) pp. 105–113.

Given the chart above, at first blush, one would naturally think that there is a relationship between Paul's eschatology and Matthew 24. However, the evidence of this fact has support beyond first blush to include grammatical, textual, and theological evidence, as well.

Grammatically, Paul begins 2 Thessalonians 2 with the same kind of question as Matthew 24:3. Second

Thessalonians 2:1 begins, "Now regarding the arrival of our Lord Jesus Christ and our being gathered to be with him."[clxxvi] The Greek construction involving the Greek article, noun, connective, and noun is the exact same grammatical construction as in Matthew 24:3. The Greek allows the possibility that "the coming of the Lord Jesus Christ" and "our assembling to him" are (1) the same event; (2) two different events; (3) the first event is a subset of the second; or (4) the second event is a subset of the first.

Dr. Daniel D. Wallace, an expert on this particular Greek construction, concludes:

> The antecedently probable alternatives are narrowed down to two in this context. Either the two terms are viewed as referentially discrete or else the second is regarded as a part of the first.[clxxvii]

Wallace's rejection of options one[clxxviii] and three[clxxix] leaves the possibility of options two and four. Option two: that the two events are different or distinct seems less likely. The fact that one article covers the two events suggests an association of one kind or another. Therefore, since we have demonstrated that the term *parousia* is the term of choice regarding our Lord's return (which is particularly significant in light of Matthew's use of this term and since we also demonstrated that the *parousia* of Christ is a multi-phased event), option four is the better choice. Our "assembling to Him" is a subset of the Lord's *parousia,* with an emphasis on its beginning.

Paul's "gathering" in 2 Thessalonians 2:1 and Matthew's "gathering" in Matthew 24:31 both occur in the same context—the eschatological end when Christ returns to gather His elect. The reader should notice that neither passage speaks explicitly of a resurrection, yet as with 2

Thessalonians 2:1, it is implicit in the illustration. The gathering in 2 Thessalonians 2:1 is defined as *ours to Him* (ἡμῶν ἐπ' αὐτὸν)—in other words, the gathering of Paul and the Thessalonians (of which some had already died). They are expecting to be a part of this great evacuation to heaven.[clxxx]

The gathering is said to cover "from the four winds, from one end of the sky to the other." *From the four winds* is easily identified as to its referent. It is a referent to the four cardinal points of the compass of the earth.[clxxxi] Clearly, the author intends a gathering that involves the entire earth.[26] This gathering involves only the elect. There is no indication that the wicked are among those gathered. The only reference to the wicked occurs in Matthew 24:29, where they mourn at the appearances of the sign of the Son of Man. This makes sense in light of the distinction between the *parousia* of the Lord and the end of the age. By definition, the end of the age has not begun at this point. The separation that is the harvest is not equal to the *parousia*. Therefore, with the appearing of the glory of God, the wicked run and hide. Then the gathering of God's elect occurs. Finally, the great separation comes, which is the end of the age in which God separates a remnant of national unsaved Israel from the remaining Gentiles. This harmonizes Matthew 13, Matthew 24, 1 Thessalonians 4, 2 Thessalonians 2, and Revelation 6. Consequently, we are satisfied that Matthew 24:31 refers to the assembling of all elect of Christ prior to God's wrath falling upon the earth to removed every last man, woman, and child who are wicked.

---

[26] The absence of a reference to raising the dead or to evacuating the elect into the air has served pretribbers well at this point. However, they do not allow this same reasoning to undermine their convictions regarding 1 Corinthians 15:51–52, where there is no mention of an evacuation to heaven. Nor does the absence of a resurrection in John 14:1–3 undermine their claim that the rapture is in focus.

Matthew 24:29–31 and the Eschatological Evacuation

With all cosmic light sources darkened, only the glory of God remains to light the universe. It is out of this dark womb that the Lord Jesus will deliver God's elect. This mass assembly we understand to be the rapture. This conclusion accords with the teachings of our Lord two nights after teaching the Olivet Discourse, when He spoke with His disciples in the Upper Room. There He told them,

> "Do not let your hearts be distressed. You believe in God; believe also in me. There are many dwelling places in my Father's house. Otherwise, I would have told you, because I am going away to make ready a place for you. And if I go and make ready a place for you, I will come again and take you to be with me, so that where I am you may be too." (John 14:1–3)

If this is a rapture passage, as many believe, then what elements of the rapture are present? The promise to come and take the disciples to a specially prepared place in the Father's mansion requires a removal to the Father's house and perhaps a resurrection if the Lord's return involves a delay.[27] Thus, John 14:1–3 implies the Lord's return, a possible resurrection, and a gathering of the saints to God's house. In light of this, it is strange that some deny that Matthew 24:29–31 is a rapture passage. A comparison

---

[27] Some see this as nuptial language involving the Jewish custom of the groom leaving the bride for up to one year, during which he prepares a home for his new bride on his father's estate. Once completed, the bridegroom then comes to receive the bride and takes her back to their new home.

of 1 Thessalonians 4:13–18—the primary rapture passage—
with 1 Corinthians 15:51–52; John 14:1–3; and 2
Thessalonians 2:1 reveal several interesting facts.

Notice the chart below:

A Comparison of the Rapture Passages

Characteristic	1 Thess. 4:13–18	1 Cor. 15:51–52	John 14:1–3	2 Thess. 2:1
Resurrection	X	X	X?	X?
Trumpet	X	X		
Angels	X			
Evacuation	X		X	
Assembling	X			X
Lord's Descent	X		X	X

One notices immediately that none of the passages
stated above has more than two explicit defining traits of the
primary rapture passage. However, notice what happens
when we add Matthew 24:29–31 to the chart.

**A Comparison of the Rapture
Passages and Matthew 24:29-31**

Characteristic	1 Thess. 4:13–18	1 Cor. 15:51–52	John 14:1–3	2 Thess. 2:1	Matt. 24:29–31
Resurrection	X	X	X?	X?	X?
Trumpet	X	X			X
Angels	X				X
Evacuation	X		X		
Assembling	X			X	X
Lord's Descent	X		X	X	X

Matthew 24:29–31 has more in common with 1
Thessalonians 4:13–18 than any other passage considered to
be a rapture passage. There is nothing in Matthew 24:29–31
to disqualify it from consideration as a rapture passage. In
context, the placement, timing, nature, and outcome of the
event is exactly where it should be to picture the

eschatological removal of God's elect before the wrath of God falls on the earth.[28]

The Format of Matthew 24:4–31

A final support for the conclusion that Matthew 24:29–31 refers to the eschatological evacuation of God's elect concerns the theological format of Matthew 24:4–31. Matthew develops the answer to his reformulated question regarding the sign of the Lord's *parousia* and the end/consummation of the age by utilizing a literary device found in the seventh chapter of the book of Daniel. The structural similarities between Daniel 7 and Matthew 24:4– 31 are also present in Revelation 4–20. The authors first give a broad overview of the events that eventuates into the coming of the millennial (temporal) kingdom of God to earth. Then a detailed look at the last three-and-a-half year career of Satan and his Antichrist follows. The final snapshot covered by all three authors concerns the coming of the Lord to reign on the earth.

---

[28] It is also important to recognize that the concept of the wrath of God is absent in Matthew 24:4–31. His people have suffered and finally experienced deliverance with no detailed explanation of the outcome of the wicked. The rest of Matthew 24 concerns warnings to the righteous to watch and wait.

In the chart of Matthew 24:3–31, each element is present. The chart follows:

A Chart of Matthew 24:3-31

	Beginning Birth Pangs	Hard Labor	Deliverance	
Question: What will be the sign of the end of the age?	Beginning birth pangs (Matt. 24:4-8)	Hard labor pangs (Matt. 24:9-12)	Deliverance (Matt. 24:13-14)	
	Messianic deception, Wars Famines, Earthquakes	World hatred, Great apostasy, Prophetic deception, Love grows cold	Gospel of the kingdom preached worldwide	The End of the Age
Question: What will be the sign of your coming?		Matt. 24:15-28 Abomination of desolation, Unparalleled persecution, Messianic and Prophetic Deception	Matt. 24:29-31 *Parousia* Son of Man	

This same scenario works out in Daniel 7 as follows: (1) broad overview (Dan. 7:1–14); (2) a focused look at Satan and his Antichrist's final campaign (Dan. 7:15–25); and (3) a picturesque representation of the Son of Man's rule on earth (Dan. 7:26–27). A very similar structure occurs in the book of Revelation: (1) broad overview (Rev. 4–11); (2) a focused look at Satan and his Antichrist's final campaign (Rev. 12–18); and (3) a picturesque representation of the King/Lord's rule on earth (Rev. 19–20). Matthew 24:4–14 covers the broad overview of the particular events that eventuate into the reign of the Lord and His saints on earth. Matthew 24:15–28 deals with Satan and his Antichrist's last campaign on earth. Matthew 24:29–31 highlights the initiation of the reign of the Son of Man on earth.

The broad overview is always given from the perspective of the saints who await their Lord's rescue. No specific timeframe is given. Regarding Satan and his

Antichrist's final campaign, each author presents their rule from the perspective of heaven. A specific timeframe of three-and-one-half years is given. The violence of the period against God and those who belong to Him is the essence of each account. The final thrust of each account is the victorious reign of God's representatives on earth.

Matthew deals with the broad overview first by answering his reformulated question. Having altered the original second question, Matthew obviously is committed to answering it. His second question involves one sign that signals two events: the *parousia* of Christ and the end of the age during which God's elect are separated from the wicked.

In reverse order of the questions asked, Matthew answers the last question first. He concerns himself initially with the end of the age. That the term *telos* ("end") occurs three times in Matthew 24:4–14 is strong support for this conclusion. Its absence from the rest of the chapter provides even more support for our position.

Matthew 24:6 has the first occurrence of the term outside Matthew's reformulated question. The phrase is *to telos* ("the end"). The term itself basically denotes "fulfillment,"[clxxxii] or completion of something. Regarding the particular usage in Matthew 24:6, Spiros Zodhiates states,

> With the def[inite] neut[or] art[icle] *tó*, *télos* usually means end, goal, or the limit, either at which a person or thing ceases to be what he or it had been up to that point or when previous activities ceased (2 Cor. 3:13; 1 Pet. 4:7). It does not, as is often supposed, mean the extinction, end or termination in time. It simply means the goal reached and conclusion of the activity that went before.[clxxxiii]

In a similar sense, Louw and Nida suggest (an idiom, literally "the end") a marker of a conclusion to what has preceded.[clxxxiv] Thus, Matthew 24:6 affirms that the beginning birth pangs do not complete or conclude events connected with the *parousia* or the end of the age. There are other activities that must fill out the time until the ultimate end comes.

The second occurrence in Matthew 24:13 is *eis telos* ("into end"). The preposition *eis* ("into") generally has the meaning of movement *into from without*.[clxxxv] However, with the verb *hupomenō* ("to remain"), the stative idea dominates. Thus, one remains in place instead of fleeing—in other words, one "endures" in trouble, affliction, or persecution,[clxxxvi] which cancels the notion of movement that is inherent to *εis*. Thus, in this case, *eis telos* defines the time limit regarding how long one will have to endure—into the end. For Matthew, the end of the age is the great separation. Thus, whoever endures and physically makes it to the end of the age will experience God's deliverance, the great separation.

The final example of *telos* in Matthew 24 occurs at verse 14. *To telos* ("the end") is repeated from verse 6. However, it appears in a different context this time. With the completion of all requirements, "then the end shall come." In context, this can only refer to the eschatological end of the age. With Matthew's trice reference to the *end*, having reformulated the initial question to Jesus about the end of the age, surely he is utilizing the Lord's answer to answer his own question. Perhaps Matthew recognized that believers would have a difficult time determining when history will have moved into the final phase that gives rise to the Lord physically ruling on the earth. While the events outlined in Matthew 24:4–14 will lead to the end of the age, it is immediately clear that a large-scale awareness that this time period has started will be difficult to determine. For example, who will make and how will the determination be made that the gospel of the kingdom has circled the earth?

With a heightened concentration of events common to human history (wars, famines, and earthquakes), given the world's present abilities to make single events larger than life, deception or misguided speculation could easily lead to error. The point is this: whether two thousand years ago or during the twenty-first century, if human recognition alone determines what is or is not the fulfillment of Matthew 24:4–14, then we are in trouble. Matthew 24:4–14 outlines events that will lead to the end of the age, but the sign of the end of the age has yet to be named.

In a normal pregnancy, the time frame between the onset of beginning birth pangs and the final delivery of a baby is a matter of hours. Therefore, to suggest that Matthew 24:4–14 signals events that will transpire over decades or centuries totally misses the analogy. Based on our Lord's prediction, at some point in the future, death, desertion, and destruction will become the agenda of the day, with such apparentness that no one will have to ask, "Is this it?" The primary sign that marks history's entrance into this unique period will be the establishment of a Jewish worship site with a restored sacrificial system on the temple mount in Jerusalem.[29] The basis of this claim follows in Matthew 24:15 where our Lord refers to the abomination of desolation—an event which must occur in Jerusalem in connection with a Jewish holy site.

---

[29] We shall expound on this point when we discussion Matthew 25:15 specifically.

Chapter Six

It Gets Worse Before It Gets Better

And answering, Jesus said to them, "Watch out
that no one misleads you. For many will come in
my name, saying, 'I am the Christ,' and they will
mislead many." (Matt. 24:4–5)

For the sake of clarity, let us state something that
may be obvious. The relationship between Matthew 24:4–14
and Matthew 24:15–28 is often confused. For many of those
who see the events of Matthew 24:4–31 couched in the
framework of Daniel's Seventieth Week, Matthew 24:4–14
is the first three-and-a-half years, with Matthew 24:15–28
covering the second three-and-a-half years. Others force
Matthew 24:4–14 to cover human history from the New
Testament times to the modern era, during whenever the
second half of Daniel's final week begins. Still others force
Matthew 24:4–28 to cover the period from the Lord's
ascension to the destruction of the second temple in
Jerusalem—a little over thirty-plus years.

Our position is that Matthew 24:4–14 covers the
entire period of Daniel's final week. Matthew 24:15–28
covers the second half of this week until the persecution is
cut short by our Lord's appearance. With that in mind (and
now that we have established the big picture), we need to
focus on the details of Matthew 24:4–14. In this chapter, we
concern ourselves with the nature of this period. Since the

birthing analogy controls this section, we can expect things to move from the first signs ("beginning birth pangs") indicating that a birth is imminent to the final painful delivery of a child. This is exactly the way Matthew builds this section.

The First Birth Pang: Deception

The first "birth pain" to be on the lookout for is deception. Be watchful for deceivers who claim: "I am the Christ." Within close proximity to either the presence of a literal, tangible, restored Jewish worship site (along with its attendant sacrifices) or the serious talk of bringing them about will come messianic pretenders. This is our Lord's first indicator that the events that signal the beginning of the remaining few years of human history have begun. But it will not be the appearance of deception alone that enables the Lord's wait-watchers to clearly identify the end times. As we discussed earlier, this—taken with what follows—are the prophesied birth pangs that move us forward and intensify until the arrival of a new life in the kingdom age.

A critical question at this point concerns the audience. To whom is the Lord talking? Matthew indicates that the Lord is speaking directly to those who asked the question—the disciples, His followers. Ultimately, His disciples will find themselves at the epicenter of the storm—the abomination of desolation—and they will need to flee once the real danger manifests itself. To limit the application of this text to ethnic Israel only is a theological presupposition. It is not an exegetically required conclusion. The very same verse occurs in Mark and Luke without indication of any application to ethnic Israel or any suggestion that the application limits itself to ethnic Israel. The text can have no application except to those who follow Jesus and are familiar with His teachings. The text applies to all disciples who are faithful to the Lord and living in Jerusalem at the time of fulfillment.

"To watch" (*blepō*) has the basic sense of being on the lookout for some event, with the implication of preparedness to respond appropriately.[clxxxvii] Only the Lord's faithful are characteristically on the lookout for deception (πλανάω). The term basically means "to wander about." In relation to the end times, it refers to the purposed attempt to deceive. The program of deception will involve many imposters. Jesus states, "For many will come in my name." This phrase contains the proposition *epi*. "Its basic meaning is on [with] further meanings [of] *at, near, to, during, because.*"[clxxxviii] However, with the Greek dative case it can mean "on," "while," or "over." If the particular usage is answering the question, "where?" then possible translations might be "on," "in," "over," "close by," or "at." If, however, *epi* is expressing an aspect of time, then possible translations are "during," "in," "at the time of."[clxxxix] It can also function in a figurative sense and mean "sovereignty or oversight *over.*[cxc]

The correct sense is not readily apparent. One would think the Lord would have said, "Many will come in their own authority." Or perhaps, "Many will come in Satan's authority." On the surface, the text seems to say that the imposters will come in Jesus' name and, at the same time, claim to be Jesus—the Christ. In essence, they come saying, "Jesus sent me. I am Jesus." Those who know scripture would naturally reject this claim. However, the Greek noun ὄνομα (name) has various nuances. It can refer to a person, a person's name, person's reputation, or a person's character or title.

The idea appears to be that many imposters will come in view of the Lord's reputation, claiming, "I am the Christ." What our Lord is saying is this: These imposters will seek to talk and act as He originally did for the purpose of deceiving people. Evidently, they will do a credible job because indications are that many will be deceived.[30] We will discuss Satan's program of deception in great detail later in the book, but suffice it to say here that only God's elect will not fall victim to Satan's plan.

Second Birth Pain: Political Upheaval

> You will hear of wars and rumors of wars. Make sure that you are not alarmed, for this must happen, but the end is still to come. For nation will rise up in arms against nation, and kingdom against kingdom. (Matt. 24:6–7)

The second birth pain marking the beginning of the end is political upheaval. *Wars and rumors of wars* indicates a very tense time on earth between certain nations. The command, "Make sure that you are not alarmed" suggests that the "wars" are not world wars, or at least will not directly involve the elect of God. *Throeō* (Θροέω = "be disturbed, be alarmed, be startled") means "to be in a state of fear associated with surprise."[cxci] The Lord's people should register no surprise when these particular events occur because "It is necessary to happen" (δεῖ γὰρ γενέσθαι). *Dei* occurs over one hundred times in the New Testament. Regarding this verb, *The Exegetical Dictionary of the New Testament* states,

> Δεῖ designates an unconditional necessity; sentences with this [verb] have fundamentally an absolute, unquestioned, and often anonymous and deterministic character...In the NT statements

---

[30] We shall look in great detail at the methods of deception that will be utilized by Satan, Antichrist, the false prophet, and others later in this chapter.

with δεῖ are normally understood more or less as divine decrees.^{cxcii}

In essence, such events marked by this term are the sovereign will of God. It is no surprise to us that a very close parallel to this Greek expression occurs in Daniel 2:28. It reports, "However, there is a God in heaven who reveals mysteries, and he has made known to King Nebuchadnezzar *what will happen* [it is necessary] in the times to come" (italics added). Of particular interest is the fact that Nebuchadnezzar's dream indicates wars in connection with the final kingdom of human history.[31]

The obvious point is this: The beginning birth pains are not random acts of mankind, but divinely directed events that are certain to occur. Thus, while this period will be difficult, God's people should not fear. He is in control, having ordained the events Himself.

Third Birth Pain: Natural Disasters

And there will be famines and earthquakes in various places. All these things are the beginning of birth pains. (Matt. 24:7–8)

Along with wars, a third mark of this unparalleled period involves *famines and earthquakes in various places.* The text does not indicate the source of these disasters. Are they the works of God or of Satan and his Antichrist? Since the Lord's faithful are not to fear these things, we think these "birth pains" are God's indirect or permissive works. That is, He allows these things, which without His suppression would occur continually.

---

[31] In the book of Daniel, the wars of chapter seven.

However, it is imperative that the reader recognize that these events are not universal. Famines and earthquakes occur in *various places* (Matt. 24:7). Where they occur will largely be determined by what God is doing with humanity at a given time. If God is driving men towards dependence on one man to solve the world's problems, then events in the large urban centers would be logical. Since the text does not say explicitly, we can only speculate. All these matters are merely the beginning of birth pangs. They signal the end of the pregnancy, but are not to alarm one's faith. No actions on the part of the faithful are required. Birth pangs signal that delivery is imminent, but not necessarily occurring without delay.

Is it possible to prove that the events detailed in Matthew 24:4–8 will begin three-and-one-half years before the hard labor pains of Matthew 24:9–14 begin? There are those who insist that Matthew follows the original script reflected in Mark and Luke. They insist that the events of Matthew 24:4–8 signal that the Lord's return is not near. We disagree. To spread the events of Matthew 24:4–8 out over centuries robs them of any significance for the final generation that will witness the beginning of the hard labor pains. Take, for example, earthquakes. With more than eight thousand earthquakes occurring yearly, how could one know that instead of the randomly occurring events of history, a certain group of earthquakes signal the beginning of the end? The same could be said of messianic imposters, wars, and famines. To serve as signs of the end, these things must occur in such a way that the final generation that will witness those things will know, "This is it." Beginning birth pains mean one thing: The end has started. Hard labor means one thing: Time to evacuate to safety.

First Hard Labor Pain: Persecution

"Then they will hand you over to be persecuted
and will kill you. You will be hated by all the
nations because of my name. (Matt. 24:9)

A rather sudden and significant shift occurs at verse 9.
The disciples are suddenly exposed to the possibility of death.
At this point, Matthew is still concerned with the broad
overview and thus does not call for action on the part of Jesus'
disciples. As discussed in the previous chapter, verse 9 begins
a discussion of those events that indicate that hard labor has
begun. The birth into a new age is imminent.

However, no one would stand by and do absolutely
nothing to escape murder. The fact that the Lord does not
give instructions at this point does not mean no action should
be taken. Matthew's point here is to simply tell the readers
what will happen. The appropriate response will come in the
detailed focus that begins at verse 15. In response to the
unparalleled distress, not only will Jesus' disciples have an
appropriate response, but so will the Lord.

Tote (τότε = "then") is one of Matthew's favorite
correlative adverbs. Here, it indicates what is next in
sequence. What happens next is very disheartening. The
faithful followers of Jesus Christ are exposed to death. The
verb that describes the fate of the faithful is *paradidōmi*
(ραραδίδωμι = "to give over"). It "designates the act
whereby something or someone is transferred into the
possession of another."[cxciii] A quick review of the
occurrences of this term in the New Testament reveals that it
is often associated with a tone that threatens the existence of
the person given up. This is certainly the case here. We are
not told who the persecutors are, but their hostility to the
Lord Jesus will find outward expression in the sufferings of
those who follow Him. *Eis thlipsis (Εἰς θλῖψιν = "to*

tribulation" or "to trouble") indicates the purpose of being given up. Clearly, the intent is to cause physical and mental misery—persecution. For some, the persecution will lead to death, which is indicated by the term *apokteinō* (ἀποκτείνω = "to kill"). This word carries with it the sense of causing death through violent means, with or without intent or legal justification.[cxciv] In other words, some will suffer martyrdom. As is evident from other scriptures, not all believers will be killed, but many will.

Second Hard Labor Pain: Hatred

The Lord Jesus lists another hard labor pain: *and you will be hated by all nations because of my name*: (καὶ ἔσεσθε μισούμενοι ὑπὸ πάντων τῶν ἐθνῶν διὰ τὸ ὄνομά μου). Hatred is the reason the Lord's followers will be killed. This hatred exists because of *the name*—Jesus. That the Lord indicates that this is the cause of the world's hatred clearly removes any doubt about the application of this text. These are faithful followers of Jesus Christ.

The only people hated for the name "Jesus" are those who make it their brand. If Daniel's Seventieth Week applies to the future, then it guarantees that the salvation of the nation of Israel cannot and will not occur before that week ends. In other words, the salvation of the nation of Israel cannot occur until the end of the last seven years; that is the prophecy (Dan. 9:24–27). Surely, no one believes that the nation of Israel is hated because of the name of Jesus today. The Jews are hated because they refuse to give up Jerusalem and the land. Therefore, Matthew 24:9 does not refer to national Israel or Messianic Jews alone.[32]

---

[32] Some might argue at this point that the rapture has already occurred and the people in focus at Matthew 24:9 are either the left behind or new

Only those who believe in Jesus are called by His name. John 15:21 records the words of our Lord, "But all these things [persecution] they [the world] will do to you for My name's sake." The Greek διὰ τὸ ὄνομά μου (*dia to onoma*) literally means "on account of my name." Loyalty to the name "Jesus" will bring persecution. It happened in the book of Acts. The council of Jewish leaders requested that the disciples of Jesus should "speak no more to anyone in this name." It was the name of Jesus that the apostle Paul fought against before his conversion. He wrote, "So then, I [Paul] thought to myself that I had to do many things hostile to the name of Jesus of Nazareth." Only true believers wear this brand.

Third Hard Labor Pain: Apostasy

"Then many will be led into sin, and they will betray one another and hate one another. And many false prophets will appear and deceive many, and because lawlessness will increase so much, the love of many will grow cold." (Matt. 24:10–12)

With verse 10, we begin a section of scripture that is unique to Matthew in many respects. Neither Mark nor Luke include verses 10–12, which focus on the response of God's people to the persecution that characterizes the hard labor pains prior to the *parousia* of the Lord at the end of the age. "And then" (*kai τότε*) indicates that the sequence of events continues. The first consequence of persecution (hard labor) is *skandalisthasontai polloi* (σκανδαλισθήσονται πολλοὶ = "many will fall away"). The NET Bible translates the text as,

---

believers after the rapture. However, this is an assumption that as yet does not have biblical support to our knowledge.

"many will be led into sin." The footnote adds, "many will fall away." This could also refer to apostasy. *Skandalizo* (Σκανδαλίζω) literally means "to cause to stumble." However, in the New Testament, the figurative sense is often used, in which case the emphasis is on the result—the one who stumbled.

In light of what follows in verse 11 as a result of the work of false prophets leading many astray, we understand the verb *skandalizo* to mean an abandonment of the faith. The *Exegetical Dictionary of the New Testament* states, "In the pass[ive] σκανδαλίζω more often means... 'fall away from faith.'"[cxcv] Naturally, there are serious questions about this conclusion.

Conservative scholars who hold to the security of the believer will quickly add that true believers will not or cannot "fall away from the faith" in the sense of losing their salvation. Thus, those who commit apostasy are not true believers. This idea is reflected in the definition of apostasy offered by Dr. Charles C. Ryrie, who writes, "Apostasy is a departure from truth previously accepted and it involves the breaking of a professed relationship with God.[cxcvi] Clearly, for Ryrie and many others, apostasy involves those who *profess*, but do not *possess* a true relationship with God.

Sadly, this definition places the cart before the horse. It assumes a consequence that scripture does not explicitly state. That is, apostasy is considered an abandonment of the faith on the part of man, which brings an immediate reciprocal abandonment of man by God. This is conventional wisdom. However, it is clear that one who merely professes can commit apostasy. The Lord depicts this in the parable of the sower. The seed (God's Word) fell upon rocky ground (a person who receives the Word with joy until persecution comes), but did not produce fruit. This person "falls away." This is the same verb used in Matthew 24:10. Since fruit production is the goal of sowing the Word and since this soil did not produce fruit, we are on good ground to conclude that this soil never achieved the desired goal. In other words, the person never became a true possessor. In a sense, he falls away.

Just as an unbeliever may commit apostasy, so may a true follower of Jesus Christ. Apostasy is an abandonment of one's commitment to God. The nature of one's commitment and the consequences of one's actions can only be assessed once the person who committed the act is known. A passage that deals with this situation occurs in the book of Hebrews.

Hebrews 10:26–31 states,

> For if we deliberately keep on sinning after receiving the knowledge of the truth, no further sacrifice for sins is left for us, but only a certain fearful expectation of judgment and a fury of fire that will consume God's enemies. Someone who rejected the law of Moses was put to death without mercy on the testimony of two or three witnesses. How much greater punishment do you think that person deserves who has contempt for the Son of God, and profanes the blood of the covenant that made him holy, and insults the Spirit of grace? For we know the one who said, "Vengeance is mine, I will repay," and again, "The Lord will judge his people." It is a terrifying thing to fall into the hands of the living God.

It is our understanding that this passage is dealing with a true believer who has committed apostasy. The author of Hebrews concerns himself with those members of the body who sin presumptively or defiantly. The author describes these people as those who received "the knowledge of the truth." By arguing from the lesser to the greater, the author points out three sins of some members of his audience and what will happen to those who commit them.

First, this person "has contempt for the Son of God." The NET Bible gives the significance of the figure of speech.[33] This person adopts an attitude towards the Lord Jesus contrary to the Lord's true nature. An illustration of this would involve a true believer who, because of circumstances or situations, adopts a position that Jesus *cannot* (rather than will not) deliver him or her from a particular sin. The second sin of this person is that he "profanes the blood of the covenant that made him holy." The remark should settle any debate that the person talked about here is not a true believer—he is! Hebrews 13:20 affirms, "Now the God of peace, who brought up from the dead the great Shepherd of the sheep through the blood of the eternal covenant, even Jesus our Lord." Thus, this is no mere covenant produced by the blood of animals. Jesus Christ produced this covenant with His life. *To profane* has the basic idea to "regard as common." The New Covenant made the man holy, but he treats it as common. The third and final sin is that the person "insults the Spirit of grace." The idea is that the person overtly speaks against the Holy Spirit. Perhaps the issue involves an abandonment of grace for the works of the Old Testament law, such as trusting in self rather than in the Spirit of God.

Of particular importance here are the consequences of these actions in terms of what God does. The author of Hebrews does not list specifics. He sets forth a warning. God will take vengeance and judge His people. However, exactly what form or to what extent that takes is not specified. The author quotes from Deuteronomy 32:35–36. A check of the context reveals that these quotes occur in a context that parallels Hebrews 10.

Deuteronomy 32 is a song of Moses performed just days before his death. This song is a prophetic testimony of

---

[33] To "trample under foot" refers to a spoiling, defeating, or treating contemptuously.

Israel's past and future dealings with God. The primary theme is rebellion against God. Israel experienced the bountiful goodness of God, which made them fat (v. 15); but afterwards, they responded by deserting God and treating Him with contempt. Both of these ideas are at the heart of apostasy. This is clear when taken with verses 16–17 that indicate that the people angered God because of their worship of other gods, idols, and demons. God's response is important. God states, "I will hide my face from them" (v. 20), which implies that He will withdraw His favor and expose Israel to natural law.

The consequences of God's removed favor involve (1) directing favor towards a "nonpeople" (v. 21); (2) increased disasters (v. 23); (3) starvation (v. 24); (4) pestilence (v. 24); (5) plague (v. 24); (6) wild beasts (v. 24); (7) vipers (24); and (8) war (v. 25). It is important that the reader not miss the critical fact that God disciplines Israel because they belong to Him. God does not cast them away. Israel, as a nation, did not stop being the people of God. For the believer, apostasy is a one-way street. The person may abandon God, but God does not abandon him. He responds with discipline up to and including physical death. Neither Israel nor a true believer loses a father. They gain a judge, whose wrath comes forth. In the context of the hard labor pains just prior to the *parousia* of Christ at the end of the age, our Lord indicates that *many* will abandon their commitment to Jesus Christ.

Interestingly, Matthew 24:13 promises physical deliverance (salvation) only for those who persevere. True believers who abandon their faith will lose the very thing they are attempting to save—their physical lives.

Fourth Hard Labor Pain: Family Betrayal

The intense persecution will have another chilling effect on believers—betrayal within the family of God. This verb occurs in Matthew's gospel thirty-one times. *To betray* translates a Greek verb that means "to deliver a person into the control of someone else involving either the handing over of a presumably guilty person for punishment by authorities or the handing over of an individual to an enemy who will presumably take undue advantage of the victim."[cxcvii] This is the intended meaning our Lord underscored in the parallel passage in Mark 13:12. The spirit of betrayal will extend up to and include family members.

Most likely, both blood and spiritual family members are in focus here. This may explain the statement to follow that "the love of many will grow cold." The level of betrayal will be at an all-time high. A lack of faith will always produce mistrust in the family of God.

Fifth Hard Labor Pain: Hatred

The final element of this triplet is hatred within the family of God. This is a hatred that retaliates. The idea is not one of dislike, but overt hostilities towards others. The sense of the text is a hatred that will create circumstances as a pretext to do harm to others.

Sixth Hard Labor Pain: False Prophets

To add to the already difficult situation, the Lord adds that many false prophets will arise. Since they are designated as false, their purpose is clearly to mislead people, which is exactly what they do. Matthew does not tell us what the consequences will be for those misled. However, of importance to us is the fact that many will be misled. This can only be because the people failed to require proof of authenticity or because the false prophets do works that appear authentic. We shall discuss this later in great detail.

Seventh Hard Labor Pain: Loveless Society

The final hard labor pain characteristic of the world just prior to our Lord's appearance involves love. Notice the Lord's statement, "and because lawlessness will increase so much, the love of many will grow cold." A final hard labor pain concerns *lovelessness*. In one of the few occurrences in the New Testament, the cause is put before the effect. Normally, the purpose statement follows. The sentence typically reads, "and the love of many will grow cold because lawlessness will increase so much." Lawlessness is going to cause lovelessness.

Louw and Nida define *lawlessness* "to behave with complete disregard for the laws or regulations of a society."[cxcviii] It involves the total breakdown of law and order. Injustice will characterize the world. Fairness, justice, rights, and all the other concepts that sane and civil people live by will be gone. The inability to get justice will drive people to care about others less and less. The NET Bible's translation *lawlessness will increase so much* catches the sense of the Greek text. It is not that lawlessness merely increases steadily over time, but that it is exponentially multiplied. The law will be lawlessness. As a result of the complete abandonment of justice and protection from the law, love will cool.

Love (ἀγάπη) is a mental attitude. To think well of others is the biblical notion of this kind of love. However, *tōn pollōn* (τῶν πολλῶν = "the many" or "majority") will not think well of others. Matthew 24:9–12 depicts a world unparalleled in its inhospitality. Faithful believers will find little help, if any, from their fellow man, or even from some members of God's family. Family, authorities, and the world will line up against them. There will be few sources of help for those who wait on the Lord.

Life Through Suffering

"But the person who endures to the end will be saved." (Matt. 24:13)

Given the absolutely inhospitable circumstances that faithful followers of Jesus Christ will experience during the hard labor, the Lord offers hope. Deliverance will come. Just as the hard labor of a mother giving birth brings new life, those who persevere (ὑπομένω = "remain under") will be delivered to their new life—ruling in the temporal kingdom of God—without having to experience physical death.

Biblical salvation from sin has but one condition: faith in the finished work of Jesus Christ at Calvary. But verse 13 is a promise for physical deliverance and has the support of verse 9. There are those who will be killed as a result of the sovereign will of God. They will not suffer the loss of eternal salvation because they were killed, but will receive a greater reward.

Here in Matthew 24:13, is the Lord stating the obvious that those who remain faithful to Him will experience physical deliverance? Naturally, if a person survives the treachery, internal hatred, lies, and lovelessness, such a one will experience God's deliverance. Such faithfulness is naturally worthy of the Lord at His *parousia*. If physical deliverance is uniquely what the Lord intended by this verse, it just seems a bit unnecessary to state the obvious.

Yet, having the privilege to be alive on this earth when the heavens split apart and reveal Almighty God coming in unspeakable glory and proving wrong all the wicked of all the ages—what a day of rejoicing that will be!

The End

One would think that the promise of deliverance would appear last. However, verse 14 is the last verse. Verse 13 is the end or goal for those who faithfully follow Christ. Verse 14 is the end or termination for those who are enemies of Christ.

God's grace will deliver those believers who persevere, according to verse 13. God's wrath will be delivered to the wicked, as seen in verse 14. The *parousia* of Christ will initiate the end of the age. The *parousia* will end the time of persecution for the surviving faithful followers of Christ at that time and begin a time of persecution for the wicked. Since the end of the age, which is the harvest, is a subset of the *parousia* of Christ, God will deliver the righteous first, followed by the punishment of the wicked. The *parousia* delivers and destroys.

Verse 14 is absent from both Mark and Luke. Why does Matthew include this verse? We understand its inclusion because of the reference to *the gospel of the kingdom* [of God]. An understanding of the meaning of this key phrase will prove helpful in understanding Matthew's inclusion of it here. This is one of the most misunderstood phrases in the whole Bible. Therefore, we shall discover its meaning before we answer the previous question.

The term "gospel" in popular culture has come to refer to something that is "undoubtedly true." However, the modern term "gospel" is derived from the Old English term *godspel*, which literally means "good tidings." This is how the term is used predominately in the New Testament. The reader is no doubt aware that the New Testament was originally written in the ancient Greek language. The ancient Greek term that corresponds to the English word "gospel" is *euaggelion*. The prefix *eu* means "well" and *aggelion* is the Greek word for "message." The significance is "glad tiding" or "good news."

A close reading of the English New Testament will reveal that the term "gospel" carries two possible nuances. The gospel of Mark, thought to be the first recorded biography of Jesus Christ, begins, "The beginning of the gospel of Jesus Christ, the Son of God" (Mark 1:1). In the title, the "gospel of Mark," the term "gospel" represents a document or body of information. Clearly, when Jesus first began His public ministry, His message was entitled,"the gospel." Not the "gospel" in the technical sense that has come to represent the message of Christian preaching, but merely the "good news." Only later in the history of the church did the term "gospel," instead of describing Jesus' message, come to embody it. Ultimately, it came to represent the document that biographically tells the story of Jesus' ministry on earth.

In the English Bible, the term "gospel" appears more than ninety times throughout the New Testament. A natural assumption might be to assign the same meaning to it each time it appears. Most readers of the New Testament would assign the sense "good news" of salvation. This, however, would be a great mistake. The New Testament announces more than one set of "good news."

During the time Jesus lived on the earth, any "good news" was considered a gospel. Therefore, when the New Testament uses the term "gospel," we must pay close attention to the context. The writers of the first three books (Matthew, Mark, and Luke) agree that when Jesus began His earthly ministry, He came preaching. Matthew, Mark, and Luke describe the content of the Lord's message in three different ways. Matthew declares, "And he [Jesus] went throughout all Galilee, teaching in their synagogues and proclaiming *the gospel of the kingdom*" (Matt. 4:23, italics added). Concerning this very same event and the context of the Lord's message, Mark's account records, "Now after John was arrested, Jesus came into Galilee, proclaiming *the gospel of God*, and saying, 'The time is fulfilled, and the kingdom of God is at hand; repent and believe in the gospel [of God]'" (Mark 1:14–15, italics added). Now notice what Luke adds: "I must preach the *good news [gospel] of the kingdom of God* to the other towns as well; for I was sent for this purpose" (Luke 4:43, italics added). A simple comparison of these passages yields the following conclusion: the gospel of the kingdom (Matthew's title); the gospel of God (Mark's title); and the gospel of the kingdom of God (Luke's title) are the same message. The exact nature of the gospel of the kingdom, which is the gospel of God, which is the gospel of the kingdom of God, will be discussed later.

The gospel of the kingdom of God was the message of Christ as He began His ministry. It was a ministry with a message designed to demonstrate the radical change the earth experiences when God physically dwells upon the earth. However, about two years into His ministry, Jesus changed His message, as stated explicitly in Matthew 16:21–23:

> *From that time* Jesus began to show to His disciples that He must go to Jerusalem, and suffer many things from the elders and chief priests and scribes, and be killed, and be raised again the third day. Then Peter took Him aside and began to rebuke Him, saying, "Far be it from You, Lord; this shall not happen to You!" But He turned and said to Peter, "Get behind Me, Satan! You are an offense to Me, for you

are not mindful of the things of God, but the things of men." (italics added)

Notice the key phrase, "from then" (ἀπὸ τότε = apo tote), which is a temporal marker or line in the sand from which a completely new set of circumstances exist. That this usage indicates a sharp distinction between what Jesus will now preach and what He was preaching before this period in His ministry finds support back in Matthew 4:17.

There we are told that the Lord Jesus began His ministry of preaching. The text states, "*From that time* Jesus began to preach and say, 'Repent, for the kingdom of heaven is near'" (italics added). Based on the meaning of this phrase, we should understand Matthew to be indicating that prior to this, the Lord did not preach such a message. In fact, Jesus was not preaching publicly at all. Looking back at Matthew 16:21, the Greek language is very precise— Matthew is speaking of a very *definite* point in time. As best as can be determined, Jesus uttered this statement *near the end* of His Galilean ministry, which would be about *two years after* John baptized the Lord in the Jordan River. "From that time" (from approximately the midpoint of our Lord's public ministry), He began to clearly set forth the gospel of Christ—His death, burial and resurrection for the sins of the world.

Peter's response indicates that this is the first time that he either heard or understood this message. It is our belief that this was the *first time* in Jesus' ministry that He clearly sets forth what was to become the gospel of His death, burial and resurrection for sin. Two facts support this conclusion. First, the phrase "from that time" means a point in time before which Jesus did not reveal this truth to His disciples. Second, Peter rebukes Jesus for teaching the death, burial, and resurrection motif, which after that time became the essence of the gospel of Christ.

But Matthew 4:23 tells us that "Jesus went about all Galilee, teaching in their synagogues, preaching the gospel of the kingdom (of God)," which occurred *long before* He established the gospel of His death, burial, and resurrection. There is no indication in scripture that Peter rebuked the Lord for teaching the *gospel of the kingdom*. Instead, Luke 9:2 indicates that Jesus sent the Twelve out to preach "the kingdom of God." It was Jesus' comments about being put to death that set Peter's teeth on edge. The difference between Peter's initial acceptance of the *gospel of the kingdom* and his initial rejection of the *gospel of Christ* argues strongly that *they are not one and the same.*

That *the gospel of Christ* concerns the death, burial, and resurrection of Jesus Christ is confirmed in Galatians 1:6–9:

> I am astonished that you are so quickly deserting him who called you in the grace of Christ and are turning to a different gospel—not that there is another one, but there are some who trouble you and want to distort *the gospel of Christ*. But even if we or an angel from heaven should preach to you a gospel contrary to the one we preached to you, let him be accursed. As we have said before, so now I say again: If anyone is preaching to you a gospel contrary to the one you received, let him be accursed.

Paul preached "the gospel of Christ." First Corinthians 15:1–4 explicitly states the content of Paul's gospel. He indicates, "Moreover, brethren, I declare to you the gospel which I preached to you...that Christ died for our sins according to the scriptures, and that He was buried, and that He rose again the third day according to the scriptures." This is the gospel that saves. Thus, in context, when Paul declares that there is only one "gospel," he is speaking of the gospel of salvation. As Peter affirms, "there is salvation in no one else, for there is no other name under heaven given among men by which we must be saved" (Acts 4:12). The fundamental distinction between the gospel of God and the gospel of Christ is this: The gospel of God condemns, but the gospel of Christ saves.

The final verse in Matthew's overview is most enlightening. He writes:

> And this gospel of the kingdom [of God] will be preached throughout the whole inhabited earth as a testimony to all the nations, and then the end will come. (Matt. 24:14)

Now that we know what the phrase "gospel of the kingdom [of God] does not mean, we are prepared to discover Matthew's meaning and reason for including it here. Matthew begins this verse with his typical connector, which indicates a continuation of his previous point. The phrase *this gospel of the kingdom* does not have a parallel in Mark or Luke's gospel, which means we are left to discover Matthew's intended meaning from the content and context of his book.

Normally, "this" (τοῦτο = the near demonstrative pronoun) points to that which either immediately precedes or follows it. In this case, it points back to verse 13, which promises physical deliverance that only the faithful can claim when the Lord comes to physically rule on the earth. The Lord began His ministry preaching the need for repentance in light of God coming to physically rule upon the earth. The simple message of the gospel of the kingdom of God is this: God through the proxy of the Son is going to come and physically rule on the earth at which time all that is unlike God will be removed. Thus, only the faithful can possibly hope to survive Christ's visible, spectacular, and awesome return to physically live on the earth in God's kingdom.

It is the message of God's rule (reign) upon the earth that will be preached or heralded to the whole inhabited earth (ἐν ὅλῃ τῇ οἰκουμένῃ) *for a testimony to all the nations (Εἰς μαρτύριον πᾶσιν τοῖς ἔθνεσιν)*. At this point, we must play close attention to the purpose of the universal proclamation of gospel of the kingdom of God. *Marturion (Μαρτύριον =* testimony) emphasizes the objective means of proof.^{cxcix} In other words, Matthew's emphasis here is not evangelistic preaching so people can get saved, but establishing an objective basis of their condemnation. The preaching of the testimony (the good news of God's coming rule on the earth) will be the basis of the world's conviction of guilt. All who heard and did not repent are condemned by what they heard.

This is similar to I. Howard Marshall's conclusion in the gospel of Luke. He writes, "*Μαρτύριον* does not mean the *activity* of bearing witness but the *evidence* that will be available on the Day of Judgment for the disciples and their enemies."^{cc} The point is this: The proclamation of God's coming rule on the earth is not so people will be saved, but that the guilt of the wicked will be clearly established.[34] The sense of verse 14 is that the proclamation of the good news of God's coming rule to the whole earth should produce repentance, but for those who will not repent, it will ultimately form the basis for the guilty conviction of the nations.

With this done, *then the end will come (καὶ τότε ἥξει τὸ τέλος)*. This is not the end of the world, but the end of the age. In a very broad way, Matthew has answered his own question (cf. 24:3). The birth of a new age will come through the hard labor pains, which God's people must experience. However, their experience will prove the wicked guilty and therefore worthy of receiving God's judgment during the end

---

[34] It is unfortunate that this passage has been used by mission agencies as a motivation to spread the gospel of Christ to the world. The goal is a good one, but their basis for doing so is built on an incorrect interpretation of this text.

of the age, which is the harvest—the separation of the righteous and the wicked.

Matthew 24:4–14 covers the entire period that will give way to the new age when God will rule upon the earth. Matthew 15–28 will take another look at the hard labor pains. However, this time the emphasis is on the cause of the hard labor pains. Matthew 24:4–14 explains the "what." Matthew 24:15–28 explains the "why." We know what will happen immediately preceding the *parousia* of the Lord. Now Matthew will tell us why the hard labor pains precede our Lord's glorious return as King of kings.

Because many scholars misunderstand the structure and focus of Matthew 24:3–31, false conclusions are often presented as fact. Therefore, in the next chapter, we will look at Matthew 24:15–28 in detail.

Chapter Seven
The Time Frame Established

Up to this point, the Lord has outlined what is most necessary to happen, but there is no indication how long these events will take from start to finish. Are we talking six weeks, six months, six years, or sixty years? Nothing remotely answers this question up to verse 14. Then Matthew 24:15 gives the first time marker for the events explained as the beginning birth pains, hard labor pains, and eventual deliverance that the faithful must experience before God's physical rule on earth manifests itself.

> "So when you see the Abomination of Desolation—spoken about by Daniel the prophet—standing in the holy place (let the reader understand)." (Matt. 24:15)

Before we look at the details of this section, the historical situation requires comment. At present, there is no holy worship site for Jews where they could offer sacrifices in Jerusalem. The only place where sacrifices would be acceptable to orthodox Jews is the original site of the first and second temple in the old city of Jerusalem. Therefore, the fulfillment of Matthew 24:15 requires the re-establishment of a holy site in Jerusalem. Given the hostilities that exist between the Arabs and the Jews and the presence of a heathen temple located in close proximity to where such a holy site would logically go, a significant change is necessary to see a Jewish worship site on the temple mount. As the situation presently stands, the establishment of a Jewish worship site on the temple mount would necessitate serious consideration.

It is our belief that such an event will only occur in the context of the fulfillment of Daniel's prophecy to which the Lord alludes in Matthew 24:15. Since Matthew places the prophetic abomination of desolation of Daniel 12:11 in close proximity to the Lord's *parousia*, we have no other choice but to expect a rebuilt holy place in Jerusalem in the future. Since Matthew reformulated the second question of the disciples and transformed the Lord's discourse into an eschatological description of the event that precedes the Lord's return, and since the fulfillment of Daniel's prophecy that the then-standing second temple had a time limit on its duration, a third temple must have been anticipated. This conclusion informs our understanding of Matthew 24:15.

The first thing we notice in verse 15 is Matthew's indication of the relationship between verses 14–15. The phrase, "so when" (Ὅταν οὖν = *Hotan ouv*, literally "when therefore) as a translation suggested by the NET Bible is a bit deceptive. Many English readers may not comprehend the intended meaning. If verse 15 is a mere continuation of the sequence begun in verse 4–14, we would expect this verse to begin with *tóτε* (tote = "then"), which is Matthew's characteristic signal of continuation. Yet, verse 15 begins with *oun* ("therefore"). *Oun* (οὖν)[cci] is a Greek conjunction that can function "inferentially, to introduce a logical result or inference from what precedes [and in this sense is translated] *therefore, so, consequently.*"[ccii]

A majority of New Testament versions translate *oun* by "so,"[cciii] suggesting a logical result or inference from what precedes it. The logical and most natural inference one should draw from Matthew 24:4–14 is a question: What should one do? Not since verse 6 has the Lord offered any instructions on the attitude of His followers in the face of "the pains of child birth." The reader is finally able to take a breath. Having warned His audience to ignore the beginning birth pains, the audience is now given the signal when other actions are warranted. Matthew will now signal the appropriate response of those located at the epicenter of the hard labor campaign. This change comes in light of the Lord's modified focus. Having reflected the events of the unparalleled time yet to come from the perspective of God's elect, He turns to the perspective of those responsible for the persecution.

Contextually, the outcome of the murder and mayhem among God's elect depicted in Matthew 24:9–13 is no different than the murder and mayhem connected with the appearance of the abomination of desolation in Matthew 24:15–28. Both produce intense suffering for God's people. Consequently, *oun* functions to indicate the logical and most appropriate actions to be taken at the first sign that intense persecution of God's elect is about to begin. Appropriately, the time to react is not after the events start, but as the events start. However, instead of restating the outcome of the events as in Matthew 24:9–13, here the first signal that the events are about to start is given.

Having warned his audience to ignore the beginning birth pains, Matthew now gives the signal that hard labor is about to start. He will now give the appropriate response of those located at the epicenter of the hard-labor campaign. This change comes in light of the Lord's modified focus. Having reflected the events of the unparalleled time yet to come from the perspective of God's elect, Matthew turns to the perspective of those responsible for the persecution.

The intensifying event between the beginning birth pains and the hard labor pains occurs with the abomination of desolation *(to bdelugma tās erāmōseōs = τὸ βδέλυγμα τῆς* ἐρημώσεως), about which Daniel the prophet spoke. Note that this is *the* abomination of desolation. The article indicates that the Lord is speaking of the well-known abomination. He further defines it as the one spoken of by Daniel the prophet.

The Greek phrase here is taken directly from the Greek Old Testament at Daniel 12:11,[cciv] where the Hebrew has a verbal idea connected with it. The Greek translates the literal Hebrew, which says, "an abomination that makes desolate." The sense seems to be that the abomination itself causes or makes desolate. Daniel makes clear that the cessation of sacrifices and the abomination are not the same. The sacrifices are stopped and followed by an abomination that produces desolation.

However, the desolation is the divine viewpoint regarding the place that suffered the abomination. From the standpoint of the desolator, the place is open for business. Matthew 24:15 indicates that the place of desolation is *topō hagiō* ("a holy place"). The absence of a definite article indicates that the place is not the famous one. This limits the application and does not require a temple per se, but a place dedicated to God like a tent.

In the three occurrences of βδέλυγμα ἐρημώσεως in the book of Daniel, two contain a reference to a period of time to follow. Daniel 9:27 calls it a half-week (forty-two months). Daniel 12:11 refers to 1,290 days (forty-three months). It certainly seems likely that some amount of time will follow this event. The enigmatic phrase "let the reader understand" signals a need on the part of the reader to pay close attention.

Unlike Matthew 24:4–8, wherein most of the events are reported to the audience as hearsay, the Lord instructs that the reader will *hear* of wars, famine, earthquakes and the like. However, at Matthew 24:15, the readers will *see* the abomination of desolation. We must remember that Matthew

24:9–14 covers the same events and timing as Matthew 24:15–18. The abomination of desolation is the signal that those living at the epicenter must seek safety.

It is clear that the Lord's original focus for this material concerned the destruction of the then-standing temple in Jerusalem. However, since Matthew changed the focus of his concern for this material and since the A.D. destruction of Jerusalem is complete, we must look for another historical destruction of Jerusalem that eventuates into the eschatological salvation of Judah. Only a literal fulfillment of Daniel 12:11 will satisfy Matthew's reformulated question because Matthew put the Daniel quote on the lips of the Lord in the context of His *parousia*.

God's Elect Must Flee

The appearance of the abomination of desolation has but one God-commanded response for the elect living in Judea: flee. That God directs those living in Judea to flee warns us that God will allow these events, and His people must not try to stop them. If the Lord allowed Gideon and three hundred men to put to flight a host of men stated to be too numerous to count, then God could easily deliver His people and the city. However, this will not be the case.

The Lord declares:

> "Then those in Judea must flee to the mountains. The one on the roof must not come down to take anything out of his house, and the one in the field must not turn back to get his cloak. Woe to those who are pregnant and to those who are nursing their babies in those days! Pray that your flight may not be in winter or on a Sabbath." (Matt. 24:16–20)

This is the only indication about how God's elect should respond to the events connected with the abomination of desolation in Judea. So as to leave no doubt that this event is a divine necessity, again, we say that there is no suggestion that believers should resist, fight, or try to undermine this event.

Since the abomination of desolation will occur in Jerusalem (Dan. 9:27), those living in Judea must "flee to the mountains." That this is a figure of speech is easily proven. There are no mountains around Judea that could possibly provide protection for a large group of people. Are there mountains near Judea high enough, with enough land mass or enough secret caves to hide a large group of people? Both Mount Lebanon and Harmon in the north have snowcaps. Survival would be difficult without heat and food. To the south and east, there are no mountain ranges sufficient to hide four or five hundred people, let alone thousands.

It is our belief that the command to "flee to the mountains" is a figure of speech meaning to seek safety. Perhaps the most powerful reminder echoed in our Lord's command comes from the story of Lot in Genesis 19:17. The angel told Lot, "Escape for your lives! Do not look behind you, and do not stay anywhere in the valley! Escape to the mountains or you will be destroyed!" The danger of lingering is obvious. As indicated by the fate of Lot's wife, the mountains were only safe if one trusted and obeyed the Lord.

Jeremiah, in an opposite sense, envisioned God's sending the Babylonians into the hills and mountains to hunt down the Israelites hiding there (Jer. 16:16). Thus, one can only hide in the hills and mountains of Judea if it is the will of God. That this is the intent here finds confirmation in Revelation 12:6, where those who flee Judea into the wilderness will find God's protective custody for forty-two prophetic months (1,260 days).

A Map of Israel's Mountains

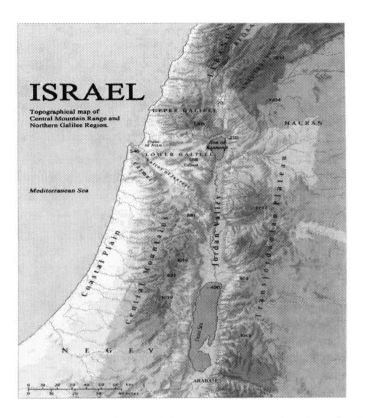

To expose the need for urgency once the abomination of desolation occurs, the Lord encourages Judea's inhabitants to run for their lives (vv. 17–18). Whether on the roof or working in the fields, returning to one's home will prove disastrous. One must flee with nothing but what is on his or her back. The need for swift action to escape is imperative! Personal items will not save anyone. In fact, pregnant women will find it difficult to escape because of the need to care for infants (v. 19). Equally, Sabbath and wintry travel should be prayed against (v. 20) due to the difficulty of travel, which might result in one losing his or her ability to flee swiftly. Yet if one is to leave home without clothing, food, money, or anything else, how then is survival possible?

As extreme as this call is, it seems a matter secondary to the immediate need to take flight and must be left with God.

Some point out that since the Lord mentions Sabbath travel, this limits the application of this text to the Jews only, as if the only people in Jerusalem are Jews who respect and honor the Sabbath. At issue is not the Sabbath, however, but the difficulty that certain situations will pose for those trying to escape from the epicenter of the persecution. Winter is not just a Jewish problem. Pregnant women will not be a problem just for Jews. However, these will be problems if one needs to flee quickly if one actually sees "the abomination of desolation" go up in the holy place.[35] What follows is an explanation regarding why swift travel is necessary.

The Cause of It All

> "For then there will be great suffering unlike anything that has happened from the beginning of the world until now, or ever will happen. And if those days had not been cut short, no one would be saved. But for the sake of the elect those days will be cut short." (Matt. 24:21–22)

With Matthew 24:21, the Lord spells out plainly why swift departures are necessary. For (this word introduces the reason to escape with nothing) there will be "tribulation a great one (*thlipsis megalā*) (author's translation of the Greek). Notice the absence of an article. Perhaps this is the first time the Lord has designated this period by this specific description, which emphasizes its importance. He indicates that this period of persecution will be unparalleled in all of

---

[35] Even so-called "left behind" people will have problems traveling if they are in Jerusalem when the event occurs. This is not just a Jewish problem.

human history. It will come upon the world as a consequence of the abomination of desolation, which triggers the wrath of Satan and his Antichrist (Rev. 12:12) due to resistance on the part of those who follow Christ or who have yet to be forced to serve Antichrist.

The fact that the Lord Jesus warns His people to flee is proof that these activities (the unparalleled persecution) are not the wrath of God. Repentance is the only appropriate response to the threat of God's coming judgment. It is unfortunate that many have misidentified the eschatological day of the Lord as being the unparalleled wrath connected with the abomination of desolation and thus calling it the time of Jacob's trouble (Jer. 30:7).

However, there are two unexampled or unparalleled times coming in the future. One is for the righteous and one is for the wicked. The great tribulation is directed at the righteous—it is Satan's and his Antichrist's wrath against those who refuse to participate in their campaign to overthrow the rule of God on earth once and for all (Rev. 12:1–17). In contrast, the time of Jacob's trouble is exclusively aimed at the wicked—it is God's eschatological day-of-the-Lord wrath against the wicked, which includes unrepentant Judah and Israel (Jer. 30:1– 31:40).[36]

The level of brutality that will characterize the unparalleled persecution of Satan and his Antichrist cannot be overstated. The unexampled persecution the elect of God will experience during this time of distress has but one purpose—death. If as we believe, the second temple destruction in Jerusalem was a pattern that will find ultimate fulfillment at the eschatological end, then the writings of

---

[36] This is the purpose and outcome of the trumpet judgments in Revelation 8–9. Only 144,000 Jewish men are protected from the trumpet judgments and just one-third of the Jews living in the land of Judea survive the judgment (Zech. 13:7–9), which is God's sacrifice taken from the earth.

Josephus about the destruction of Jerusalem in show just how abhorrent this future period will be. We will quote the entire section so that the reader can get a full appreciation of the context:

> **1.** (527) Accordingly Simon would not suffer Matthias, by whose means he got possession of the city, to go off without torment. This Matthias was the son of Boethus, and was one of the high priests, one that had been very faithful to the people, and in great esteem with them: (528) he, when the multitude were distressed by the zealots among whom John was numbered, persuaded the people to admit this Simon to come in to assist them, while he had made no terms with him, nor expected anything that was evil from him. (529) But when Simon was come in, and had gotten the city under his power, he esteemed him that had advised them to admit him as his enemy equally with the rest, as looking upon that advice as a piece of his simplicity only: (530) so he had him then brought before him, and condemned to die for being on the side of the Romans, without giving him leave to make his defense. He condemned also his three sons to die with him: for as to the fourth, he prevented him, by running away to Titus before. And when he begged for this, that he might be slain before his sons, and that as a favor, on account that he had procured the gates of the city to be opened to him, he gave order that he should be slain the last of them all: (531) so he was not slain till he had seen his sons slain before his eyes, and that by being produced over against the Romans; for such a charge had Simon given to Ananus, the son of Bamadus, who was the most barbarous of all his guards. He also jested upon him, and told him that he might now see whether those to whom he intended to go

over, would send him any succors or not; but still he forbade their dead bodies should be buried.[ccv]

(548) Hereupon some of the deserters, having no other way, leaped down from the wall immediately, while others of them went out of the city with stones, as if they would fight them; but thereupon, they fled away to the Romans:—but here a worse fate accompanied these than what they had found within the city; and they met with a quicker dispatch from the too great abundance they had among the Romans, than they could have done from the famine among the Jews; (549) for when they came first to the Romans, they were puffed up by the famine, and swelled like men in a dropsy; after which they all on the sudden over-filled those bodies that were before empty, and so burst asunder, excepting such only as were skillful enough to restrain their appetites, and, by degrees, took in their food into bodies unaccustomed thereto. (550) Yet did another plague seize upon those that were thus preserved; for there was found among the Syrian deserters a certain person who was caught gathering pieces of gold out of the excrements of the Jews' bellies; for the deserters used to swallow such pieces of gold, as we told you before, when they came out; and for these did the seditious search them all; for there was a great quantity of gold in the city, insomuch that as much was now sold [in the Roman camp] for twelve Attic [drams], as was sold before for twenty-five; (551) but when this contrivance was discovered in one instance, the fame of it filled their several camps, that the deserters came to them full of gold. So the multitude of the Arabians, with the Syrians, cut up those that came as supplicants, and searched their bellies. (552) Nor does it seem to me that any misery befell the Jews that was more terrible than this, since in one

night's time about two thousand of these deserters were thus dissected.

5. (553) When Titus came to the knowledge of this wicked practice, he had like to have surrounded those that had been guilty of it with his horse, and have shot them dead; and he had done it, had not their number been so very great, and those that were liable to this punishment would have been manifold, more than those whom they had slain. (554) However, he called together the commanders of the auxiliary troops he had with him, as well as the commanders of the Roman legions (for some of his own soldiers had been also guilty herein, as he had been informed) (555) and had great indignation against both sorts of them, and spoke to them as follows:—"What! have any of my own soldiers done such things as this out the uncertain hope of gain, without regarding their own weapons, which are made of silver and gold? (556) Moreover, do the Arabians and Syrians now first of all begin to govern themselves as they please, and to indulge their appetites in a foreign war, and then, out of their barbarity in murdering men, and out of their hatred to the Jews, get it ascribed to the Romans?"—For this infamous practice was said to be spread among some of his own soldiers also. (557) Titus then threatened that he would put such men to death, if any of them were discovered to be so insolent as to do so again.[ccvi]

(567) And indeed, why do I relate these particular calamities?—while Manneus, the son of Lazarus, came running to Titus at this very time, and told him that there had been carried out through the gate, which was entrusted to his care, no fewer than a hundred and fifteen thousand eight hundred

and eighty dead bodies, in the interval between the fourteenth day of the month Xanthicus [Nisan], when the Romans pitched their camp by the city, and the first day of the month Panemus [Tamuz]. (568) This was itself a prodigious multitude; and though this man was not himself set as a governor at that gate, yet was he appointed to pay the public stipend for carrying these bodies out, and so was obliged of necessity to number them, while the rest were buried by their relations, though all their burial was but this, to bring them away, and cast them out of the city. (569) After this man there ran away to Titus many of the eminent citizens, and told him the entire number of the poor that were dead; and that no fewer than six hundred thousand were thrown out at the gates, though still the number of the rest could not be discovered.... [ccvii]

1. (1) Thus did the miseries of Jerusalem grow worse and worse every day, and the seditious were still more irritated by the calamities they were under, even while the famine preyed upon themselves, after it had preyed upon the people. (2) And indeed the multitude of carcasses that lay in heaps one upon another, was a horrible sight, and produced a pestilential stench, which was a hindrance to those that would make sallies out of the city and fight the enemy: but as those were to go in battle-array, who had been already used to ten thousand murders, and must tread upon those dead bodies as they marched along, (3) so were not they terrified, or did they pity men as they marched over them; nor did they deem this affront offered to the deceased to be any ill omen to themselves.[ccviii]

Josephus depicts betrayal, murder, and the unparallel slaughter of the Jews. If this time yet to come is unparalleled—if it could be worse than this—we shudder to think of it.

The Promise of Deliverance

After the description of this unparalleled time, the Lord offers a word of hope for God's elect. Matthew 24:22 promises deliverance. God promises to "amputate" or "cut short" this unparalleled time of persecution. Without this measure, "no one would be delivered." This clearly refers to physical deliverance. Nothing can prevent the salvation of God's elect. Furthermore, God has numbered those who will die at the hands of these tyrants of history (Rev. 6:11). Clearly, Satan and his Antichrist gain no benefit from killing all the wicked, thus depleting Satan's kingdom of citizens. Yet, they gain every benefit from killing the righteous. Therefore, God in His mercy will cut short the days of persecution for the sake of His elect.

Daniel 9:27 and 12:11–12 make clear that forty-two to 44 ½ months are the determined extremes of the rule of Satan and his Antichrist. However, the length of their persecution against God's elect is a *time, times*, and *half a time*, which because of its use in Daniel 7 and Revelation 12 in close proximity to forty-two months and 1,260 days leads many to conclude the same length of time for *time, times*, and *half a time*. This is everywhere implied, but not explicitly stated. It is our conviction that this designation is used specifically to allow God room to fulfill His promise without breaking His Word.

At no time in scripture has the last half of the final week of Daniel's prophecy been depicted to last more than forty-two months. The final week is the same length as each week of the first sixty-nine. Therefore, if God promises to cut short the persecution of God's elect by Satan and his Antichrist, it must be shorter than forty-two months. To say that God cut short the persecution of the elect to forty-two months requires proof that Daniel's final half (forty-two months) of the final week was originally longer than three-and-one-half years, but there is no biblical basis for this conclusion. Therefore, God will cut short the length of this persecution, even though He will not cut short the amount of time Satan and his Antichrist will rule on the earth— forty-two months. In other words, the persecution is cut short, but the length of Satan's and his Antichrist's rule will not be. God will remove the primary object of their hatred—His elect—and finish out the week with His day-of-the-Lord wrath.

Do Not Believe the Lies

The intense and unparalleled persecution of the elect by Satan and his Antichrist will signal the imminent arrival of Jesus Christ from heaven. It is at this time that God's elect must look to the sky, for their redemption will soon draw near. This is the only scenario in which one can speak of imminence with respect to the Lord's return. Knowing this, Satan and his Antichrist will attempt to mislead the elect. To counter this deception the Lord gives His church specific details regarding His coming in the air. The Lord states,

> "Then if anyone says to you, 'Look, here is the Christ!' or 'There he is!' do not believe him. For false messiahs and false prophets will appear and perform great signs and wonders to deceive, if possible, even the elect. Remember, I have told you ahead of time. So then, if someone says to you, 'Look, he is in the wilderness,' do not go out, or 'Look, he is in the inner rooms,' do not believe him. For just like the lightning comes from the

east and flashes to the west, so the coming of the Son of Man will be. Wherever the corpse is, there the vultures will gather." (Matt. 24:23–28)

A systematic campaign to deceive God's elect will occur in concert with the unparalleled persecution happening on the earth. Any claims made by false messiahs and prophets, regardless of how authentic they sound and what miraculous works are demonstrated to prove their authenticity, the elect must not buy their lies. Matthew 24:27 makes clear that the return of the real and authentic Messiah—our Lord Jesus Christ—will not be a secret. The *parousia* of the Son of Man will be visible for all to see. He compares it to lightning, which never needs an introduction. His point is that lightning breaks the darkness. Therefore, His return will break into darkness with the light of glory, which everyone will see. Under these circumstances, no one will need to be told that the Lord has come.

Jesus concludes this section with the enigmatic: "Wherever the corpse is, there the vultures will gather." A comparison of the only other occurrence of this saying in scripture (Luke 17:37) reveals a different situation. Matthew's context establishes the intended meaning of the proverbial statement. Having committed four verses to the idea that the Lord's return will be so obvious that those looking and expecting it will have no reason to be deceived, Matthew includes this statement immediately following the reason that deception will be impossible for faithful followers of Jesus. His return will be visible for all to see. This is the intent of Matthew 24:28. Vultures come to their kill from the air. Similarly, the Lord will come for us. We will not need to go to Him.

Chapter Eight
The Arrival of the Son of Man

"Immediately after the suffering of those days,
*the sun will be darkened, and the moon will not
give its light; the stars will fall from heaven, and
the powers of heaven will be shaken*. Then the
sign of the Son of Man will appear in heaven,
and all the tribes of the earth will mourn. They
will see *the Son of Man arriving on the clouds of
heaven* with power and great glory. And he will
send his angels with a loud trumpet blast, and
they will gather his elect from the four winds,
from one end of heaven to the other." (Matt.
24:29–31, italics in NET)

Matthew 24:29 begins the general description of the
parousia of the Lord. *Eutheōs* (*Εὐθέως* = "immediately")
after the suffering of those days signals the next event in
Matthew's sequence. After the suffering is cut short, the sign
of the eschatological day of the Lord immediately follows.
Some have falsely concluded that Matthew intends to
communicate that all the events connected with the Lord's
return climax at this point. But this cannot be true, given that
Armageddon has yet to occur. Others argue that the great
tribulation concludes at this point, based upon Matthew's
sequence indicator, *εὐθέως* ("immediately").

However, Matthew 24:29 indicates that τὴν θλῖψιν
(*tān thlipsiv* = "the tribulation") is followed by the

eschatological cosmic disturbances as the sign of God's imminent wrath. Given all that happens up until this point, is strange that Matthew does not report the occurrence of God's wrath either explicitly or implicitly. The best explanation for this is the fact that tribulation (v. 9) and great tribulation (v. 21) are the same. The great tribulation's focus is upon the elect of God, but we have the promise that those days of tribulation shall be cut short. So we should understand Matthew 24:29 as referring to the day when God will cut off this grievous affliction. On that day, when the womb opens (so to speak), the light of God's glory will break forth with deliverance for the righteous and destruction for the wicked. This beautiful portrayal occurs in Matthew 24:29–31.

The 'Parousia' of Christ

Matthew, unlike the other gospel writers, uses a unique term "Your *parousia*" in 24:3 to inform us of the Lord's future return in the end times. The word also appears in verses 27, 37, and 39.

The Term 'Parousia' in Matthew 24

Matthew 24:27	Matthew 24:37	Matthew 24:39
For just as the lightning comes from the east and flashes even to the west, so will the coming of the Son of Man be.	For the coming of the Son of Man will be just like the days of Noah.	And they did not understand until the flood came and took them all away; so will the coming of the Son of Man be.

Jesus is the Son of Man, and it is His *parousia* that will occur in the eschatological future.

Matthew 24:27 reveals that the Lord's return will be a visible event.[ccix] Thus, there will be no need for prophetic announcement that He has returned. Matthew 24:37 reveals that the Lord's *parousia* will occur suddenly, catching the wicked unprepared. The *Bible Knowledge Commentary* states,

> People then were enjoying the normal pursuits of life, with no awareness of imminent judgment. Life continued normally for the people of Noah's day for they were eating, drinking, marrying, and giving in marriage. But the Flood came and took them all away. It was sudden and they were unprepared.[ccx]

Matthew 24:39 follows up with a final remark regarding the Lord's *parousia*. The unpreparedness of the wicked will result in their separation and removal from the earth. However, the sequence of the events (i.e., the separation and removal of the wicked) follows in Matthew 24:40–41. At the *parousia* of Christ, the righteous are taken away first, with the judgment of the wicked to follow.[37]

---

[37] Michael H. Burer, in an article entitled, "Matthew 24:40–41 in the NET Bible Notes: Taken for Salvation or Judgment?" argues, "There is debate among commentators and scholars over the phrase *one will be taken and one left* about whether one is taken for judgment or for salvation. If the imagery of Noah and Lot is followed, the ones taken are the saved. Those left behind are judged. The imagery pictures the separation of the righteous and the judged (i.e., condemned) at the return of the Son of Man, and nothing more. This passage has been frequently debated concerning what it means to be "taken" and what it means to be "left." Are those taken away saved and those left behind judged, or is the opposite the case and those taken away judged and those left behind saved?"

The NET Bible prefers the former interpretation, as indicated in the note, for the following reasons:

(1) Both interpretations must draw upon the prior context, which speaks of the days of Noah and the flood. Verses 37–39 read as follows: "For just like the days of Noah were, so the coming of the Son of Man will be. For in those days before the flood, people were eating and drinking, marrying and giving in marriage, until the day Noah entered the ark. And they knew nothing until the flood came and took them all away."

The verse speaks of two groups of people: Noah, whom God allowed to enter the ark, and those who remained on the earth and were destroyed by the flood. (a) On a first reading in English, the text seems to use "take away" in a specific sense to imply judgment; some form of the verb "take [away]" is used in v. 39 to describe the effects of the flood upon those who remained on the earth in Noah's day and then again in vv. 40 and 41 to describe what happens to one of the people in each pair. This would arguably support the interpretation that people are "taken away" for judgment. This argument does not hold up, however, when examined from a lexical standpoint. The underlying Greek words used in each case are different. In v. 39, a form of the verb ai[rw (*airw*) is used, while in v. 40 and 41, a form of the verb paralambavnw (*paralambano*) is used. This is a case where one English word overlaps in sense with two different Greek words. Since they are different words, similarity in English translation has to be carefully sifted for interpretive value. (b) The imagery itself lends the most credence to the interpretation that those taken away are taken for salvation. In the original narrative about Noah, God was gracious to save Noah from judgment by taking him off the earth and placing him in the ark. He was "taken away" from the place where God's judgment was poured out to a place of safety in the ark. Thus the reference to Noah lends more credence to the interpretation that those taken are taken for salvation.

(2) The verb *paralambanō* used to describe those who are taken away in vv. 40 and 41 is used by Matthew sixteen times in his gospel. It is used twice in chapter one to refer to the positive event of Joseph taking Mary to be his wife (1:20, 24) and four times in chapter two to mean "take to safety" (2:13, 14, 20, 21). Seven other occurrences have a neutral meaning of "take with/along" and refer simply to accompaniment (4:5, 8; 12:45; 17:1; 18:16; 20:17; 26:37). The sole reference that can be taken negatively is in 27:27 where the guards take Jesus into the palace to beat and mock Him. It is within the general contours of Matthew's use to see *paralambanō* as having a positive nuance here. Thus, those who are taken would be taken for salvation.

(3) The verb *aphiēmi* (*afihmi*) used to describe those who are left behind in vv. 40 and 41 often means "abandon" or "forsake"; Matthew uses it that way in 4:20, 22; 8:22; 19:27, 29; 23:23, 38; 26:56; and 27:50. When it has a positive nuance, it takes on the technical meaning of "forgive," usually of sins (see 6:12, 14, 15; 9:2, 5, 6; 12:31, 32; 18:21, 27, 32, 35) but also of debt (18:27, 32). There is no mention of sins or debt in conjunction with *aphiēmi* in this context, so it is difficult to see this verb as fitting the contours of Matthew's positive use of the word. Most likely,

A comparison of Luke's passages where Matthew's insertion of the term *parousia* occurs reveals nothing similar to Matthew's unique saying.

A Comparison of
Matthew and Luke's Usage of 'Parousia'

Matthew 24:27	Matthew 24:37	Matthew 24:39
For just as the lightning comes from the east and flashes even to the west, so will the coming of the Son of Man be.	For the coming of the Son of Man will be just like the days of Noah.	And they did not understand until the flood came and took them all away; so will the coming of the Son of Man be.
Luke 17:24	Luke 17:26	
For just like the lightning flashes and lights up the sky from one side to the other, so will the Son of Man be in his day.	Just as it was in the days of Noah, so too it will be in the days of the Son of Man.	

In the two places where he parallel's Matthew, Luke has either "Son of Man...in his day" or "in the days of the Son of Man." Since the term *parousia* does not occur in the gospel of Luke at all, we are incline to see Matthew creating a unique saying that helps to make his point that Jesus is the regal ruler who will establish His kingdom after returning from the heavens.

---

the verb fits Matthew's negative use meaning "abandon" or "forsake." This would imply that those left behind are left for judgment.

These factors combine to produce in the judgment of the NET Bible editors a favorable opinion towards the interpretation mentioned in the note—namely, that in Matthew 24:40–41 those who are taken away are saved and those who are left behind are judged.

Chapter Nine
Satan's Campaign of Deception

One of the most challenging aspects of the unparalleled persecution of Satan and his Antichrist concerns the level of deception. The theme of deception runs throughout the New Testament in connection with the final days just prior to the Lord's *parousia*. Scripture repeatedly warns the faithful followers of Jesus Christ to watch out for this deception. False messiahs, false prophets, and false members of the family of God will make it increasingly difficult to discern who is and who is not truly a committed follower of Jesus Christ.

In Matthew 24, the Lord Jesus tells of a rather heightened period of deception to occur in or around the final week of Daniel's prophecy. Those identified in scripture as the primary purveyors of deception in descending order of importance are (1) Satan (Rev. 12:9); (2) Antichrist (2 Thess. 2:10); (3) the false prophet (Rev. 13:14); (4) Jerusalem (Rev. 18:23); (5) false messiahs (Matt. 24:4–5); and (6) false prophets (Matt. 24:11). As to the identity of the deceivers, it is easily discovered from scripture. What is not easy to discover is the nature of their deception. Scripture seems to go out of its way to convince the reader that true miracles will be the means of deception. Yet, most conservative scholars reserve the miraculous to be a prerogative of God alone. Are the works of Satan and of those who work in conjunction with his energy (ἐνέργειαν = "operative power") true miracles or are they part of his deception? In essence, they look and feel authentic, but are they real?

Satan's Powers Manifested

An explicit statement regarding the miraculous works seen by God's elect can be found in Matthew 24:24. The Lord Jesus states that many will be mislead by false prophets and false messiahs. The Lord specifically says, "False christs and false prophets will arise and will show *great signs and wonders*" (*sāmeia megala kai terata*, italics added). On only two other occasions in the New Testament are similar combinations of these Greek words used: Acts 6:8 and 8:13.

In Acts 6:8, the writer informs the reader that Stephen, who proved that he was a faithful follower of Jesus Christ by his death, "was performing great wonders and miraculous signs among the people." The two expressions occur in opposite positions, but the two phrases occur exactly as they do in Matthew 24:24. There is absolutely no doubt that these are works that God did through his instrument Stephen. A similar report occurs in Acts 8:13. There Philip, the human instrument of God, has "the signs and great miracles" associated with his work. The phrases are not exactly as in Matthew 24:24, but they are so close as to make little difference. The reaction of Simon the magician locates these works in the arena of the truly miraculous. Having engaged in false works, Simon knew about their reality.

The apostle Paul also confirms that miraculous works by Satan and his workers will be evident during the end times. In 2 Thessalonians 2:9, Paul writes, "The arrival of the lawless one will be by Satan's working with all kinds of miracles [δυνάμει = *duvamei*] and signs [σημείοις = *sāmeiois*] and false wonders [τέρασιν ψεύδους = *terasin pseudous*]." The particular words Paul uses here are significant.

The apostle John records in Revelation 13:13–14 regarding the beast (the false prophet) that comes up out of the land, "He performed momentous signs [σημεῖα μεγάλα = sāmeia megala], even making fire come down from heaven in front of people and, by the signs [σημεῖα = sāmeia] he was permitted to perform on behalf of the beast, he deceived those who live on the earth."

Revelation 16:14 indicates that demons that represent the spirit of Satan, Antichrist, and the false prophet will go out to convince the kings of the East to come and fight against Christ at Armageddon. The tool used to convince the kings is σημεῖα (sāmeia = "signs"). A final reference in the book of Revelation occurs at 19:20, where the false prophet is once again identified as a worker of σημεῖα (sāmeia = "signs"). The result of the works of the false prophet is the deception of the world.

Biblical Miracles

A comparison of the terms used to describe true biblical miracles reveals no difference from those used to describe the works of Satan and those who do his works. In fact, every word used to describe the works of Satan and his followers is also used to describe the works of Christ and the apostles. The individual words, as well as the same combination of words, occur throughout the New Testament. What is even of more of interest is the fact that no miraculous work of Satan is ever ascribed as magic or witchcraft. John reports, "many believed in His name [Jesus], observing His σημεῖα (sāmeia = "signs"). Peter reports in Acts 2:22 that Jesus did δυνάμεσι (dunamesi = "powerful deeds"), καὶ τέρασι (terasi = "wonders"), and καὶ σημείοις (sāmeiois = "signs"). Acts 2:43 makes clear that the apostles were also workers of τέρατα (terata = "wonders") and καὶ σημεῖα (smeia = "signs"). The apostle Paul states,

"Indeed, the signs [σημεῖα] of apostle were performed among you with great perseverance by signs [σημείοις] and wonders [τέρασιν] and powerful deeds [δυνάμεσιν]."

Satanic Works at the End Time

There are those who believe that Satan and his minions are not able to work authentic miracles in the tradition of Jesus and His followers. The two explicit examples of the works of Satan during the end times—calling down fire from heaven (Rev. 13:13) and giving breath to the image of the beast (Rev. 13:15)—are usually regarded as tricks. However, these conclusions are nothing more than personal prejudices. There is nothing in the text that allows one to conclude that Satan is playing tricks on people as far as the miracles are concerned. His goal is to deceive. How he deceives is not a case of smoke and mirrors.

Perhaps the greatest feat of Satan during the end times will be that of resurrecting the Antichrist from the dead. Revelation 13:1–4 states,

> Then I saw a beast coming up out of the sea. It had ten horns and seven heads, and on its horns were ten diadem crowns, and on its heads a blasphemous name. Now the beast that I saw was like a leopard, but its feet were like a bear's, and its mouth was like a lion's mouth. The dragon gave the beast his power, his throne, and great authority to rule. One of the beast's heads appeared to have been killed, but the lethal wound had been healed. And the whole world followed the beast in amazement; they worshiped the dragon because he had given ruling authority to the beast, and they worshiped the beast too,

saying: "Who is like the beast?" and "Who is able to make war against him?" (Rev. 13:1–4)

The critical phrase occurs in verse 3. Notice the possible translation options:

- *NB*: "One of the beast's heads appeared to have been killed, but the lethal wound had been healed."
- *NASB: "I saw* one of his heads as if it had been slain, and his fatal wound was healed."
- *NIV*: "One of the heads of the beast seemed to have had a fatal wound, but the fatal wound had been healed."
- *ESV*: "One of its heads seemed to have a mortal wound, but its mortal wound was healed."
- *KJV*: "And I saw one of his heads as it were wounded to death; and his deadly wound was healed."

Are we to discern from these translations that one of the heads was put to death? Each seems to come just short of explicitly stating this. "Appeared to," "as if," "seemed to," "seemed to," and "as it were" all leave room for the possibility that the head only appears to have suffered a deadly blow. The Greek literally says, "As slain to death" (*hōs esphagmenān eis thanaton*). The critical question concerns the intent of *hos*. This word occurs in the New Testament more than five hundred times. It has a wide use. One use is "to introduce a characteristic quality that is real, claimed, or supposed."[ccxi] Thus, it is possible that the head only appears to have been slain.

Earlier in the book of Revelation, John used this identical phrase to speak of the Lamb of God. In Revelation 5:6, the Lamb is described "as slain." The Lamb is Jesus Christ. In the case of our Lord, the phrase definitely means having been put to death. This would seem to be a rather strong case that in Revelation 13:3, it refers to actual death also. In Revelation 13:12, the second beast that comes from the earth makes the world worship the first beast, "the one whose lethal wound had been healed (οὗ ἐθεραπεύθη ἡ πληγὴ τοῦ θανάτου αὐτοῦ).[ccxii] The word *plēgē* ("blow, wound or plague") occurs twenty-two times in the New Testament. Setting aside its usage in Revelation 13 (three times), this word is not used to refer to death resulting from it. There were those who received beatings (Luke 10:30, 12:48; 2 Cor. 6:5 and 11:23), but those beatings did not result in death. Acts 16:33 speaks of those who needed to wash their wounds. Acts 16:23 speaks of those who received many blows. None of these examples involves a wound that resulted in death.

Yet, Revelation 13:3 and 12 both speak of the death of the beast from his wound. *Hā plēgē tou thanatou autou* is best understood to mean, "the wound which produces his death."[ccxiii] Revelation 13:14 adds to this discussion this fact: "the one who has the wound of the sword and came to life"; this beast came back to life. The Revelation gives us the fact that the beast's wound was caused by a *machairās* ("sword").

The aorist verb *zō* ("to live") occurs three times in Revelation. In Revelation 2:8, it refers to the resurrection of Jesus Christ. It is translated in such a way so as to emphasis the ingressive idea: He came back to life. In a similar circumstance, Revelation 20:4–5 speaks of the future resurrection of those who were beheaded. In both cases, the subject was dead. Scholars do not doubt the meaning of this term in these two texts. However, there is doubt about Revelation 13:14. The primary problem that most conservative scholars have with Revelation 13:3, 12, and 14 is the notion that Satan has the power to raise the dead. The text does not say that Satan raised the beast from the dead. However, that is the assumption that drives most objections to what is plain and clear.

A Possible Solution

If the miracles and resurrection of the beast are authentic, who is ultimately responsible for them? The apostle Paul makes a very interesting statement in 2 Thessalonians 2:11: "Consequently God sends on them a deluding influence so that they will believe what is false." There is much debate about the meaning of this verse, and 2 Thessalonians chapter two has contributed greatly to it. Primarily, Paul points out the role that the man of lawlessness will play. Verses 1–12 have much affinity with both Matthew 24 and the Revelation of John. In verse 8, Paul informs the reader that the man of lawlessness will be brought to his ultimate "end by the appearance of His [Jesus] coming."

The man of lawlessness works through "the activity of Satan." "Activity" [ἐνέργειαν = *energeian*] is better translated "power" here. The man of lawlessness works according to the power of Satan. We can discern the sense of the term from its use in Colossians 1:29. The verse states, "Toward this goal I also labor, struggling according to his power [ἐνέργειαν] that powerfully works in me." Paul was very much aware of God's power working (*energeian*) in him. The mighty works we see demonstrated by the apostle must ultimately find their source in Jesus Christ.

As Paul works through the power of Jesus, so the man of lawlessness will work through Satan with all power, signs, false wonders, and with all deception "for those who perish." Paul instructs that people perish "because they did not receive the love of the truth so as to be saved." It is important that the reader pay close attention to Paul's words. It is not that they did not hear the truth, but that they found no place in their hearts for it. Second Thessalonians 2:11 explains the consequences of their actions. Verse 11 begins, "Consequently." This picks up the thought of the second half of verse 10. A future generation of men and women will perish because they will not receive the love of the truth. Because they found no place in their hearts for the truth, God will send upon them a deluding influence so that they will believe what is false.

The idea that God sends upon them a deluding influence (ἐνέργειαν πλάνης) [i.e., for those individuals mentioned in v. 10] so that they will believe the lie is very interesting and at first, appears to be contradictory to the nature of God. However, if one does not observe the sequence highlighted in these verses, he or she might draw such a false conclusion about the role God plays here. The sequence is important. First, they refuse the truth. It is only then that God influences them to believe what is false. This is not a new idea that God helps people who rebel against His law to cast off all restraint and forge ahead with abandonment.[ccxiv] During the eschatological end-times, people will swallow the "false wonders" of Satan and his Antichrist. In response, God will send a "deluding influence" that those people will believe the ultimate lie that the man of lawlessness is God. This aspect of the verse is clear. However, the meaning of a "deluding influence" remains unclear.

The translation of ἐνέργειαν πλάνης by the phrase "deluding influence" is an attempt by Bible translators to soften the original sense of the text. This is done primarily to lessen the idea that God sends *deception* upon mankind. *Πλάνη* occurs ten times in the New Testament. It is consistently translated "error" or "deception."[ccxv] If the phrase is translated as the individual words are throughout the New Testament, possible translation options are (1) power of deception; (2) working of deception; (3) working of error; or (4) power of error. Taken in this way, we conclude that God is sending on the wicked a power of deception.

The people's movement towards wickedness did not begin with God, but as verse 10 teaches, to perish is the destiny of the wicked. It is in light of this that God sends a power of deception. The deceptive power causes unbelievers to cast themselves with abandonment at the feet of Satan and his Antichrist.

Conclusion

It is our conviction that Satan will work and perform true miracles. He received this ability from God.

Chapter Ten
Confusion, Confusion, Confusion

> So when you see the Abomination of
> Desolation—spoken about by Daniel the
> prophet—standing in the holy place (let the reader
> understand), then those in Judea must flee to the
> mountains. (Matt. 24:15-16)

Both because our Lord initially connected the fulfillment of Daniel's prophetic abomination of desolation with the destruction of Jerusalem and because Matthew retained that connection, but emphasized the eschatological destruction of Jerusalem in the context of our Lord's return, we need to examine chapters 9–12 of the book of Daniel. With what is now a 1900-year gap between weeks sixty-nine and seventy, we must determine if such a gap was anticipated by Daniel. Since Daniel refers to this event on three separate occasions in these chapters, we must also determine if one or all three of these references form the basis of our Lord's prophetic promise. However, the most important reason we need to examine Daniel 9-12 concerns the actual timing of Daniel's initial prophecy. It is our conclusion that many futurists have incorrectly understood the intent of Daniel's prophecy and therefore, have introduced elements into its fulfillment that are not textually supportable. There is no easy way to expose you, the reader, to all these issues without asking you to patiently and prayerfully wade through the next few chapters.

Our Lord's reference to Daniel's abomination of desolation comes with a command. Judeans are to flee for safety after seeing the abomination of desolation (τὸ βδέλυγμα τῆς ἐρημώσεως = *to bdelugma tās erāmōseōs*) standing in the holy place. With the article τὸ (to = "the"), the Lord declares that this is the well-known abomination. In other words, this is something about which His Jewish audience should have known.

In Matthew 24:15, the Lord quotes a phrase from Daniel 12:11,[ccxvi] which states:

> From the time that the daily sacrifice is removed
> and the abomination that causes desolation is set
> in place, there are 1,290 days.

With a direct quote from Daniel 12:11, the Lord touches upon a host of issues that create great difficulty for many who try to correctly interpret Matthew's Olivet Discourse—not the least of which is the matter of the timing of its fulfillment. Since our Lord quotes from Daniel 12:11, but Daniel 9:24–27 contains the prophecy about the seventy weeks, we must clearly establish the relationship between these two passages since there is much disagreement about whether Daniel's Seventieth Week has any relevance for the church. Some see all of Daniel's Seventieth Week as already fulfilled; others insist that only the first half of the week was fulfilled; and still others argue that none of Daniel's final week has found fulfillment. Who is right? A correct answer will determine whether a future generation of our Lord's bride will or will not experience the great tribulation.

To discover a biblical answer to this question, we want to examine Daniel's record without any preconceived notions other than the fact that our Lord quoted from it. Of great interest to us is the fact that Daniel mentions an "abomination" three times in a prophetic context: Daniel 9:27; 11:31; and 12:11. We shall look at each reference to discover whether one is able to set a specific point in the past for fulfillment or whether an eschatological[38] fulfillment is yet to be expected.

Daniel's Abomination of Desolation

Daniel 11:31

Of the three verses, Daniel 11:31 is perhaps the easiest to identify: "His forces will rise up and profane the fortified sanctuary, stopping the daily sacrifice. In its place they will set up the abomination that causes desolation."[ccxvii] Even secular chronologists believe that fulfillment occurred in 167 B.C., when in connection with a rather famous event (the coming of Antiochus Epiphanes), the Jewish temple suffered a desecration that extended over a three-year period.

Concerning Daniel 11:31, Leon Wood writes,

> Antiochus Epiphanes (175–164 B.C.), the "little horn" of chapter eight and type of the Antichrist, is now presented.... The text concerns him for the following fifteen verses. The reason for so much attention is that, as in chapter eight, he prefigured the Antichrist, and there was a need for telling more about him in this capacity.[ccxviii]

---

[38] This term simply means having to do with the events of the very last days. It applies to the days just prior to the Lord's coming to physically rule upon the earth.

Daniel specifically identifies the work of Antiochus Epiphanes as "the abomination of desolation." This expression is the same as that found in Daniel 9:27, with the exception that here it is singular and has the article. This abomination is historically verifiable and can help us with later fulfillments of a similar nature. (See Daniel 8:12–14, 24–25.)

Daniel 12:11

Daniel 12:11 has the next level of certainty because the context in which it occurs is clearly yet future. Daniel 12:1–2 puts verse 11 clearly in the yet eschatological future. Daniel 12:1–2 indicates that the Jews will experience an unparalleled time of distress followed by a resurrection of the dead. The text says:

> At that time Michael, the great prince who watches over your people, will arise. There will be a time of distress unlike any other from the nation's beginning up to that time. But at that time your own people, all those whose names are found written in the book, will escape. Many of those who sleep in the dusty ground will awake—some to everlasting life, and others to shame and everlasting abhorrence.

In connection with these events, Daniel learns that forty-three months separate the beginning from the end of the events connected with this abomination of desolation. Only those who accept a less-than-literal interpretation of Daniel 12 will argue for any type of past fulfillment.

The fact that the Lord Jesus quotes this verse and signaled a yet future fulfillment from His day strongly supports our conclusion that this text yet awaits a literal fulfillment, notwithstanding the fact some argue for a fulfillment in connection with the destruction of the second temple by the Roman general Titus. However, with the annihilation of six million Jews during World War II, there is no sense in which the second temple destruction by Titus can be the worst persecution the Jews will ever experience. Any realistic fulfillment of Daniel 12:1 must await the future, which should cause all to pause when one compares the destruction of Jerusalem by Titus and the World War II extermination of six million Jews to a possible future fulfillment. How can it be any worse?

Daniel 9:27

This final text is the most difficult to understand and locate in time. Depending on one's understanding of Daniel 9:27 and its relationship to Daniel 9:24–26, one could draw the conclusion (as we do) that "on the wing of abominations" in verse 27 refers to things that will happen in Jerusalem after the destruction depicted in verse 26. This would require both destruction and a subsequent re-inhabiting of the city. Our thinking is this: Daniel 9:26 indicates the second temple destruction of Jerusalem by Titus. Therefore, Daniel 9:27 must refer to the desecration of a rebuilt temple.

Thus, the second temple destruction of Jerusalem occurs between Daniel's sixty-ninth and Seventieth Week. This precludes that either Daniel 9:27 or 12:11 has anything to do with the second temple destruction. Therefore, it is our belief that only Daniel 9:26 found fulfillment with the destruction of Jerusalem and the temple by Titus.

Premillennial scholars uniformly believe that Daniel 9:27 and 12:11 have a yet future fulfillment. Preterists,[39] on

---

[39] The word "preterism" comes from two Latin words: *praeter* ("beyond") and *ire* ("to go"). Preterism looks at certain biblical

the other hand, see a fulfillment for these prophecies in connection with the destruction of Jerusalem/temple by Titus. Given the division that exists among believers about the fulfillment of Daniel's prophecies, several questions come to mind, including: (1) Were any of Daniel's prophecies fulfilled in the second temple destruction by the Romans? (2) Do Daniel's prophecies have multiple referents or fulfillments? (3) How literal should we expect the fulfillment of Daniel's prophecies to be?

Since Daniel 11:31 and 12:11 are contextually clear regarding the timing of their fulfillment, we need only look in detail at Daniel 9:24–27. It remains enigmatic as to referent and fulfillment. Daniel 9:24–27 states,

> Seventy weeks have been decreed for your people and your holy city, to finish the transgression, to make an end of sin, to make atonement for iniquity, to bring in everlasting righteousness, to seal up vision and prophecy and to anoint the most holy place. So you are to know and discern that from the issuing of a decree to restore and rebuild Jerusalem until Messiah the Prince there will be seven weeks and sixty-two weeks; it will be built again, with plaza and moat, even in times of distress. Then after the sixty-two weeks the Messiah will be cut off and have nothing, and the people of the prince who is to come will destroy the city and the sanctuary. And its end will come with a flood; even to the end there will be war; desolations are determined. And he will make a firm covenant with the many for one week, but in the middle of the week he will put a stop to sacrifice and grain offering; and on the wing of

---

predictions as having already been fulfilled. See Stanley D. Toussaint, "A Critique of the Preterist View of the Olivet Discourse," *BSac* 161 (Oct 2004) p. 469, for details.

abominations will come one who makes desolate, even until a complete destruction, one that is decreed, is poured out on the one who makes desolate. (NASB, 1995)

This passage forms the basis of several significant truths, according to most conservatives. In their thinking, this passage predicts the death of the Messiah; the number of years until He is put to death; the number of years until the destruction of Jerusalem and the second temple; and the final seven-year period during which all the end-time events will occur, with the exception of the thousand-year reign of Christ upon the earth.

However, due to an interpretive judgment (which we believe does not have textual support) and a misunderstanding concerning the starting point for the 490 years Daniel prophetically reports in chapter nine, we are of the opinion that Daniel 9 requires reexamination. In the hope that you the reader will appreciate out conclusions about Daniel's Seventieth Week, it is necessary to look at this chapter in great detail. One issue of paramount importance concerns the historical date of the events depicted there. To accurately determine when to begin counting the years necessary to fulfill Daniel's prophecy, we must know when Daniel actually gave the prophecy. This is necessary before we examine what influence Daniel's final week has on Matthew 24.

The Date of Daniel 9:1:
Jewish vs. Western Calendar

The ninth chapter of Daniel opens with Daniel identifying the year during which this prophecy occurs. It is "the first year of Darius, the son of Ahasuerus, who was of Median descent and who had been made king over the kingdom of the Chaldeans" (Dan. 9:1).

It would first appear that Daniel has done us a great service. He lists the year and the king on the throne of Babylon, which should greatly aid us in knowing the time of Daniel's writing. Instead, the reference creates a major problem. Historical records and archeological evidence provide no proof of a king by the name of Darius ruling over the Chaldeans. There is also a problem with the chronology of the Persian period.

The primary problem seems to be that the rabbinic tradition only accounts for a fifty-two-year length of the Persian Empire, while secular chronologists indicate 208 years as the length of the Persian Empire. That's a 156-year discrepancy!

The Jewish Calendar

According to the Jewish calendar, we are 5,767 years removed from the day of creation. If we follow a strictly Jewish chronology, the destruction of Jerusalem by the Romans occurred in the year 3828. In the year 3338, the first temple was destroyed. One sees that from the Jewish year 3828 (second temple destruction) back to 3338 (first temple destruction) is exactly 490 years. In the Jewish chronology, the first temple stood for 410 years and the second temple stood for 420 years. Between these two periods is the seventy-year exile.

The Jewish chronology requires that the time period of Daniel 9 cover the period from the destruction of the first temple to the destruction of the second temple by the Romans. As stated earlier, to make the numbers fit, some Jewish chronologists make the length of the Persian period fifty-two years. The most obvious question is this: Does scripture support this conclusion? We believe it does not.

The Jewish chronology suggests that only four kings ruled Persia. This is patently contradicted by Daniel 11:2–3, which states,

> Now I will tell you the truth. Three more kings will arise for Persia. Then a fourth king will be unusually rich, more so than all who preceded him. When he has amassed power through his riches, he will stir up everyone against the kingdom of Greece. Then a powerful king will arise exercising great authority and doing as he pleases.

Taken at face value, this passage implies at least five kings of Persia. Since Cyrus reigns during the time of this prophecy and he was the first Persian king, then only four more would follow him. The fifth and final king, it appears from this text, would fall to Alexander the Great. However, most scholars believe at this point that Daniel left out five kings who would rule after the Persian king of great wealth who merely antagonized "the kingdom of Greece." That Daniel would list only five kings, when in reality there were would be ten, seems extremely uncharacteristic. It is possible, but not probable.

Unfortunately, the Persians are of little help in settling this question. Alexander the Great destroyed the majority of Persian records during his conquest. Secular historians of antiquity are no help either. They do not agree about the length of the Persian period. Modern historians have built their case by taking facts from different historians of antiquity. No two agree among ancient sources.

Finally, we must add that there is no concrete evidence that the Jews are attempting to hide 150-plus years of history. Given modern archaeology, such a feat would be impossible.

The Jews understand Daniel 9:24–27 to begin with Jeremiah's prophecy and to end with the second temple destruction. They accomplish this by indicating that the first seven weeks (forty-nine years) occurs between the destruction of Jerusalem in the year 3338 and the decree of Cyrus the Great, whom Isaiah calls "an anointed prince" (see Isa. 45:1) in the year 3390. Then they count from the decree of Cyrus to an agreement between the Romans and the Jewish leadership. Three-and-a-half years later, the Romans broke their promise, began a siege of Jerusalem, and finally completely destroyed Jerusalem and the temple a little over four years later.

All told, from Cyrus' decree to the destruction of Jerusalem is 441 years. In this scenario, Daniel 9:24–27 has nothing to do with the birth and death of Jesus of Nazareth. Jewish chronologists consider Cyrus the "anointed prince" of Daniel 9:25 and the Aaronic priesthood the "prince cut off and alone" of Daniel 9:26. Thus, the Jewish view understands that all 490 years of Daniel's prophecy have been fulfilled totally.

Inherent Problems with the Jewish View

There are clearly four problems with the Jewish chronology. First, from all appearances, it seems that Daniel intended the 490 years to be counted using a modified Egyptian solar calendar that marks time by counting twelve 30-day months as one year. This fact makes it impossible to count forty-nine years between the prophecy of Jeremiah and the decree of Cyrus because the actual period is closer to fifty-two years.

Second, Daniel's prophecy of 490 years looks forward from the issuing of a decree to restore Jerusalem. Now it is possible that a decree to rebuild the city could have been issued before the destruction of the city, but one would think the order would be the opposite. If Jeremiah issued a decree to rebuild Jerusalem, then Daniel should have known this, given that he was thoroughly familiar with the writings of Jeremiah.

The third problem with the Jewish chronology is that the modern way of counting time, the lunisolar calendar,[40] is inconsistent with how the seventy-year captivity was counted. As we shall see, the seventy-year captivity was counted using a pure lunar calendar of 354 days. Since the development of the sophisticated modern lunisolar calendar was a later addition to the Jewish chronologists relative to the Old Testament, to use it to calculate biblical dates prior to its development will most certainly introduce errors into the timeline.

---

[40] The lunisolar calendar is the modern way Jews count their year. It involves both a lunar calendar of twelve 29- and 30-day months, alternating based on the new moon with an additional month added periodically to keep the year constant with a solar calendar of 365.25 days per year. See the next chapter for a detailed understand of the lunisolar calendar.

The fourth problem is that the modern Jewish chronology fails to accurately account for Daniel 11:2–3. The true length of the Persian and Media Empire is closer to 116–131 years. Thus, the Jewish timeline is sixty-four to seventy-nine years too short. The Jewish chronology does not conform to nor confirm the biblical data in the book of Daniel. Therefore, we reject it.

The Western Calendar

Secular and many biblical chronologists, on the basis of one historian of antiquities by the name of Claudius Ptolemy (A.D. 70–161), accept the notion that the Persian Empire lasted 208 years. The following chart lists the ruling kings of Persia:

Traditional List of Persian Kings

King	Number of Years Ruled
Cyrus	539–530
Cambyses	530–522
Darius I	522–486
Xerxes I	486–464
Artaxerxes I	464–423
Darius II	423–404
Artaxerxes II	404–359
Artaxerxes III	359–337
Arses	337–335
Darius III	335–331

The reader should know that of all the other ancient lists of Persian kings, not a single one agrees with Ptolemy's list. The Jewish historian Josephus lists only six kings for the Persian period: (1) Cyrus, (2) Cambyses, (3) Darius Hystaspes, (4) Xerxes, (5) Cyrus, son of Xerxes, (6) Darius.

Most Jewish chronologists count only four: (1) Darius the Mede, (2) Cyrus, (3) Cambyses, and (4) Darius. One Persian poet, Firdausi, offers a list that contains only six kings of Persia. Concerning the whole matter of conventional chronology of the ancient world, James B. Jordan writes,

> The consensus chronology, used by secular scholar and Christian scholars alike, is built on fiction, creates huge problems with the history of every culture of the ancient world, and is collapsing today. Believing Christians can rejoice at this development, but students must be aware that many Bible Dictionary articles, Bible Encyclopedia articles, and Old Testament commentaries written in this century are replete with error wherever they discuss links between Bible history and the history of the ancient world.[ccxix]

While many westerners act as if the modern dating of the ancient world is set in stone, in actuality, there remains much uncertainty. The fact that Daniel says 483 years will pass between the command to restore Jerusalem and the second great destruction is sufficient evidence for us that the Western calendar is between seventy-seven to ninety-two years too long.[41]

We believe this to be the case for three reasons. First, the modern Western calendar counts according to a 365.25-day year when the Old Testament chronology is based on

---

[41] Conservative scholars are able to accommodate the extra seventy-seven to ninety-two years by starting the date of the fulfillment of Daniel's 483 years by accepting the 444 B.C. decree of Artaxerxes to Nehemiah as the beginning of the fulfillment. This is an issue we shall deal with later.

either a pure lunar calendar of 354 days or a modified Egyptian solar calendar of 360 days per year.

Second, there is at least a seventy-seven-year gap in Persian history that no historical or archaeological evidence has yet to confirm. The kings of this seventy-seven-year gap have only one Greek historian to support their existence. In other words, if we did not have the record of Ptolemy, the Greek historian, there would be no record of this seventy-seven-year period of the Persian Empire.

Third, and finally, the objective basis of the Western calendar are very subjective opinions about a particular lunar eclipse and comparative dates in a fifth century B.C. document found at a Jewish colony in Elephantine, Egypt. Ptolemy's historical account is supposedly confirmed by a reference to a solar eclipse in a recently discovered Persian document. Scientists have supposedly confirmed that the reference to a solar eclipse during a certain period in the ancient past is correct. This taken with historical references found in a document discovered in Elephantine, provides for some conclusive evidence that Ptolemy's records are historically accurate. However, the matter has much uncertainty about it.

There is only one objectively verifiable point in the ancient past that can form the basis of a reliable calendar for the Bible—the day of the creation of the world. The date of the world's creation is an objectively verifiable point, in our opinion, because the Bible specifies events with the day and month in which such events occurred from the very first day of creation until the destruction of the second temple by Titus. There are more than three hundred of these types of dated events in the Old Testament. As the reader will see later, we utilize this method to date the fulfillment of Daniel's prophecy.

Making Sense of the Nonsense

Taking Daniel 11:2–3 as the reason that Persia would have five kings before the Greeks conquered them, and the fact that Daniel seems to indicate that both a Median and a Persian king would rule simultaneously for the entire Persian empire, we disagree with both the Jewish and Western calendars regarding the length of the Persian empire.

This is not conventional wisdom. In fact, it flies in the face of the majority of scholarship about this period of history. Yet, allow us to present our case for our conclusion.

The Case for Simultaneous Kings

Daniel 8:20 indicates, "The ram that you saw with the two horns stands for the kings of Media and Persia." Notice that Daniel wrote, "The kings of Media and Persia." On its face, this statement requires us to understand that the horns do not represent the Medes and the Persians. The horns represent kings. This fact is incontrovertible.

Thus, there are several ways to understand Daniel's statement. First, it is possible that the Medes and Persians each had only one king since the ram had only two horns. A second possibility is that Media and Persia both had a number of kings during the whole period of their rule. Which of these two possibilities is supported by Daniel?

If only one line of kings ruled over two kingdoms, one would expect the text to read, "The king of Media and Persia," which is the way most scholars interpret this passage. Since we have the benefit of history, we know that Persia did have more than one king. However, we also know from Daniel that the Medes had at least one king. Therefore, it is more probable that the "two-horned ram" depicts two kingdoms, each with its own set of kings.

On three separate occasions, Daniel explicitly states that the great kingdom to follow the Babylonians would be composed of two peoples. In the statue of Nebuchadnezzar's dream, the silver portion (which represented the Medes and Persians) had two arms (Dan. 2:32).[42] In Daniel 5:28, Daniel must interpret the handwriting on the wall of the palace of Belshazzar. In so doing, Daniel relates to the king that "thy kingdom is divided, and given to the Medes and Persians." The kingdom was not divided in the sense of two equal halves, but divided in the sense that two peoples would control it.

We are not of the opinion that Daniel indicates that the Medes would have the kingdom for a short time to be followed by the Persians. For in Daniel 8:3, we learn that the second kingdom would have two kings—this, in light of the fact that the "ram" had two horns. Daniel 8:20 explicitly says, "The ram that you saw with the two horns stands for the kings of Media and Persia."

To be fair, there is a textual problem that gives some scholars the right to conclude that only one line of kings ruled over both the Medes and the Persians. The three versions of the Hebrew Bible have "king" (singular) instead of "kings" (plural) here.[ccxx] Only the Massoretic (original Hebrew) text of the Old Testament has the plural reading.

We are very comfortable with the Massoretic reading due to the extended discussion of this kingdom at Daniel 8:3. Clearly, two separate kingdoms are the focus of the ram image. While the Medes and the Persians were committed to the same agenda, they were separate people.

The sense of Daniel 8:20 would seem to be lost if the singular term *king* were read there instead of the plural term *kings*. If the word "kingdom" had been used here, then

---

[42] This, in and of itself, does not prove our point, since the fourth beast empire represented by the legs did not consist of two separate peoples.

maybe a singular term would be correct. After all, the Medes and Persians were one kingdom. But since the emphasis is not on the kingdom of the Medes and Persians, it seems that "two horns" require two "kings."

In comparison, when describing the kingdom of Greece, Daniel indicated that the male goat had one horn (Alexander the Great), which signifies that the third beast empire began with only one line of kings. However, that line of kings was broken off and in its place "four conspicuous horns" came up in its place. In the kingdom symbolized by the ram and the kingdom symbolized by the goat, the horns represent a line of kings.

Now it is very interesting that Daniel does not indicate that one of the horns of the ram was broken off, as was the great horn of the goat (Alexander the Great). Rather, in the case of Media and Persia, the Persian line of kings became the stronger, but the Media line of kings continued. Perhaps this explains the Jewish chronology. The Jews focused on the Persian line of kings. There were, in fact, four lines of kings that constituted the Medo-Persian Empire:

Darius, the Mede	Cyrus, his son Cambyses, Persian
Pseudo-Smerdis	Darius, his son Xerxes,
	Grandson, Artaxerses

Daniel 5:31 explicitly says, "Darius the Mede received the kingdom, being about sixty-two years old." This is undeniable proof that the Medes did have at least one king. Daniel also states that he (Daniel) "lived on until the first year of Cyrus the king" (Dan. 1:21) and that he "prospered during the reign of Darius and the reign of Cyrus the Persian."[43] We understand this to mean that some parts of the rule of Darius and Cyrus occurred at the same time.

---

[43] Some would translate this portion, "during the reign of Darius, even the reign of Cyrus the Persian," thus, giving the idea that Darius and

In light of these factors, it is our belief that during the rule of the Medes and Persians, there were two kings ruling simultaneously, each having a king on the throne, even when the Persians became the strongest as the scripture predicted. This would answer the question of why the different lists do not add up. Darius was the first king of Media to rule over Babylon. Cyrus was the first king of Persia to rule over Babylon. Daniel 11:2–3 affirms that, after Cyrus, there were to be only four Persian kings before the coming of Alexander to conquer the Persians. Thus, some of the kings in the secular lists were probably kings of the Medes who ruled from Babylon. A possible division of the kings might go something like this:

Suggested List of Median and Persian Kings

Media	Persian
Darius	Cyrus
Pseudo-Smerdis	Cambyses
	Darius Hystaspes
	Xerxes
	Artaxerxes

While we are not at all prepared to be dogmatic about this issue, we do feel that a scenario similar to what we suggest above will ultimately prove true. Chronologists are of very little help at this point. Still, as with so many other difficulties, future discoveries will confirm the biblical account.

Cyrus were the same person. However, to do so would require that Daniel made a mistake in identifying this person of Median ancestry. While we may not be able to prove that Daniel is correct, as we understand it, we must reject any notion that Daniel made a mistake in his report of the historical facts. We are well aware that scholars have called into question other historical facts reported in the book of Daniel only to be silenced by archeological discoveries.

It is worth mentioning at this point that some secular and biblical scholars excoriated Daniel regarding the identity of Belshazzar. They repeatedly accused Daniel of making an error because there were no records in Babylonian history of a king by the name Belshazzar. Then archeologists discovered writings that identified Belshazzar as the son of Nabonidus, who spent most of his time out of the capital of Babylon, leaving Belshazzar to co-rule. Archeology proved Daniel right and the critics wrong.[ccxxi] Another point of great interest is this: The rule of Belshazzar was simultaneous with that of his father, Nabonidus. Therefore, Daniel could speak of Belshazzar without reference to Nabonidus. Since Cambyses was the son Cyrus the Great, since Xerxes was the son of Darius, and since Artaxerxes was the son of Xerxes, it is more than likely that just as in the case of Belshazzar and Nabonidus, there was overlap in their reigns. This would explain why the Western calendar perhaps is seventy to ninety or more years too long.

An example of this phenomenon concerns the reign of Xerxes and his son Artaxerxes. A comparison of Nehemiah and the Jewish historian Josephus reveals an overlap of the reigns of these two kings, with the result that the same number of years is counted twice. Nehemiah 2:1, 6 declares, "It came to pass in the month Nisan, in the twentieth year of Artaxerxes the king.... It pleased the king to send me" to Jerusalem. Yet, Josephus indicates that Nehemiah came to Jerusalem in the twenty-fifth year of the reign of Xerxes. Secular chronologists report the reign of Xerxes to have lasted twenty-two years and that of Artaxerxes to have lasted forty-one years. Thus, it is possible that the reigns of these two kings overlapped to some degree.

History, once again, will have to confirm Daniel as being right concerning the identity of Darius the Mede. Also, history will eventually prove the correct understanding of the Persian period. Because of the confusion resulting from the duplication of names for certain kings (for example, Darius) and, in other instances, only titles such as Ahasuerus and Artaxerxes (Great Shah) were used; for these and other reasons, until archeologists uncover evidence to confirm or disprove chronologists, the Bible is the authority as far as this author is concerned.[44]

Therefore, Daniel 9:1 remains the most authentic reference to be trusted for the actual existence of Darius, the son of Ahasuerus, who was of Median descent and who had been appointed king over the Babylonian empire.[45] If Daniel 11:2–3 is taken as we have suggested, then the Persian empire had five kings:

Persian Kings and Length of Rule

King of Persia	Length of Rule
Cyrus	Nine years
Cambyses	Eight years
Darius	Thirty-six years
Xerxes	Twenty-two years
Artaxerxes	Forty-one years

This scenario puts the length of the Persian empire at 116 years and allows the chronology of Daniel 9 to end with the destruction of the second temple just one year after 434 years from the rebuilding of the walls of Jerusalem by Nehemiah. This complies with Daniel's prophecy that the destruction of Jerusalem and the sanctuary would occur after sixty-nine weeks and not during it.

---

[44] Whatever may come to light, it will only prove the Bible correct once again.

[45] If "Ahasuerus" is a title that means "Great Shah," then Daniel's identification of Darius as the first king of the Medes will require a whole new understanding of the historical references in the book of Daniel.

Chapter Eleven
Reconciling the Timelines

The major events of the Babylonian, Persian, Greek, and Roman empires are, for the most part, historically certain to have occurred; they are not in question. The primary problem is the absence of day, month, and year references for them. When one reads of an event as having occurred on January 1, 590 B.C., that date represents a modern attempt to count back to accurately pinpoint the date of the event using all the data of human history. However, whether we can assign a specific date to an event three thousand years ago depends on one Greek historian and a reference to a solar eclipse found in another ancient document.

We have days and months and years from one major event to the next, but no ancient source has given us a reference point that allows us to identify a point in ancient history as January 1, 1650 B.C. from the very beginning of time, except the Bible.

Secular and most biblical chronologists are certain that the Western dating system is, for the most part, accurate. This is primarily due to the dating system derived from an Assyrian eponym (pronounced ep-*uh*-nim),[46] which

---

[46] In this case, an "eponym" is any ancient official whose name was used to designate the year. In other words, during certain periods, each year

mentions a solar eclipse. This particular eclipse has been identified by astronomical calculations to have occurred on June 15, 763 B.C.

Perhaps the best-known biblical chronologist of modern times is Edwin R. Thiele. In his book, *The Mysterious Numbers of the Hebrew Kings*, he argues strongly that the modern dating system is accurate in light of the positive identity of this particular solar eclipse.

He writes,

> Since Ptolemy's canon gives precise and absolutely dependable data concerning the chronology of a period beginning with 747 B.C., and since the Assyrian eponym canon carries us down to 648 B.C., it will be seen that there is a century where these two important chronological guides overlap and where they may be used as a check on each other. The canon of Ptolemy provides the date 709 B.C. (year 39 of Nabonassar era) when Sargon, king of Assyria, became king of Babylon. From Assyria come two tablets, K 5289 and K 2588, that provide the information that the eponymy of Mannu-ki-Ashur-Li', the thirteenth year of Sargon as king of Assyria, was his first year as king of Babylon...Now on the basis of Ptolemy's canon we are able to provide dates to all the other eponymies of the Assyrian lists, and we thus secure 763 for the eponymy of Bur-Sagale—the same date as was secured for that eponymy by the evidence of the solar eclipse that took place that year in the month Simanu. So

was named for a person. So instead of designating January 1, 2007 as the year, January 1, the sixth year of Bush would be given. Thus, "Bush" is the eponym. In ancient times, each year a different person or king or official or governor was designated as that year's eponym. Instead of the year being designated by a number, the year was named after the person who was eponym for that year.

the date 763 for the eponymy of Bur-Sagale has been established not only by the astronomical evidence of Assyria but also by that Ptolemy's canon. We thus have complete assurance that 763 is the correct date for Bur-Sagale and that the other dates of the eponym lists, whether reckoned backward or forward from that date, are likewise correct.[ccxxii]

It would certainly seem from Thiele that the matter is settled. However, we are highly suspicious of using one astronomical event as the sole basis for the Bible's dependability. The simple fact that no one knows whether the eclipse in question was total or partial renders the whole discussion speculative. The lack of certainty about this fact demands anything but certainty. With regard to the solar eclipse of 763 B.C., there is evidence just as convincing that event could have occurred in the years 791, 771, 770, or maybe a whole century later. The problem concerns the year. No ancient people used a number to designate the year in the modern sense.

A More Excellent Way

Since we are absolutely committed to scripture and believe that there were no errors in the original manuscripts, we look to the Bible first to answer questions of historical chronology as it relates to the Old Testament period. If historical references confirm the biblical record, all the better. But if there is doubt or contradiction, we accept the biblical record as is. The Bible gives a host of data concerning chronology. Our primary problem concerns our ability to understand the significance of the data. If one trusts the Bible, he can set forth a chronology of the Old Testament from the first day of creation to the destruction of the second temple by Titus, the Roman general. Doing so will result in about a one-hundred-year discrepancy between the biblical record and the modern Western calendar.

In the first pages of the Old Testament appears a genealogical list that begins with Adam, the first man, and stops with the sons of Noah: Shem, Ham, and Japheth. However, scholars have long debated the chronology depicted in Genesis 5. Depending on which version of the Old Testament one uses, the number of years represented by the genealogy of Adam is either 1,556 years according to the Massoretic Hebrew Bible, 2,142 years according to the Septuagint (the Greek translation of the Hebrew Old Testament), or 1,207 years according to the Samaritan Pentateuch. Trying to reconcile these numbers has forced scholars to take many different views regarding the intent of the author. Some take the numbers literally, others symbolically. Still others take the numbers in a hybrid literal or fictional/symbolical sense. Perhaps, there is another way to understand the differences between the numbers in the different versions of the Old Testament.

A Possible Explanation

In *The Secret System: A Study of the Chronology of the Old Testament*, Gerhard Larsson offers a suggestion for how one might appreciate the differences in Old Testament chronology.[ccxxiii] Larsson takes the chronological references literally, but believes that they were adjusted by a redactor of the Old Testament.[47] In Larsson's view, the redactor of the

---

[47] Redaction criticism is the belief that parts of the Old and New Testaments are the results of redactions. That is, separate written sources from several streams of tradition were joined together to make what is now considered the Pentateuch or the Gospels. The person responsible for editing the different source materials is called a "redactor." Following this line of thinking, Moses is not the final author of the Pentateuch, but

Old Testament developed an artificial scheme with the data of the Old Testament in order to hide a system that was intended to hold special information for those who find the secret system of calendar reckoning.[ccxxiv]

Larsson summarizes:

> The hypothesis is that there was one concluding redaction embracing twelve books: Genesis, Exodus, Leviticus, Numbers, Deuteronomy, Joshua, Judges, I–II Samuel, I–II Kings, I–II Chronicles (including Ezra 1:1–3:7), Jeremiah and Ezekiel. These twelve books constituted the first Bible canon. One of the connecting elements was the chronology....[ccxxv]

Additionally, Larsson adds:

> The chronological data given in the sections of the Bible concerned are taken from three calendars, whose origins were fixed at the beginning of the first day of Creation and which thereafter ran parallel. Of these calendars, one based on the ancient lunar year of 354 days, one on the Egyptian solar year of 365 days and one on the "standard" year (a solar year where 4 years = 4 x 365 + 1 day). They were employed in the normal way, the lunar year consisting of 12 months of 29 and 30 days alternatively, the Egyptian solar year

---

rather, an unknown redactor hundreds of years after the death of Moses is responsible for organizing four or more sources into what we now call the Pentateuch. Matthew is not the author of the gospel of Matthew, but rather, an unknown redactor molded and shaped the book that bears his name. This method is largely accepted by liberal scholars who reject the Bible, just as conservatives know it to be the inspired Word of God. We reject redaction criticism as a method of biblical study and the conclusions that it fosters.

consisting of 12 months of 30 days followed by 5 intercalary days, and the standard year with one extra intercalated day every fourth year...In the luni-solar calendar, special months were intercalated with the aid of direct observations, in order to compensate the differences between the lunar and the solar years; however, this compensating process was not employed in the chronological system of the original OT, which was quite natural, as corrections did not follow a regular pattern at this time.[ccxxvi]

Larsson believes three calendars are the basis for references that occur in much of the Old Testament. He is specifically focused on events from the creation to the end of Judah's exile. Following Larsson's system, the events of the Old Testament from creation to the end of Judah's exile would date as reflected on the chart on the opposite page.

Larsson's system does provide an explanation for the textual difficulties in the Bible involving chronological references. For example, Genesis 5:32 indicates that Noah was five hundred years old at the birth of his son Shem.

The text states, "After Noah was 500 years old, he became the father of Shem, Ham, and Japheth." Yet, at the birth of Arpachshad, the son of Shem and grandson of Noah, Genesis 11:10 reports that Shem was one hundred years old. The text states, "This is the account of Shem. Shem was 100 [years] old when he became the father of Arpachashad, two years after the flood."

Three-Calendar Dates for
Major Old Testament Events

Event	Lunar Calendar	Solar Calendar	Impr. Solar Calendar
Creation of Adam	6–7.1.1[1]	7.1.1	7.1.1
Death of Adam	7.1.931	2.13.902	17.5.902
Birth of Noah	7.1.1057	11.3.1025	1.7.1024
Birth of Shem	7.1.1557	16.2.1510	4.2.1509
End of the Flood	11.3.1658	3.4.1608	27.2.1607
Birth of Arpachshad	11.3.1660	11.3.1610	4.2.1609
Birth of Eber	11.3.1725	26.3.1673	4.2.1672
Death of Noah	11.3.2008	18.9.1947	17.5.1946
Abram departs Haran	11.3.2025	11.3.1964	11.11.1962
Birth of Aaron	11.3.2362	14.1.2291	22.6.2289
Birth of Moses	11.3.2363	3.1.2292	11.6.2290
Manna Begins to Fall	18.10.2445	15.2.2372	3.7.2370
Death of Moses	3.12.2486	3.1.2412	11.5.2410
Temple Destruction	7.5.3352	10.5.3251	18.2.3249
Mitigation of Jehoiachin	25.12.3377	20.3.3276	27.12.3273
End of Seventy Years subjugation	29.6.3403	20.12.3300	16.9.3298

[1] The numbers in the chart reflect the day, month, and year of a particular event. For example, the death of Adam on the lunar calendar is 7.1.931, which means Adam died on the seventh day of the first month of the year 931 after the first day of creation. Since a solar year has more days than a solar year, lunar years are shorter than solar years and thus pile up faster. Thus, by the death of Adam, there is a twenty-nine-year difference between the lunar and solar calendars in terms of the number of years since the first day of creation.

The Bible specifically states that the birth of Arpachshad occurred two years after the flood. The flood is reported to have occurred when Noah was six hundred years old. The text specifically states, "In the six hundredth year of Noah's life, the second month, on the seventeenth day of the month," which is sufficient information to date this event from the first day of creation. Thus, Shem should be 102 years old at the time of Arpachshad's birth. Critics and unbelievers naturally point to this as an example of an error in the Bible.

Larsson believes that birth dates follow a pure lunar calendar in Genesis as do all other events, with the one exception that Genesis 11:10 gives dates according to "an improved calendar."[48] Thus, Shem was one hundred *lunar*

---

[48] The Old Testament potentially uses three different calendars to calculate time: (1) a lunar calendar of 354 days per year, (2) an Egyptian solar calendar of 360 days per year, with an additional five days added at

years old at the beginning of the flood, but according to the improved calendar, he was one hundred *improved solar years* old at the birth of Arpachshad.[ccxxvii] Thus, "Shem was 100 *lunar years* at the beginning of the Flood but also 100 *improved years to the very day* at the birth of Arpachshad."[ccxxviii]

In connection with the Exodus of the Jews from Egypt, Larsson writes,

> I will take another example with a partly different type of chronological construction: the Exodus and the connected events. Many dates are given but, viewed superficially; they do not seem to present any special problems. After more careful study, however, we find a rather confusing picture of exact dates of events mixed with round and somewhat contradictory lengths of periods. Aaron, for example, died 40 years after his and Moses' meeting with Pharaoh (Exod 7,7; Num 33,38–39). Moses should then be 120 years old. But at his death considerably later he is still only 120 years old. While further still a couple of months remain until 40 years have passed since the Exodus and even less time has passed since the people reached the desert, he declares that they have now been wandering for 40 years in this big desert (Deu 2,7).
>
> Later we are told that manna—which started to fall only one month after Exodus and was to fall for 40 years (Exod 16,35)—did not cease to fall before the people had crossed Jordan.

---

the end of each year, and (3) an improved calendar consisting of 365.25 days per year.

All these discrepancies may be explained by assuming that 40 years was just a round figure and not should be considered as an exact period. More difficult is to accept that it in Num 14,33–34 is declared that—after the spies had returned from Canaan—the children of Israel would wander in the desert in 40 years as a punishment for their disobedience. But later we are told that the punishment just took 38 years (Deu 2,14).[ccxxix]

Larsson explains these chronological difficulties in the following manner:

We find for example that Aaron's death date—the first day of the fifth month in the fortieth year according to the text and also according to the solar calendar in the solution above—corresponds surprisingly enough to the date of 11.3 in the lunar calendar, His birth date will be the same but 123 years earlier. This means that *all forefathers after the Flood up to Aaron will have this connecting date for their births and deaths.* And, remarkably enough, in the same time the birth day of the first High Priest "happens" to fall in the Passover day, the most important feast day, in the solar calendar.

Moses will also have the birth date 11.3. But the length of his life—120 years—is reckoned in solar years, not lunar years. This solves the contradiction compared with Aaron. In the lunar calendar the death date agrees with the Bible text that the crossing of Jordan took place the tenth day of the first month (Josh 4,19) after 30 days of mourning and a few days reconnoitering and preparation.

We also find from the table that the period of manna is 40 years to the day in the solar calendar, that the period from the day of the 40 years condemnation after the return of the spies up until the desert is abandoned is as said (Num 14,34) 40 years to the day in the lunar calendar in the same time as the period between this last day and the day when Kadesh was left (and the desert wandering started) is in the improved solar calendar also exactly 38 years—as told in Deu 2,14. The table thus gives an exact solution to all the different time periods and dates mentioned in the text at the same time that it emphasizes the inner connection with the forefathers from the Flood to the Exodus.[ccxxx]

At the outset, we must make a critical distinction. We do not agree with Larsson about how the text came to reflect the three-calendar system (in other words, that a redactor made the changes to the text two-hundred-plus years before Christ). We believe the individual books of Old Testament were written by those who claim to have written them. Yet, we are satisfied that a three-calendar system best explains what would otherwise be considered errors in the biblical text. The explanation for how this system came to be reflected in the Old Testament, if true, is best credited to the Holy Spirit rather than man's creativity.

Now if one starts three calendars from the very first day of creation, as Larsson does: (1) a lunar calendar of 354 days per year, (2) an Egyptian solar calendar of 360 days per year, with an additional five days added at the end of each year, and (3) an improved calendar consisting of 365.25 days per year—what are the chances that the historical references connected with the Exodus would fall on a specifically verifiable date on at least one of those calendars?

Larsson, who is a professor of mathematics at the Royal Institute of Technology in Stockholm, Sweden, writes,

> In this case there is an accumulation of different chronological data—ages, the date of Aaron's death, the period of wandering in the wilderness, the dates when the Israelites began to eat manna and when they stopped eating manna, etc.... In this case there was an extremely small chance, from a statistical point of view, that there could be a solution which was in agreement—to the day— with all this chronological information from different biblical books. But nevertheless there was a solution.

> Working in this way and testing all the possibilities of using different calendars, different alternatives given in the text, etc, it can be shown mathematically and statistically that, merely for these groups of events, the chance of finding a solution which satisfies the given conditions is very small indeed, in fact only a fraction of a million. A solution has nevertheless emerged.[ccxxxi]

Utilizing the three-calendar-system, we shall return to the timing of the ninth chapter of the book of Daniel and the fulfillment of Daniel's 490-year prophecy.[49]

---

[49] Whether the three-calendar system accurately explains all the textual issues in the Old Testament will continue to be debated and examined. When we applied the method to the prophecy of Daniel 9, we found it compelling.

The Book of Daniel and Three-Calendar System

If we apply this system to the book of Daniel, the deportation of the first group of Jews to Babylon by Nebuchadnezzar occurs on:

Three-Calendar Date for Judah's Deportation

Lunar Calendar	Solar Calendar	Improved Calendar
29.6.3333	25.1.3233	13.11.3230

Using these dates as reference points, we can specifically date the historical references given in the book of Daniel pertaining to both the Babylonian and Persian empires.

The books of the Old Testament most related to the Persian Empire are Ezra, Nehemiah, Esther, Haggai, and Zechariah. The following chart lists the historical references to Persian kings in each book:

Historical References to
Persian Kings after Judah's Restoration

Ezra	Nehemiah	Esther	Haggai	Zechariah
Cyrus first year, 1:1	Twentieth year [of King Artaxerxes]	Days of Ahasuerus, 1:1	Second year of Darius the king,	Second year of Darius, 1:1
Cyrus to Darius, 4:5 Ahasuerus 4:6 Artaxerxes, 4:7	Twentieth year of King Artaxerxes 2:1	Third year of Ahasuerus, 1:3	Second year of Darius the king, 1:15	Second year of Darius, 1:7
Darius second year, 4:24 Cyrus, Darius, Artaxerxes, 6:14	Twentieth year to thirty-second year – King Artaxerxes 5:14	Twelfth year of King Ahasuerus, 3:7	Second year of Darius, 2:10	Fourth year of King Darius, 7:1
King Darius sixth year, 6:15	Thirty-second year of Artaxerxes king of Babylon, 13:6			
Artaxerxes 7:1 Seventh year of Artaxerxes, 7:7				

We find four of the five kings of Persia mentioned in these books. The book of Daniel acknowledges one king of the Medes—Darius. A list of the Babylonian, Mede, and Persian kings that appear in the book of Daniel follows:

Historical References to Kings
in the Book of Daniel

Nebuchadnezzar	Dan 1:1	First year of reign
Cyrus the king	Dan 1:21	Until first year of reign
Nebuchadnezzar	Dan 2:1	Second year of reign
Belshazzar	Dan 5:1	No date given
Belshazzar	Dan 5:30	Chaldean king slain
Darius the Mede	Dan 5:31	First year of reign
Darius	Dan 6:28	No date given
Cyrus the Persian	Dan 6:28	No date given
Belshazzar	Dan 7:1	First year of reign
Belshazzar	Dan 8:1	Third year of reign
Darius	Dan 9:1	First year of reign
Cyrus	Dan 10:1	Third year of reign
Darius the Mede	Dan 11:1	First year of reign

The three-calendar-system would offer the following chart of dates for the book of Daniel:

Three-Calendar Dates for
The Book of Daniel

Event	Lunar	Solar	Improved
Judah's Captivity Begins	29.6.3333	25.1.3233	13.11.3230
Nebu'nezzar's Second	3334	3233	3231
Cyrus' First Year Begins	30.9.3402	25.3.3300	26.12.3297
Judah's Captivity Ends	29.6.3403	20.12.3300	16.9.3298

From the chart, we discern that the seventy years of captivity were to be counted in lunar years. This is not unexpected, since much of the Old Testament marks time by a pure lunar calendar. However, with the prophecy of Daniel 9, as we shall see, time will follow the solar calendar modeled after the Egyptian solar year—twelve 30-day months without the intercalary of five additional days.

Perhaps the reason God chose the Egyptian calendar system is because the Jews would be without their sacrificial system for a number of years during the 490-year prophetic period. It is also clear that during the fulfillment of Daniel's prophecy, the Romans used a calendar closer to the Egyptian model. Why God utilizes the Egyptian calendar system we can only speculate, but that the Egyptian calendar is the one of choice to mark the spacing of Daniel's 490 years is not guesswork. This we will prove in the next chapter.

Putting It All Together

Isaiah prophesied that Cyrus, God's anointed, would initiate the rebuilding of Jerusalem and lay the foundation of the temple (Isaiah 44:5–45:1) more than 150 years before it happened. Ezra confirms (Ezra 1:1) that Isaiah's prophecy did come true. Two years after Cyrus allowed exiled Jews to return to the land, the foundation of the temple was laid (Ezra 3:10).

Ezra then reports,

> Then the people of the land discouraged the people of Judah, and frightened them from building and hired counselors against them to frustrate their counsel all the days of Cyrus King of Persia, even until the reign of Darius king of Persia. (Ezra 4:4–5)

About fifteen years later, during the second year of the reign of Darius king of Persia, the Jews finished the temple. Scripture indicates that Cyrus, the Persian king, would send the Jews home to build God a house (Ezra 1:1; 2 Chron. 36:22, Isaiah 44:28–45:1). This decree is generally believed to have occurred during his first sole regnal year. However, it is with certainty that the temple in Jerusalem was not completed until about twenty years after Cyrus' decree.

Daniel 9:2 states, "[I]n the first year of his [Darius'] reign I, Daniel, came to understand from the sacred books that, according to the word of the LORD disclosed to the prophet Jeremiah, the years for the fulfilling of the desolation of Jerusalem were seventy in number." Jeremiah 25:11 specifically states, "This whole area will become a desolate wasteland. These nations will be subject to the king of Babylon for seventy years."

This verse refers specifically to the subjugation of nations (among which Judea was one) for seventy years. Babylon's *subjugation* of the nations would last seventy years. However, as reflected in Daniel's prayer, the subjugation of the nations was not Daniel's primary concern. Closer examination of Daniel's prayer finds Jerusalem and God's holy hill to be the center focus of his requests before God in the ninth chapter (Dan. 9:3–19).

The time of Jeremiah 25 coincides with the year when Nebuchadnezzar defeated Pharaoh Necho at Carchemish. One year later, the subjugation and first deportation of Jews occurred. Seventy pure lunar years later, Cyrus, the first Persian king, issued a proclamation allowing all those deported by the Babylonians to return, including the Jews (Ezra 1–4). Jeremiah 29:11–12 reaffirms God's promise that Babylon's subjugation would last seventy years.

The reader should keep clearly in mind that the restatement of Jeremiah 29 came almost ten years after the first deportation of Jews to Babylon. In other words, the first Jews were taken to Babylon ten years before Jeremiah's reminder in chapter twenty-nine. Following the three-calendar system for the events connected with the events of Daniel 9, we suggest that the first year of Darius the Mede would be 3400 (lunar), 3298 (Egyptian solar), and 3295 (improved) years from the first day of creation.

According to the three-calendar system, the first deportation occurred in the year 3333 (lunar). The complete ruination of the temple occurred in the year 3352 (lunar), just less than nineteen years after the subjugation of the land by the Babylonians. We believe Daniel understood that, just as the subjugation lasted seventy (lunar) years, the ruined state of the temple would last seventy (lunar) years, as well. However, the starting points for the two events are not the same. The total ruin of Jerusalem occurred in the year 3352 (lunar). Therefore, not until the year 3422 (lunar) would that curse be lifted, which is exactly when the temple was completely restored in fulfillment of both Isaiah's and Jeremiah's prophecies. Please notice that this is a full seventeen years after the decree that the Jews could return to Judea.

As Daniel is praying, confessing, and beseeching God to grant favor to Jerusalem and His Temple Mount, Gabriel shows up with information regarding the Jews, Jerusalem, and the sanctuary. Daniel will soon learn that the future of both Jerusalem and God's holy hill will be restored, only to experience another period of destruction later—before final restoration and eternal peace comes.

Chapter Twelve
490 Years (Daniel 9:24)

> Seventy weeks have been decreed upon your people and upon your holy city to put an end to rebellion, to bring sin to completion, to atone for iniquity, to bring in everlasting righteousness, to seal up vision and prophecy, and to anoint a most holy. (Dan. 9:24)

Daniel 9:24 promises Daniel that his longed for hopes of peace and prosperity for Jerusalem and God's holy hill must await another seventy-week season of heartache and pain. Only after seventy weeks will the Jews and Jerusalem be free of their burden of sin, rebellion, and brokenness. A new age marked by righteousness will come.[50]

Seventy weeks is the decreed length of Daniel's prophecy. Scholars have continued to devote attention to its meaning. It is our understanding that the seventy weeks represents 490 years. *Shabu'îm* is the Hebrew word "weeks." It basically means "sevens." It is primarily the context of Daniel 9 that influences scholars to conclude that the angel

---

[50] Daniel's six outcomes divide evenly. Three outcomes ([1] to put an end to Israel's rebellion nature; [2] to bring Israel's sin of unbelief to an end; and [3] for Israel to atone for her iniquity by serving a sentence of punishment [the time of the Gentiles]) are completed during the 490-year period. Three outcomes ([1] to bring in everlasting righteousness by God changing their hearts through a new covenant; [2] to prove once and for all, God's faithfulness to His prophetic word; and [3] to anoint the most holy place) are the result of the end of the weeks.

intends "weeks of years." Since either days or months would yield a time period far too short for the fulfillment of the prophecies outlined in both chapters two and seven, years are the only reasonable solution in this author's opinion.

Equally, taking the term to refer to a spiritually perfect space of time leaves the text open to mere speculation. In this rare case, we allow history to confirm that "years" is the angel's intended meaning. That said, we must busy ourselves with the issue of how to correctly count the years and when to start to clock to move towards fulfillment.

The three-calendar system has demonstrated that certain portions of the Old Testament have three possible calendars by which to date events. Therefore, it is possible that Daniel's 490-year period could consist of:

173,460 days (354-day lunar year x 490 years)
178,360 days (360-day Egyptian year x 490 years, plus 5 days x 490 years)
178,972.5 days (365-day improved year x 490 years, plus .25 day x 490 years)

Since Judah's captivity was counted using a pure lunar calendar, we know Daniel had this option available. Yet, it would appear that the best system for counting the days necessary to fulfill Daniel's 490-year prophecy is the Egyptian calendar of twelve 30-day months per year. It's true that 360-day years would be easy to count, but would not maintain the months in their proper seasons. So the Jews must have used more than one calendar. Is there any biblical or extra-biblical support for this claim? Yes! The idea of the Jews using at least two methods to reckon time—one strictly for counting time between events and another for maintaining seasonal feasts—is not farfetched. In the books of Enoch 78:15–16, an indication is given that during the second century before the Lord Jesus, the Jews clearly used both a lunar year of 354 days and a solar year of 365 days.[51]

Over many years, the Jews came to use a twelve-month year with a twenty-nine or thirty-day alternating cycle, which required a thirteenth month every so often to keep the seasons in their correct months. This system was continually refined until it acquired the present modern-day lunisolar calendar format.

What Does a Modern Jewish Year Look Like?

The modern Jewish way of reckoning a year is remarkably consistent. An ordinary (non-leap) year has 353, 354, or 355 days.[52] A leap year has 383, 384, or 385 days.[53]

---

[51] The Books of Enoch is a group of pseudepigraphic writings ascribed to Enoch the son of Jared and father of Methuselah. The works are usually dated near the beginning of the second century B.C. Zondervan *Pictorial Encyclopedia of the Bible* states, "Book III is the so-called Book of the Heavenly Luminaries and covers chapters 72–82. It is an almost purely scientific treatise, showing virtually no interest in ethical questions. The author seeks to construct a uniform astronomical system from the data of the Old Testament and argues that the measurement of time should be solar rather than lunar. Interestingly, however, the author's solar year is 364 days though he is aware of the 365 1/4 day year." (Zondervan *Pictorial Encyclopedia of the Bible*, Vol. 2 (Grand Rapids: The Zondervan Corporation, 1976) pp. 309–310.

[52] A year consisting of 353 days is called a "deficient" year. It is one day less than a regular year, which has 354 days, and two days less than a complete year, which is composed of 355 days. A normal lunar year is 354 days. The Jewish calendar finds it necessary to either add an extra day or subtract a day from a regular year (354 days) to prevent the first day of a new calendar year from falling on a Sunday, Wednesday, or Friday.

[53] The Jewish lunisolar calendar requires the addition of a thirteen-month every two to three years. Thus, a deficient leap year would have 383 days; a regular year would have 384 days, with a leap complete year having 385 days. This prevents the New Year from occurring on Sunday,

The three lengths of the years are termed "deficient," "regular," and "complete," respectively. An ordinary year has twelve months and a leap year has thirteen months. Every month starts (approximately) on the day of a new moon. Under this scenario, the years and months are as follows:

Months on the Modern Jewish Calendar

Name	Length in a deficient year	Length in a regular year	Length in a complete year
Tishri	30	30	30
Heshvan	29	29	30
Kislev	29	30	30
Tevet	29	29	29
Shevat	30	30	30
Adar I	30	30	30
Adar II	29	29	29
Nisan	30	30	30
Iyar	29	29	29
Sivan	30	30	30
Tammuz	29	29	29
Av	30	30	30
Elul	29	29	29
Total	353 or 383	354 or 384	355 or 385

Given the modern Jewish lunisolar calendar, no combination of "deficient," "regular," and "complete" years adds up to 1,260, 1,290, or 1,335 days, which mark the fulfillment of the latter half of Daniel's final week.

The closest cycle of years would consist of 1,269 days,[54] 1,285 days,[55] or 1,300 days.[56] Given the following: (1) the preciseness of the numbers given in the book of Daniel—1,260, 1,290, and 1,335; (2) that no combinations of lunisolar years equal these numbers, and (3) the difficulty the

---

Wednesday or Friday. The leap month is called Adar 2 and always has 29 days.

[54] This combination is composed of a complete year, a deficient leap year, a complete year, and half a complete leap year.

[55] This combination is composed of a complete leap year, a regular year, a complete year, and half a deficient leap year.

[56] This combination is composed of a deficient leap year followed by a complete year, followed by a complete leap year and half of a following complete year.

---

average Jewish person most likely would have had trying to figure out Jewish lunisolar years in the modern sense, we conclude that Daniel did not intend for the Jewish people to follow a lunisolar-year calendar to mark the passing of time to see the fulfillment of his prophecy.

Until we are given better evidence, we conclude that Daniel's Seventieth Week prophecy requires the simple method of the Egyptian calendar when counting (360 days per year without the intercalary five days). One thousand two hundred and sixty days is exactly three-and-a-half Egyptian solar years. One additional mouth is one thousand two hundred and ninety days. Two and half additional months equals one thousand three hundred and thirty-five days.

That nations were counting the year as twelve 30-day months without the addition of intercalary days perhaps is confirmed by a parenthetical note in the writings of Herodotus, the Greek historian. In his book, *Histories: The 28 Logoi, Book III*, Herodotus recounts the list of provincial governorships, which were called "satrapies." All governorships were responsible to pay an annual tribute to Darius I, the Persian King, during Daniel's time. Concerning the tribute of the fourth governorship, Herodotus writes,

> The Cilicians paid 500 talents of silver, together with 360 white horses (one for each day in the year); of the money, 140 talents were used to maintain the cavalry force which guarded Cilicia, and the remaining 360 went to Darius.

In Herodotus' complete list, the number *360* appears five times as the sum of the talents of gold paid by individual governorships.

It is our belief that the time from the subjugation of the southern tribe to Babylon until their release by Cyrus is seventy lunar years. We also believe that the time from

Cyrus' release until the destruction of Jerusalem by Titus is 483 Egyptian solar years, without the necessary intercalary days added. This, we shall defend in the following chapter.

Chapter Thirteen
Jerusalem's Timeline (Daniel 9:25)

And know and understand: From the issuing of a word to restore and rebuild Jerusalem until an anointed one, a prince, seven weeks [49 years]. And sixty-two weeks [434 years] it will return and be built with plaza and moat, and in distressful times. (Dan. 9:25)

In this chapter, we will look at key details raised in Daniel 9:25. Before we do that, however, keep in mind a fundamental difference between typical futurists whose timeline for the fulfillment of Daniel's 490-year prophecy follows this pattern. The prophecy began in 444 B.C. and ended just days before the Lord's death in Jerusalem in A.D. 33 (483 years). A final seven years will begin either near or just after the rapture (pretrib) or just after the great tribulation (posttrib). Between these two events is the church age.

A better way of thinking about this time in our opinion is to see the beginning of Daniel's 490-year prophecy associated with the decree of Cyrus allowing the Jews to return and concluding with the destruction of the second temple in Jerusalem. The final seven years are still to come with the period between these two events comprising the desolation of the Jews. What follows is a defense of this position.

Please keep this in mind as you read the following chapters. However, before we look at the timeline in detail, we must first deal with a translation matter in verses 25–26. Daniel 9:25 states:

> So you are to know and discern *that* from the issuing of a decree to restore and rebuild Jerusalem until Messiah the Prince *there will be* seven weeks and sixty-two weeks; it will be built again, with plaza and moat, even in times of distress. (NASB)

The sense is that from the time a decree is issued to rebuild Jerusalem under certain conditions until Messiah the Prince, there will be sixty-nine weeks (483 years of twelve 30-day months). As this verse appears in many Bible versions, the translators have made several critical decisions of which many readers are unaware, yet they become the basis for the formation of dogmatic theological positions in light of those decisions.

First, the translators posit "messiah" as the correct translation for the Hebrew term. The translators also placed a capital "M" on "messiah" to designate this as a reference to Jesus Christ alone. Yet, of the thirty-nine occurrences of *anointed* in the Hebrew text, Daniel 9:25–26 contains the only two examples in the English translation which use "messiah" to refer specifically to the Lord Jesus. Neither the Hebrew text (Massoretic) nor the Greek text (Septuagint) explicitly supports such a decision. All the other thirty-seven occurrences are translated by the English word "anointed," in most translations.[ccxxxii] It's obvious that the decision to refer specifically to the Lord Jesus leads the English reader to draw certain conclusions that may or may not be correct. *There is no textual basis for this decision on the part of the translators.*

Second, the translators place the article "the" before the terms "prince" and "messiah." There is no article reflected in the Hebrew text either at Daniel 9:25 or 26. *There is no textual basis for this decision.*[ccxxxiii] Third, most translators decide to ignore the Massoretic text regarding the relationship between the "seven weeks" and the "sixty-two weeks." The Massoretic text suggests that there are two time periods. While the punctuation of the Massoretic text came hundreds of years after the birth of Christ and might suffer from certain biases on the part of those who punctuated it, any decision to reject their punctuations must be defended as much as any decision to accept them. In other words, one should not pick and chose only those suggestions that agree with one's presuppositions.

The NASB takes the traditional approach and depicts the two time periods as joined together: *"there will be seven weeks and sixty-two weeks."* However, the Massoretic text places an *athnāh*, which is the second greatest stop in the Hebrew text, below *shabuwa'* ("week"). It means that the verse is to be divided into at least two logical parts.

This is the way the text was translated in the original 1611 King James Bible. This is also the way the translators of the new English Standard Version chose to represent the Hebrew reading. There is sufficient historical evidence to argue for a distinction between "seven weeks" and "sixty-two weeks." Thomas E. McComiskey concludes:

> Thus, the Massoretic tradition is in full accord with Hebrew grammar and syntax in every respect. It is a valid way to understand the consonantal text. On the other hand, the arrangement of the numerals required by the messianic view, while not impossible, is without biblical parallel and suffers from a lack of precision in the numerical ordering of events. In this view, the significance of the division of the

sixty-nine weeks into seven and sixty-two is left undefined by the text itself and the rebuilding of the city is left without a time reference, that is, it could take place during the seven weeks or the sixty-two weeks or cut across both. It is suggested here that the Massoretic accentuation should be observed unless it can be demonstrated on other exegetical grounds that the time divisions of v 25 belong to the same clause.[ccxxxiv]

There is a similar acknowledgement to McComiskey's conclusion in the NET Bible. In a footnote, the NET Bible explains:

The accents in the MT [Massoretic Text] indicate disjunction at this point, which would make it difficult, if not impossible, to identify the "anointed one/prince" of this verse as messianic. The reference in v. 26 to the sixty-two weeks as a unit favors the MT accentuation, not the traditional translation. If one follows the MT accentuation, one may translate "From the going forth of the message to restore and rebuild Jerusalem until an anointed one, a prince *arrives*, there will be a period of seven weeks. During a period of sixty-two weeks it will again be built, with plaza and moat, but in distressful times."[ccxxxv]

Notice the translation of Daniel 9:25–26 reflected there:

Know therefore and understand that from the going out of the word to restore and build Jerusalem to the coming of an anointed one, a prince, there shall be seven weeks. Then for sixty-two weeks it shall be built again with squares and moat, but in a troubled time. And after the sixty-two weeks, an anointed one shall be cut off and shall have nothing.

One immediately becomes aware of the consequences of following the Massoretic text. That is, this passage does not explicitly refer to Jesus Christ or the death of the Messiah. *That is significant.* It's a point this author had failed to notice until compelled to do so as a result of this study. If the text is not a prophecy of the death of Jesus, who or what is this anointed one—cut off and alone? Who is this anointed prince who appears seven weeks after the "word" goes forth? How one understands the original Hebrew text is important for understanding the timeline of Daniel's prophecy.

Daniel 9:25 Explained

Verse 25 begins with the conjunction "and." However, it can be (and is) variously translated depending on the context. There is nothing in the grammar of this verse that determines the sense of the conjunction. It is the context and one's sense of the verse that influences what connective idea one uses. For those who see verse 25 as a beginning explanation of verse 24, they argue for an informal inference or they see verse 25 as the consequence of verse 24. Yet, it can just as easily function as the continuation of Gabriel's revelation. In essence, verse 25 is the second fact Gabriel came to communicate to Daniel.[ccxxxvi]

Since verse 25 seems to begin a breakdown of the 490 years, most are of the opinion that verses 25–27 explain verse 24. This is a logical inference and is probably right. If the verse is taken as reflected in the Massoretic text, then the first half of the verse concerns the seven weeks (forty-nine years of twelve 30-day months) before an anointed leader comes. "From the issuing of a word" (דָּבָר = *dabar*, "a word") refers to a divine communication—a word from God. Normally, *dabar* refers to a prophetic utterance from God. Of the more than fourteen hundred occurrences of this term in the Old Testament, there is not a single explicit example of its usage as a decree by a human agent.[ccxxxvii]

Daniel 9:23 indicates that a "word" went forth when Daniel began to pray. Daniel 9:2 indicates that Jeremiah the prophet sent forth a "word" of God concerning the number of years of Jerusalem desolation. Therefore, in each case, the "word" is the will of God. It is simply communicated to man by either a prophet or an angel.

Historically, scholars have identified three decrees as a possible fulfillment of Daniel 9:25. Some Jewish interpreters point to Jeremiah's "word" given in close proximity to the destruction of the first temple. In this case, Daniel's 490-year prophetic timeline began forty-nine years before the angel told Daniel the prophecy. This is necessary to bring the 490 years to completion with the destruction of Jerusalem by Titus according to the modern lunisolar calendar of the Jews.

Most dispensational interpreters point to the decree of Artaxerxes in B.C. 444 on the Western calendar in connection with Nehemiah's return to finish the work in Jerusalem. This is necessary to complete 483 years with Jesus' ministry just prior to His death in Jerusalem. They are then left with thirty-plus years between the Lord's death and the destruction of Jerusalem by Titus. While this line of reasoning is possible, it seems highly unlikely given Daniel's clear intent to give the number of years necessary to accomplish the prophetic word. We would expect this 483-year period to actually end with the destruction of Jerusalem.

To leave a thirty-plus year gap between the "cut off anointed one" and the destruction of the city and sanctuary after specifying the number of years for the whole matter is highly uncharacteristic of the general nature of this passage. On its face, it seems as if Daniel is laying out a very specific timeline that would not allow a gap of thirty-plus years near the end of the prophecy once the clock started as it relates to clicking off the 434-year portion. This would seem to make sense in light of the need for a gap between the sixty-ninth and Seventieth weeks.

The strongest support for this position is 2 Chronicles 36:23 and Ezra 1:2–4, which focus on the rebuilding of the temple exclusively. It is this fact that has led pretribulationists to argue strenuously that the 444 B.C. edict of Artaxerxes to Nehemiah is the starting point for Daniel's prophecy. Yet this line of reasoning is only necessary because Western chronologists first accepted Ptolemy's canon that demands a 208-year Persian empire. Since Cyrus' edict by the Western calendar must have occurred in 538 B.C., making Daniel's 483 years insufficient to span the time gap to the death of Christ or the destruction of Jerusalem by Titus, some scholars had to move the terminus *a quo* (the starting point) significantly forward. In their scheme, 444 B.C. is the only date that will work. However, it only works because they are willing to leave a thirty-plus year gap between the death of the Messiah and the destruction of Jerusalem in A.D. 70, and they are willing to ignore the essence of the book of Nehemiah regarding his task.[57]

Dr. Harold W. Hoehner summarizes the arguments in Nehemiah that support the 444 B.C. position:

> Several factors commend this decree as the one prophesied by Daniel (9:25) for the commencement of the seventy weeks. First, there

---

[57] Closer examination of the book of Nehemiah reveals that he did not rebuild Jerusalem. He only rebuilt the walls, and he did it in fifty-two days. Clearly, he did not rebuild the city of Jerusalem in that period of time.

is a direct reference to the restoration of the city
(2:3, 5) and of the city gates and walls (2:3, 8).
Second, Artaxerxes wrote a letter to Asaph to give
materials to be used specifically for the walls
(2:8). Third, the Book of Nehemiah and Ezra 4:7–
23 indicate that certainly the restoration of the
walls was done in the most distressing
circumstances, as predicted by Daniel (Dan 9:25).
Fourth, no later decrees were given by the Persian
kings pertaining to the rebuilding of
Jerusalem.^{ccxxxviii}

We shall examine each point Hoehner offers.
Nehemiah 2:3, 5 states,

> I replied to the king, "O king, live forever! Why
> would I not appear dejected when the city with the
> graves of my ancestors lies desolate and its gates
> destroyed by fire?... and said to the king, "If the
> king is so inclined and if your servant has found
> favor in your sight, dispatch me to Judah, to the
> city with the graves of my ancestors, so that I can
> rebuild it."

According to Hoehner, this verse declares that
Nehemiah requests permission to return to Judea and totally
rebuild the whole city of Jerusalem. However, there is no
evidence in the book of Nehemiah that he accomplished such a
feat. Nehemiah relates a story that has as its center the walls
and gates of the city. This is the heart of the report the men told
to Nehemiah: "The wall of Jerusalem is broken down, and its
gates are destroyed by fire." Therefore, Nehemiah only went
back to restore the walls and gates of the city.

There is no mention of completing the building of the
city. There is no celebration of its completion. Nehemiah
12:27 indicates that Nehemiah celebrated the restoration of

the walls only. It is beyond reason that Nehemiah could have restored Jerusalem but did not celebrate it when that was supposedly his primary purpose for leaving Persia.

Nehemiah 7:4 states, "Now the city [Jerusalem] was spread out and large, and there were not a lot of people in it. At that time houses had not been rebuilt." Eight verses earlier, in Nehemiah 6:15, which covers the same period of time, Nehemiah writes, "So the wall was finished on the twenty-fifth day of the month Elul, in fifty-two days."

Fifty-two days is far too short a time to rebuild the city of Jerusalem, and taken with Nehemiah 7:4, we know that the city was not rebuilt. Only the walls of the city were restored. This matches with Nehemiah 2:8, where we are told that Nehemiah only requested enough timber to repair the walls, gates, and possibly a house for him to live in.

There simply is no record that Nehemiah rebuilt the whole city. In fact, Nehemiah 7:73 declares, "All the rest of Israel lived in their cities." Thus, the people living in Jerusalem were primarily its leadership (Neh. 11:1). Therefore, the request of Nehemiah to return to the city of his ancestors "so that I can rebuild it," was neither properly equipped nor completed.

The second support Hoehner offers to support his conclusion that the 444 B.C. edict of Artaxerxes begins the clock of fulfillment for Daniel's prophecy concerns the materials requested by Nehemiah. This argument is counter-productive for Hoehner because it demonstrates that Nehemiah only got materials to rebuild the walls and gates. Nothing was given to rebuild the whole city. He certainly did not get materials to build houses.

That the walls and gates of Jerusalem were built in distressing circumstances, as predicted by Daniel (9:25), does not prove the whole city was restored. It only shows that one aspect of the restoration of the gates and walls meets Daniel's specifications. Hoehner's final point, that there are no historical edicts after 444 B.C., has merit only regarding his conclusions because of the amount of time necessary to fulfill Daniel's prophecy in light of his belief that Ptolemy's canon requires 208 years' duration for the Persian empire. A shorter number of years for the empire would make this point moot.

The True Terminus *A Quo*

We understand the decree of Cyrus to be the *terminus a quo* for the fulfillment of Daniel 9:25. The content of the "word" is "to restore and build Jerusalem." This is exactly what Isaiah said Cyrus would say.

Isaiah 44:28 indicated that God would commission "Cyrus…to decree concerning Jerusalem, 'She will be rebuilt' and concerning the temple, 'It will be reconstructed.'" This passage alone is sufficient to prove that Cyrus did decree concerning Jerusalem, "She will be rebuilt." Otherwise, God's word has failed, which is a conclusion we are not prepared to accept.

Some scholars are unwilling to accept Cyrus' decree as fulfillment of Daniel 9:25. They reason that Cyrus' statement in Ezra 1:2–4 says nothing about rebuilding Jerusalem, but focuses on "the temple of God which is in Jerusalem." Ezra 1:2–4 actually says,

> Thus says King Cyrus of Persia: "The Lord God of heaven has given me all the kingdoms of the earth. He has instructed me to build a temple for him in Jerusalem, which is in Judah. Anyone from his people among you (may his God be with him!) may go up to Jerusalem, which is in Judah, and may build the temple of the Lord God of Israel— he is the God who is in Jerusalem. Anyone who survives in any of those places where he is a

resident foreigner must be helped by his neighbors with silver, gold, equipment, and animals, along with voluntary offerings for the temple of God which is in Jerusalem."

Second Chronicles 36:23, which repeats Cyrus' decree, is absent any reference to rebuilding Jerusalem. Yet, Isaiah 44:28 instructs that Cyrus would decree that Jerusalem be rebuilt. Isaiah 44:28 specifically says:

"...who commissions Cyrus, the one I appointed as shepherd to carry out all my wishes and to decree concerning Jerusalem, 'She will be rebuilt,' and concerning the temple, 'It will be reconstructed.'"

In a context that has as its primary focus the restoration of Jerusalem and the cities of Judah,[ccxxxix] God reveals the instrument of his future plans. The Hebrew of this verse is unmistakable in what it asserts. Cyrus "will issue the edict that makes possible the restoration of city and temple" (v. 28)."[ccxl]

That the rebuilding of Jerusalem is the heart of Cyrus' edict is captured well by Klaus Baltzer. He writes,

What Cyrus orders according to Isa 44:28b is that Jerusalem should be built and the foundations of the temple laid. But v. 26 went much further when it talked about the founding of the city. The text therefore differentiates very precisely, making clear that the refounding of the city is Yahweh's direct command, while this is only indirectly true of the command to lay the foundations of the temple.[ccxli]

It is worth mentioning that neither decree of Cyrus was fulfilled during his lifetime. Neither the temple nor the city was finished until many years after his death. Cyrus only decreed that the Jews could return and rebuild Jerusalem and the temple. He did not say how long it would take or what obstacles the people might face.

Given the content of Daniel's visions in chapters two, seven, and eight, we know he had a general understanding about the future of his people. Three more kingdoms would arise and directly influence them. As chapter nine opens, Daniel is reading the *books* (notice: books—plural) of which one is clearly Jeremiah.[58] Daniel knew Jerusalem's desolation had a seventy-year time limit on it. Evidently, he did not know the exact date it would end. Our point is this: Daniel already had a "word" from God through Jeremiah concerning the termination of Jerusalem's desolation by the Babylonians. With Darius the Mede ruling over Babylon and Cyrus over Persia, in fulfillment of Isaiah 45:1, Daniel had to have known that it was only a matter of time (within months at most) that the people would be allowed to return to Judea.

However, upon closer examination of Daniel 9, we see that the essence of Daniel's prayer concerns Jerusalem, which is mentioned eight times. The people would be allowed to return, but what would happen to the city of Jerusalem?

Forty-Nine Years to an Anointed Leader

It is our conviction that the decree of Cyrus began the clock for the fulfillment of a new 490-year period. Since the subjugation of the Judea began 29.6.3333 (lunar calendar),[ccxlii] God kept His word to the very day and hour.

---

[58] Perhaps the other book is Isaiah, which contains the Cyrus prophecy.

Therefore, we would expect Cyrus to issue his decree on 29.6.4203 (lunar calendar). On this date, Daniel's new 483-year prophecy began.

The normal, natural, and customary sense of verse 25 is that forty-nine years from a "word" to restore and build Jerusalem (which Cyrus fulfilled), an anointed leader "will come," "appear," "go forth" or some such verb. The original Hebrew text does not have a verbal idea that explains what "an anointed leader" will do. A check of most translations of Daniel 9:25 reveals that a verb of motion is supplied. Thus, this "anointed leader" will either come or go forth to assist in the restoration of Jerusalem. It is our contention that this anointed leader is not a reference to Jesus, God's Messiah.

The Hebrew מָשִׁיחַ (mashiyach = "anointed") occurs with reference to the kings of Israel, to Cyrus the king of Persia, the high priest of Israel, and to the patriarchs of Israel. Nagid (נָגִיד = "leader, ruler, officer") is used almost fifty times and is applied to leaders in several fields—governmental, military, and religious. The word usually is singular and refers to the man at the top: the king, the high priest, and so on. But there are references to leaders and captains in the army. [ccxliii] Nagid is better translated here as "leader." There are those who understand that Daniel 9:25 applies to Cyrus the king of Persia, for he came on the scene fifty years after the destruction of Jerusalem. However, the sense of the text looks forward from the date the word goes forth, not backwards.

Daniel does not tell us explicitly what this anointed leader will do. However, the context would favor him helping to rebuild and restore Jerusalem. Since neither the temple nor Jerusalem was restored during the life of Cyrus, we understand that he merely issued the decree that the Jews could do the job. Cyrus was not personally responsible for the actual completion.

The text is not clear whether the forty-nine years would see the birth of this anointed leader or his emergence on the scene. However, since the restoration of Jerusalem is in focus, it is reasonable to conclude that this leader would be instrumental in Jerusalem's restoration. A check of Israel's history after Cyrus' announcement reveals several possibilities for fulfillment. The early church fathers saw fulfillment in Joshua the high priest, who returned in the first group of exiles with Zerubbabel.

We believe it is possible to be dogmatic regarding the identity of this anointed leader. The two well-known leaders forty-nine years after the Cyrus' "word" went forth are Ezra and Nehemiah. Ezra was a priest directly descended from Aaron (Eze. 7:1–6). However, it is with Nehemiah that the final restoration of the city of Jerusalem was begun—walls, gates, and people to live in it. The first chapter of Nehemiah reports that he was the son of Hacaliah, a name of unknown origin and meaning. Some speculate that he was of the tribe of Judah and linage of David.

There is no explicit basis to make this claim. Yet, Nehemiah was appointed governor of Judah. However, prior to his appointment, he held some position among his people in that they came to him when Jerusalem needed help. It is also clear that he had God's favor on his life. It is in this sense that Nehemiah could be considered "an anointed leader."

It is our contention that the forty-nine years of twelve 30-day months began with the issuing of Cyrus' decree on 29.6.3402 (lunar calendar) and 20.12.3300 (Egyptian solar calendar). We obtain this date by counting from the first day of creation using the pure Jewish lunar year until the last day of Judah's captivity. However, on this date, Daniel began a new clock—a modified Egyptian solar calendar consisting of twelve 30-day months. Notice the chart below and the dates computed using the three-calendar system:

Days/Creation	Lunar	Egyptian	Improved
1,204,484	29.6.3403	20.12.3300	16.9.3298

Daniel's Prophetic Fulfillment Calendar

Event	Day/Creation	Lunar	Modified Egyptian
Cyrus decree	1,204,484	29.6.3403	20.12.3300
First anointed leader	1,222,124	28.4.3453	20.4.3349

If we use the date of Cyrus' decree that the Jews could return to their land and rebuild their city and sanctuary as the starting point for the fulfillment of Daniel's first seven weeks, then count forward by 17,640 days (forty-nine years x twelve 30-day months), which places us on the twentieth day of the fourth month of the 3,349[th] year after creation by the Egyptian calendar. This equates to the twenty-eighth day of the fourth month of the 3,453[rd] year after creation on a pure lunar calendar.[59]

This is particularly interesting in light of Nehemiah 6:15, which indicates that Nehemiah finished the work on the walls and gates of Jerusalem on the twenty-fifth day of Elul, which is the sixth month of the Jewish civil year. Nehemiah 6:15 also indicates the work took fifty-two days to complete, which means that it began on the third day of the month of Av. Av is the fifth month of the Jewish civil year. Nehemiah reports that he "was there [in Jerusalem] three days [Neh. 2:11]. Then I arose in the night."

---

[59] The product of forty-nine years x 360 days is 17,640 days. The division of 17,640 days/354 (one pure lunar year) is forty-nine years, ten months, and twenty-eight days, or the twenty-eighth day of the fourth month (Tammuz), of the 3453rd year from the day of creation, which the chart above reflects.

Nehemiah must have arisen on the night before the third day of month of Av. If we subtract three days, and if the month of Av has thirty days, then Nehemiah must have arrived at Jerusalem on the twenty-eighth day of Tammuz, which is the fourth month of the Jewish civil year.

Tammuz (fourth Jewish month)

Av (fifth Jewish month)—work started third day (27 days worked)

Elul (sixth Jewish month)—work finished twenty-fifth day

The data agrees with our date. Nehemiah arrived in Jerusalem on the twenty-eighth of the month Tammuz, inspected the city's walls after three days of rest and began the work on the third day of Av.

Jerusalem's 434 Years Existence

The second half of Daniel 9:25 refers specifically to the future of Jerusalem. For sixty-two weeks (434 years of twelve 30-day months) Jerusalem literally, "will return and be built." In her restored state, Jerusalem will have "plaza and moat." She will have stressful times, but she will continue to exist for 156,240 days. This seems to be the sense of the text when taken in contrast to Daniel 9:26, where the city and the sanctuary suffer destruction.

The Hebrew at this point does not help the reader much in understanding the author's intent. The reader/interpreter must make several judgments. Depending on what decisions one makes, the meaning of the text can go several ways.

We can certainly rule out the possibility that Daniel indicates that the city will take 434 years to build. Such a conclusion makes no sense. Equally, since grammatically it is highly unlikely that this passage refers to Jesus Christ and His death, we can reject that line of reasoning. The translation in the ESV, as far as grammar, punctuation, and style go, probably best reflects the sense of the text: "Then for sixty-two weeks it [Jerusalem] shall be built again with squares and moat, but in a troubled time."

Given this sense, it may be best to take the meaning to be—Jerusalem will exist 434 years. There are two possible ways to take the final clause: either during the reconstruction, when she will experience a time of trouble or oppression, or during the 434 years she will experience trouble or oppression. Both were equally true.

If we allow history to influence our understanding of the text, while there were times of oppression during the reconstruction of Jerusalem's walls, during the 434 years of her existence before destruction, she was literally oppressed by both the Greeks and the Romans.

Next, we discover the termination of Daniel's prophecy when Jerusalem and the temple suffered destruction.

Chapter Fourteen
The Terminus *Ad Quem* of Jerusalem
(Daniel 9:26)

> And after the sixty-two weeks [434 years], an anointed one will be cut off and there is not to him. And a people of a coming prince will destroy the city and the sanctuary. And the end of him *will come* with the overflowing. And to an end war is determined, desolations are decreed. (author's translation)

The text intimates that the destruction of the city and the sanctuary will occur after the sixty-two weeks (434 years)—not during, but after. In the eyes of many, Daniel 9:26 indicates that two events will occur after sixty-two weeks: (1) an anointed one will be cut off; and (2) the city and the sanctuary will suffer destruction. Consequently, several questions require attention. First, what is the relationship between "an anointed one" and the city and the sanctuary? Second, do these events occur between weeks sixty-nine and seventy or is there a gap between the two? Third, does a literal fulfillment of Daniel 9:24 require a yet-future fulfillment of Daniel's Seventieth Week?

There are those who place Daniel's prophetic destruction within the Seventieth Week. However, the text does not say that these events occur *within* it (Daniel 9:27). As we shall see, when Daniel discusses the Seventieth Week, he says nothing about the destruction of the city.

Those who hold that the destruction of an anointed one, Jerusalem, and the sanctuary occurred during the Seventieth Week can only do so if it followed immediately upon the heels of the sixty-ninth week. Yet, it is our conviction that the destruction occurred after the termination of the sixty-ninth week, leaving the Seventieth Week to a yet future fulfillment.

Unless one is willing to limit the six promises of Daniel 9:24 to something less than literal, there is no way they are a present reality for ethnic Israel or Jerusalem. Only by spiritualizing the promises and limiting the fulfillment to the spiritual seed of Abraham can the promises have any possible fulfillment at this time. However, such a concept would have been very foreign to Daniel at the reception of the promises. Equally, assigning the fulfillment of Daniel 9:24 to the events connected with Antiochus Epiphanes would require the setting aside of a literal fulfillment of what the text promises.

Most importantly, those who died believing that God would honor His promise as it was literally told to them will rise in the resurrection only to find that God pulled a change while they were dead. Now anything is possible, but this conclusion is highly improbable. To demand that the promises of Daniel 9:24 and the circumstances detailed in Daniel 9:27 have found fulfillment requires the complete abandonment of logic, reason, and any possible consistent hermeneutic.

The number of problems created by seeing the historical fulfillment of Daniel 9:24 and 27 in connection with either the death of Christ, the A.D. 70 destruction of Jerusalem, or in association with the times of Antiochus Epiphanes are insurmountable. Rather, as we have pointed out, the death of Jesus occurred long before the sixty-ninth week. The destruction of Jerusalem occurred after the sixty-ninth week. The events connected with Antiochus occurred long before the fulfillment of Daniel 9:26. All the events connected with the Seventieth Week await a yet future fulfillment.

Therefore, when did the sixty-ninth week end? If we count from the twenty-fifth day of Elul forward 434 years utilizing our modified Egyptian calendar, we arrive at the fourth day of Shevat in the 3,894[th] year after the creation of the world. Notice on the chart below how the date matches the historical record.

The Fall of the Second Temple

Event	Day/Creation	Lunar	Modified Egyptian
Cyrus Decree	1,204,484	29.6.3403	20.12.3300
1st Anointed	1,220,124	28.4.3453	20.4.3349
Walls Finished	1,220,152	25.6.3453	12.5.3349
End of 69th Week	1,376,392	4.11.3894	2.6.3778

Four hundred and thirty-four years, when counted by the modified Egyptian solar calendar, equates to 156,240 days. If, as we argued earlier, Nehemiah arrived in Jerusalem the twenty-eight of Tammuz, 3453 years after the creation, and he completed the walls and gates on 25.6.3453, then 434 modified Egyptian solar years later (156,240 days) puts the destruction of Jerusalem and the sanctuary beyond 4.11.3894 after the creation of the world. Since the destruction was to occur after the sixty-ninth week, we understand the sixtieth week to have ended on 4.11.3894 years after creation. With the sixty-ninth week ending in the month of Shevat (January/February), less than two months later Jerusalem was surrounded by Titus and his armies. John Donahue, College of William and Mary, writes,

> Titus began an assault on the city in spring, A.D. 70. In less than four weeks, his forces had breached the walls of the so-called New City, or

suburb of Bezetha. Only the inner city and the Temple itself remained to be taken.[ccxliv]

F. F. Bruce, in his book *New Testament History*, confirms Donahue's reference to "spring, A.D. 70," when he writes,

> Josephus, Tacitus and Suetonius combine to tell how they were encouraged by an ancient oracle in their sacred writings to the effect that "at that very time" a man or men from Judaea would gain supreme world-dominion. The oracle is probably the angelic prophecy in Dan. 9:24–7 announcing that seventy heptads of years would elapse before the establishment of everlasting righteousness (i.e. under the promised kingdom of the saints which the God of heaven would set up); calculations in the sixties evidently led some to believe that this period was approaching completion. Josephus tells us how he came to the conclusion that the oracle really pointed to the Roman commander-in-chief Vespasian (sent to Judaea by Nero early in 67 to put down the revolt), who was proclaimed emperor in the summer of 69; Tacitus and Suetonius put the same construction on the oracle. But the insurgents took it to mean that the hour of Israel's liberation was at hand....

> Titus began the siege of Jerusalem in April, 70. The defenders held out desperately for five months, but by the end of August the Temple area was occupied and the holy house burned down, and by the end of September all resistance in the city had come to an end.[ccxlv]

The traditional Jewish calendar indicates the destruction of the temple occurred on the ninth day of Av in the year 3,828/30. Our calculations place it on the ninth day of Av in the year 3,895, which is sixty-five years longer than the traditional Jewish date. Earlier, we argued that the length of the Persian empire was 116 years. Thus, our date is exactly sixty-four years longer than the traditional suggested year on the Jewish calendar.

As discussed earlier, historians indicate that Vespasian arrived and began to put down the Jewish rebellion in Galilee in May. These events continued until November. By the winter of 3893, Vespasian had subdued most of Judaea and was making final preparations to attack Jerusalem when he learned that Emperor Nero had died. This event caused Vespasian to halt his attack. We explain the necessity for this by recognizing that the sixty-ninth week was not yet finished. After a year of appointments and the deaths of several emperors of Rome, finally Vespasian was appointed emperor of Rome on December 22. Vespasian sailed for Rome, but dispatched Titus to crush Jerusalem.

By our calculations, the sixty-ninth week ended on the fourth day of Shevat, 3894. By April, Titus began the actual destruction of Jerusalem. On the ninth day of Av, in the year 3895, Jerusalem and the temple fell. Thus, within one year, the destruction of Jerusalem and the temple was complete. That some Jews had knowledge of Daniel's prophecy and anticipated its fulfillment during these days suggests that Daniel's sixty-ninth week found fulfillment in close proximity to the destruction of Jerusalem and not to the crucifixion of Jesus Christ.

Confirmation of Our Timeline

A literal translation of Daniel 9:26 does not help much with understanding the meaning intended. The verse clearly refers to events after the sixty-two weeks. The first event after the sixty-two weeks concerns "an anointed one." Of the thirty-nine occurrences of this term in the Old Testament, thirty-eight references clearly mention a person (priest, prophet or king). Thirty-seven of those references have an identifying characteristic that leaves no doubt that the priest, prophet, or king associates with or belongs to God.

However, the occurrence of *mashiyach* (מָשִׁיחַ = "an anointed one") in Daniel 9:26 is unique. This verse does not have this characteristic explicitly stated. Neither the context nor the grammar helps to identify this anointed one as belonging to the Lord God. Even in the case of Cyrus (a Gentile) in Isaiah 45:1, he is specifically identified as God's anointed, even though there is no evidence that he was a believer in the God of the Jews.

Again, the specific term *mashiyach* is found thirty-nine times in the Old Testament. In thirty-eight of those occurrences, a person is clearly the referent. On the basis of usage alone, one would conclude that Daniel 9:26 also refers to a person. However, the essence of Daniel 9:26 concerns Jerusalem, the temple, and the destruction of the person responsible for the destruction of them both.

Since *mashiyach* is ambiguous as to its referent in Daniel 9:26, perhaps Daniel intended something that closely fits the context. An abstract concept is more fitting, since it "is an indefinite noun in Dan. 9:25–26."[ccxlvi] This conclusion has support in both the Septuagint[60] and Theodotion[61]

---

[60] The Septuagint (LXX) is the Greek translation of the Old Testament thought to have been completed in the third century before Christ. In connection with the book of Daniel, the modern Septuagint offers two

versions of the Old Testament. In both versions, the term *chrisma* (χρῖσμα = oil for anointing or the action of anointing), occurs for the Hebrew term *mashiyach*. (See Exodus 29:7; 30:25). "The word refers to that with which the anointing is performed, the unguent or ointment."[ccxlvii]

There are two oddities about the Greek translation. First, *chrisma* is a neuter singular noun instead of a masculine noun, as in the Hebrew Bible. This indicates that the Greek translators did not interpret the Hebrew *mashiyach* to refer to a person. If the Greek translators understood Daniel to have been referring to a person, *christos* would have been appropriate, since it refers to a person. Second, neither version has the article. Therefore, an appropriate translation is "an anointing" in an abstract or metaphorical sense. Since both the Hebrew and Greek texts of Daniel 9:26 allow for an abstract or metaphorical concept, it is our conviction that the text does not automatically have to refer to Jesus, the Messiah.

As in the case of Cyrus (Isa. 45:1), the designation "His anointed" does not require the literal anointing with oil. The idea of an actual "anointing" is not present. The expression metaphorically designates Cyrus to be God's elect to service. Similarly, Isaiah 61:1 depicts God's anointed to be a preacher of spiritual freedom. The New Testament identifies the preacher of spiritual freedom to be Jesus and clarifies that Isaiah intends a metaphorical anointing and not a literal pouring of the oil. Thus, a

---

possible translations. This decision is the result of a very poor translation of much of the book of Daniel in the original LXX. What is thought to be the original translation, also known as the Old Greek Version, the early Church set aside and adopted Theodotion's version for the book of Daniel because the translation is better.

[61] Theodotion was a Greek translator thought to have lived near the end of the second century. He completed a revision of the Septuagint. His revision of the book of Daniel completely replaced the original translation in the LXX.

metaphorical anointing simply designates one as rightly called and appointed by God—elect to service, as it were.

In a study of the very important documents found at Qumran, M. De Jonge reaches a similar conclusion about the basic meaning of *mashiyach*. He writes that *mashiyach* "denotes divine calling and appointment and cannot properly be called a title, though there may have been a tendency to use it as a standard expression for the future king."[ccxlviii] Given that the Qumran materials were written several centuries after the book of Daniel, we must allow for the development of the concept of God's anointed to have involved more than what is historically understood from the references in the Old Testament. However, that the term could refer to a metaphorical placement of God's favor on a person or thing must be allowed in light of Isaiah 45:1 and 61:1.[ccxlix]

Therefore, it is altogether possible and most likely that Daniel 9:26 is not referring to a person but to the metaphorical placement of God's favor on a person or thing. This conclusion would make sense and fit the context if the destruction of Jerusalem and the sanctuary is the focus. With the destruction of the city and the sanctuary, their special place in God's economy is lost. The correctness of our conclusion finds support in what follows.

The verse indicates nothing unique about this anointing other than what happens to it. "He shall be cut off" (*yiccarat*). This Hebrew verb can have a number of variant meanings. It can refer to making a covenant, as in 1 Samuel 20:16. It can refer to putting a person to death, as in Genesis 9:11, Psalm 37:9, and Proverbs 2:22.[62] It can express the idea of consuming food (Num. 11:33). It can mean "to cut down," in the sense of severing an object from its source. Finally, it can mean "to be cut off," as in being excluded from an association or membership (Ex. 12:15).[ccl]

---

[62] Significantly, this verb is never used to refer to the death of a righteous person.

The Greek versions of Daniel have different verbs as a translation of the Hebrew verb *yiccarat*. The LXX has the passive verb *aphistami*, which basically means "to be taken away." Theodotion, on the other hand, has *exoletreuō*[ccli] which means "to be utterly destroyed or completely cut off from."[cclii] The Hebrew text and both Greek versions indicate that an anointing shall be cut off. What is this anointing? If we allow the Greek versions to interpret the Hebrew text, we may conclude that Daniel intends a figure of speech here. The thing is put for what it represents. In this case, an anointing represents the special enablement God granted to His anointed. As Cyrus (Isa. 45:1) was God's special instrument (metaphorically anointed) to accomplish Judah's return, Jerusalem and the sanctuary were God's instruments for His presence on earth. This calling and right were to be lost after 434 years from the date of Nehemiah's restoration.

That Daniel's people, the city, and the sanctuary lost their unique position after 434 years from Nehemiah's restoration is confirmed in the New Testament. Romans 11:22 states,

> Notice therefore the kindness and harshness of God—harshness toward those who have fallen, but God's kindness toward you, provided you continue in his kindness; otherwise you also *will be cut off.* (italics added)

This verse indicates that a majority of Israel was cut off. The verb *ekkoptō* (literally, "to cut out," which is in keeping with the metaphorical language) suggests that God removed a majority of national Israel. Obviously, we must answer this question: "From what and in what sense was a majority of national Israel cut out?" After a detailed study, Dr. J. Lanier Burns concludes that Israel (the natural branches = unbelieving Jews) was cut out of God's "covenantal relationships with the patriarchs."[ccliii] The sense in which this occurred relates to their loss of spiritual and physical blessings—divine favor. Ultimately, a majority of national Israel did, in fact, lose their right to life (spiritual), the liberty of dwelling in their own city, and the light of God's presence in the sanctuary.

Interestingly, *ekkoptō* ("to cut out") in Romans 11:22 echoes Daniel 9:25's *yaccarat* ("to cut off"). A majority of God's people lost their access to the temporal blessings of Abraham, Isaac, and Jacob. While waiting for God's ultimate redemption and restoration, Jews were able to experience God's protection, peace, and prosperity. However, after the sixty-two weeks, these blessings would be lost to many.

The Lord Jesus also promised a similar judgment on Jerusalem and the sanctuary and, by implication, on the people of Israel. In Luke 13:34–35, the Lord declares,

> O Jerusalem, Jerusalem, you who kill the prophets and stone those who are sent to you! How often I have longed to gather your children together as a hen gathers her chicks under her wings, but you would have none of it! Look your house is forsaken! And I tell you, you will not see me until you say, 'Blessed is the one who comes in the name of the Lord!'

If one is not familiar with the New Testament, he or she may not know that this declaration by our Lord appears in Matthew 23:37–39.[63] However, while Matthew places this pronouncement at the end of an extended denouncement of the religious leaders of Israel, Luke places it earlier in his chronology. This explains our use of it rather than the

---

[63] A similar statement occurs in Luke 19:41–44, where the Lord again promises destruction for Jerusalem and her environs.

passage in Matthew. The destruction that Jerusalem and her environs are about to face is not a recent prophetic announcement. Rather, in a wider context, it goes back to Daniel 9. In a sense, the Lord Jesus is restating what Daniel had already promised.

The specifics of Luke's account are important. The double reference—"Jerusalem, Jerusalem"—highlights the Lord's heightened sense of remorse that Jerusalem, which stands for the people living in her, have such a flawed history. Luke uses the two Greek forms for our English term *Jerusalem*: *Jerosoluma*) and *Jerousalem*.[ccliv] The first form occurs in the writings of those who are either non-Jews or Jews writing to Greeks. The later form occurs in the writings of Jews, particularly the Septuagint.[cclv] Scholars are not in agreement concerning why Luke uses different forms of the term. However, it appears that, at least in his gospel, Luke focuses on the significance of Jerusalem as God's special city when he uses the term in the latter sense.[cclvi]

Thus, in her official capacity, Jerusalem has failed to accomplish her anointed task. Instead, she gained a reputation for murder ("you who kill the prophets and stone those who are sent to you"). The Lord depicts Jerusalem as a mother with children. He wanted to save her children, but she would not have it. The image of a mother bird protecting her baby chicks provides a simple but powerful illustration of the Lord's desire to save Israel.

However, Luke 13:35 discloses a sad and opposite outcome—a prophecy of judgment. In what is thought to be language that alludes to Jeremiah 12:7 and 22:5, the Lord solemnizes, "Look, your house is forsaken!" "Your house" refers to Jerusalem and her environs, which include both the people and the temple. Both the city and the temple suffer because the people who occupy them cause God's wrath to fall on them.[cclvii]

What the Lord promises is abandonment. Dr. Darrell L. Bock agrees that this is a "reference to the abandonment of the nation."[cclviii] Dr. I. Howard Marshall instructs that "to abandon" (αφίημι), can refer to the abandonment of Jerusalem by God absolutely (Jer. 12:7) or to its abandonment to its enemies.[cclix] It is our conclusion that God's abandonment of Jerusalem and her environs means that God will withdraw His presence from the temple and from Jerusalem.[cclx] That this is the correct interpretation of this verse finds support in next important phrase.

When this "anointed" is cut off, "there is nothing to him." What does Daniel mean by the phrase, "there is nothing to him?" The difficulty of understanding Daniel's intended meaning is made clear when one considers the wide variety of potential English translations of this phrase. The following chart offers a small sampling:

Key Phrase in Daniel 9:26

Version	Reference
NASB	"and have nothing [or no one]"
Message	"the end of him"
KJV	"but not for himself"
ESV	"shall have nothing"

The Hebrew that is the basis of the suggested translation is *wā'ayin lô*. This phrase literally mean "and [there is] not to him." Daniel 11:45 has a similar phrase in a similar context, with the possible meaning, "and there was no deliverer to him." The difficulty of understanding the phrase grows out of the absence of an object. Unlike Daniel 11:45, we are not told what or who is "not to him."

The versions of Daniel regarding this phrase are very different in terminology, but we believe the versions have the same basic meaning. The Septuagint (Old Greek Version) reads, "and it shall not be or exist." Theodotion has, "and judgment is not in it." The addition of the word *krima* (κρίμα = "judgment") by Theodotion is particularly difficult for many scholars to explain. However, we believe it is the key to understanding Daniel's original intent.

Krima is a legal term typically understood to denote the result of an action such as a judge's decision, judgment, or verdict (Ex. 18:22). It can also refer to the action of judging (2 Kings 17:26), as well as the lawsuit or case brought before a judge (Ex. 18:22). However, of great interest to us is the occurrence of this term in Daniel 7:22 in Theodotion's version. Daniel 7:21–22 states,

> While I was watching, that horn began to wage war against the holy ones and was defeating them until the Ancient of Days arrived and judgment was rendered in favor of the holy ones of the Most High. Then the time came for the holy ones to take possession of the kingdom.

What does Daniel mean by "judgment was rendered?" It is our conviction that the correct sense of the text is "dominion." Most scholars recognize that *judgment* includes *rule.*[cclxi] However, we understand Daniel's promise to involve a matter that results from God's judgment of the beast. Thus, the saints receive the benefit of God's judgment. That benefit is dominion, which Daniel 7:27 states the saints will receive when Antichrist is judged.

Therefore, *krima* possibly means the same thing in Daniel 9:26 (Theodotion) as it does in Revelation 20:4. The text states, "Then I saw thrones and they sat on them, and judgment was given to them" (NASB). This verse places in parallel to *krima* the idea of reigning with Christ in His kingdom, just as Daniel 7:22 does.

Revelation 20:4 is much stronger in its affirmation that "authority to judge rather than judgment passed in their favor" is the author's intended meaning. Proof of this is the fact that John sees throne-sitters. Therefore, the judgment of the wicked is over. The righteous have taken their seats. Consequently, it is the authority or dominion to rule for the thousand years ahead that John emphasizes here.

The *Exegetical Dictionary of the New Testament* agrees that the idea of dominion is prominent in Daniel 7:22 and Revelation 20:4 for the term *krima*. It states,

> *Krima* (Κρίμα) is used of *dominion* in Rev. 20:4 (cf. Dan. 7:22, where κρίμα is parallel to βασίλειον [LXX] or βασιλεία [Θ]).[cclxii]

If we take Theodotion's suggested understanding of Daniel's original intent regarding the phrase "and [there is] not to him," we can argue that Daniel's reference is not to a person. Rather, Daniel spoke of God's metaphorical "anointing" that rested on Jerusalem and the temple. What Daniel informs us of is this: Jerusalem and the temple will no longer serve as the place of God's presence on earth. Their dominion has been taken away.

In this case, *mashiyach* refers to God's special anointing or choice that rested on Jerusalem and the sanctuary. The sense in which Jerusalem and the sanctuary was God's anointed is very similar to the sense in which Cyrus the Persian king was God's anointed (Is. 45:1). One author states,

Cyrus was the Lord's appointee for a definite task. The Isaiah passage suggests that *māsiah* be understood as one singled out or "chosen"… for a task, characteristically one of deliverance.[cclxiii]

As Deuteronomy 12:5 indicates, God promised to establish a place of residence in the land of Israel. The verb "to elect" or "to choose" expresses the intent of God regarding His future residence on earth. Several hundred years after Moses spoke these words, we discover that God ultimately elected Jerusalem to be the site of His divine residence.

As the seat of God's presence on earth, Jerusalem and the sanctuary exercised dominion over the whole earth through God's choices and will for the earth. It is this position of privilege that was lost or cut off with the destruction of Titus.

Some conservatives are quick to apply this verse to Jesus. However, Daniel 9:26 leaves the cut-off anointed one devoid of anything. One could make an argument that during the three hours our Lord was on the cross, He had no one—He was alone. Yet, after His resurrection, He proclaimed that "all authority in heaven and earth" were His. Equally, in a sense, the Lord Jesus did not lose anything by His death. In His very death, He gained everything. Those who killed the Lord lost everything, but He lost nothing. Thus, the verse can hardly describe the Lord Jesus after the resurrection.

That Daniel 9:26 does not have messianic overtones seems clear by the fact that *no* New Testament author alludes to it as such. When the wise men came looking for the baby born King of the Jews, Daniel 9:26 was not consulted nor highlighted to our knowledge. This text was never connected with the death of the Lord Jesus by New Testament writers. The Lord Jesus Himself only used Daniel 12:11 in connection with the destruction of Jerusalem in the Olivet Discourse. He never alluded to Daniel 9:24–27 with reference to Himself. It is clear that the Lord had a wide knowledge of the book of Daniel. His use of the unique title "Son of Man" is proof positive. This does not prove that Daniel 9:26 does not apply to the Lord's death, but it does scream for caution.

The decision to see fulfillment in the Lord Jesus by the average lay person is natural, given the scarcity of other possible fulfillment options and the translational issues reflected in most English versions of scripture. Rabbinic Jews teach that the high priest is the anointed one who lost everything at the destruction of the second temple. Some have suggested the anointed one is John the Baptist. Others have suggested the Antichrist.

It is our conclusion that this "anointed" that is cut off and left with nothing is the anointing itself. In other words, the verse could be translated:

> Now after the sixty-two weeks, an anointing will be removed and there will be nothing left of it. For the city and the sanctuary, the people of the coming price will destroy them.

The remaining portion of Daniel 9:26 states, "But his end will come speedily like a flood. Until the end of the war that has been decreed there will be destruction." This translation reflected in the NET Bible suggests correctly that "the prince of the people to come" is the subject of this clause. We believe the "prince of the people to come" is not Titus, but a yet future leader of wickedness.

Only the people of the prince to come were responsible for the destruction of the second temple and Jerusalem. Nero, the emperor of Rome, sent the Roman commander in chief by the name of Vespasian to Judaea to put down the Jewish rebellion. However, Nero committed suicide in the summer of

3893. With the death of Nero, Vespasian stopped his efforts in Judaea pending the outcome in Rome. One year later, in the fall of 3894, just as Vespasian was beginning his attack on Jerusalem, he was proclaimed emperor of Rome. Vespasian's oldest son was then given responsibility to put down the Jewish rebellion, while Vespasian returned to Rome. That boy's name was Titus.

With Daniel's sixty-ninth week ending in Shevat, Titus began his attack against Jerusalem in Nissan. By August of that year, Jerusalem and the temple were in ruins. He returned to Rome in 3896 and served with his father until his father's death. Titus became emperor in 3902. Yet, he died in September, 3904 after only twenty-six months as emperor of Rome. While there are many different accounts of his death, one states that while ill, Titus was drowned with snow by Domitian, his brother.

The events surrounding the death of Titus are interesting. Suetonius, a Roman historian, reports,

[H]e [Titus] was cut off by death, to the loss of mankind rather than to his own. After finishing the public games, at the close of which he wept bitterly in the presence of the people, he went to the Sabine territory somewhat cast down because a victim had escaped as he was sacrificing and because it had thundered from a clear sky. Then at the very first stopping place he was seized with a fever, and as he was being carried on from there in a litter, it is said that he pushed back the curtains, looked up to heaven, and lamented bitterly that his life was being taken from him contrary to his deserts; for he said that there was no act of his life of which he had cause to repent, save one only. What this was he did not himself disclose at the time, nor could anyone easily divine.[cclxiv]

Based on the above accounts, it is hardly possible that Titus' death could serve as the fulfillment of Daniel 9:26. Rather, the people of the prince destroyed the second temple but the prince awaits a future return wherein he will suffer for the sins of his people.

The historical context of the second temple destruction did not end with the destruction of Jerusalem and the temple. The war against the Jews continued, just as Daniel 9:26 promised. The Roman army continued its fight against the Jewish strongholds of Herodeion, Masada, and Machaerus. The last of the three to fall was Masada, the most impregnable. Her defenders held out until May of 3899, when to the last man, woman, boy and girl, all committed suicide with the exception of one woman and two small children. As Daniel 9:26 had promised, "Until the end of the war that has been decreed there will be destruction." A glorious people, city, and sanctuary were reduced to a proverb: "O, how the mighty have fallen."

Yet, God is not finished with Jerusalem nor the people's ruler to come. Both will reunite for a short period before God finishes His judgment of both. This matter we hope to address in another book in the not too distant future.

Chapter Fifteen
The Final Act—Yet to Be (Daniel 9:27)

Daniel 9:27 is the final verse of the chapter and concerns a final week—seven years. There is much debate about the relationship between verses 26–27. If the events of verse 26 occur between the sixty-ninth and Seventieth weeks, then the events of verse 27 are distinct. If the events of verse 27 are a clarification of verse 26, then verse 27 explains how the destruction of Jerusalem is accomplished. Daniel 9:27 literally says,

> He will confirm a covenant with the many for one week [seven years]. And half of the week [3½ years] he will cause sacrifices and offerings to cease and on a wing of abominations desolation and upon end and decreed end is poured out upon the one who desolates.

We understand verse 27 not to be a clarification of verse 26. Upon closer examination, verse 27 does not explicitly indicate the destruction of Jerusalem. It indicates the desecration of the temple by a desolator who himself will be desolated. To stop the sacrifices to the one true God and, in turn, demand worship in His temple is a desecration, but it does not necessarily involve the destruction of the temple or the city of Jerusalem.

The "complete destruction" mentioned in verse 27 applies to the desolator and not to the temple or city. The English Standard Version gives a good sense of the intent of verse 27: "And on the wing of abominations shall come one who makes desolate, until the decreed end is poured out on the desolator." This agrees with the New International Version, which states, "And on a wing of the temple he will set up an abomination that causes desolation, until the end that is decreed is poured out on him." However, verse 26 speaks specifically to the destruction of the city and the sanctuary. As well, it is the people of the prince to come that is responsible for the destruction of the city and the sanctuary.

Verse 27 begins with the fact that a prince has come. He will make a strong covenant with the many for one week (seven years). Since Daniel 9:24 makes clear that God determined the seventy weeks, the one-week covenant is God's limitation and not the prince's. We are certain that this prince has no desire to limit this covenant to seven years. As will be seen, he desires to rule forever, but divine necessity limits his plans.

Therefore, it is unwise to be on the lookout for a seven-year covenant between Israel and an as yet unknown power. It will be events and circumstances beyond his control that will dictate the course of his actions. The specific details remained a secret until the Lord Jesus revealed them to John on the island of Patmos.

Daniel's Seventieth Week

Did Daniel's Seventieth Week find *the* fulfillment, *a* fulfillment, or *no* fulfillment in the second temple destruction? This is the most probative question requiring an answer in regards to this text.

The most vocal supporters of a fulfillment of Daniel's Seventieth Week are those who hold some form of preterist position, among whom are some Jewish chronologists who also see the destruction of Jerusalem as the fulfillment of this prophecy. In this regards, who or what was "the abomination of desolation"? According to Craig A. Evans, a New Testament scholar, there are four candidates espoused as fulfillments for the "desolator" of Daniel's final week. He lists:

The prefect of Judea, Pontius Pilate
Gaius Caligula
Phanni, the high priest
Titus, the Roman General.[cclxv]

On its face, none of these have gained anything near a consensus. Pontius Pilate's attempt to have Roman soldiers march into Jerusalem with standards adorned with busts of Tiberius Caesar never occurred and preceded Matthew's record of the Lord's prophecy. Therefore, there is no sense in which Pontius Pilate could be the abomination of desolation. Gaius Caligula's request that a statue of him be erected in or near the temple was never carried out. Phanni was objected to by some Jews, but accepted by others as high priest. His serving as high priest did not rise to the occasion to be considered an abomination by the nation. The widest agreement among historians holds that Titus, the Roman general responsible for the final destruction of Jerusalem, was or caused the abomination of desolation. This view has some support. However, there is an important aspect of the abomination of desolation which no one connects with Titus. The abomination of desolation consists of a man receiving worship in the one true God's holy place. There is no indication that he demanded the Jews to worship himself or anyone else in the temple. His soldiers supposedly worshiped outside the eastern gate, but there is no report that anyone worshiped in the temple.

It is possible to build a case for fulfilled prophecy between what our Lord promised and what happened in connection with the destruction of the second temple only if one is willing to play games with the text. R.C. Sproul's willingness to accept Josephus' account of events and possible cosmic disturbances as indicators of the fulfillment of the Lord's prophecy in Matthew is chilling. Only by accepting generalities, similarities, and hyperboles can one make a case for fulfillment of Matthew's Olivet Discourse in connection with the destruction of Jerusalem.

Moreover, to suggest that the destruction of Jerusalem by the Romans is the fulfillment of Matthew's Olivet Discourse is seriously undermined by Matthew's reformulation of the second question. Matthew devotes no time or attention to the destruction of Jerusalem in the first century. Sadly, preterists force Matthew to answer a question he never answered.

This is easily proven. To maintain their interpretation of Matthew 24–25, preterists and others must ignore passages that clearly contradict their positions. For example, Matthew 23:39 states, "For I tell you, you will not see me from now until you say, 'Blessed is the one who comes in the name of the Lord!'" This verse follows Jesus' chiding of the children of Jerusalem for murdering God's messengers and refusing to believe them. The Lord naturally includes Himself among those whom the people rejected. For this, He promises, "Your house is left to you desolate!" It is not immediately clear who or what the object of "your house" is. It may refer to the temple, Jerusalem, or the nation of Israel. The fact that thirty-plus years transpired between this prophecy and the destruction of the temple and Jerusalem militate against their inclusion as referent to "your house." The present tense of the verb also supports this conclusion.

The text does not say that your house *will be left* to you desolate. A stronger case for the temple or Jerusalem would need to have the support of a future tense verb. Rather, the text says, "Is left to you desolate." Thus, the desolation began long before the destruction.

"House" is used as the term "Jerusalem" is used at the beginning of verse 37. The term is a metonymy. The place (Jerusalem) is put for the people who occupy her. So "house" is put for the people who occupy it. By rejecting Jesus, the Jews are empty or destitute. They have no remedy. They have abandoned their solution. The Jews will continue in this empty or desolate state until they repent. The Lord states, "Your house is left to *you* desolate." By "you" does He mean (1) those individuals listening to Him; or (2) the nation without respect to individuals? Logically, it must refer to the nation in verse 38 just as it does in verse 37. Since the text expresses what their present situation is and not what it will be, we conclude that the nation is the focus because individual Jews will continue to experience God's grace. National Israel as a nation is locked out, but individual Jews may enter.

Verse 39 begins with the word "for," which signals an explanation. Jesus will now explain why the Jews (nation of Israel) are empty or desolate. The nation will under no circumstances (οὐ μή) see Him. The double negative rules out any possibility that the nation will see the Lord Jesus "from now on" (ἀπ' ἄρτι).[cclxvi] This expression makes clear His intent. Israel has lost a privilege. The duration is expressed by the phrase, "until (ἕως) they say, 'Blessed is he who comes in the name of the Lord.'" There is debate among scholars about the exact meaning of the phrase, "until they say." After intense study, Dale C. Allison, Jr., of Texas Christian University, concludes:

> Until you say...can be understood to signal a conditional sentence...The text then means not,

when the Messiah comes, his people will bless him, but rather, when his people bless him, the Messiah will come. In other words, the date of the redemption is contingent upon Israel's acceptance of the person and work of Jesus.[cclxvii]

Thus, the nation has no hope; it is left empty until it says, "Blessed is he who comes in the name of the Lord." The latter part of this verse is a quote from Psalm 118:26. It expresses the happiness and joy God's people experienced as God's man came to the city of God. Thus, Jesus reveals that His people will have a future, but not until they repent and welcome Him whom they now reject. This prophetic pronouncement removes any possibility that the second temple destruction saw the return of the Lord Jesus in any way.

Matthew 23:38–39 cannot have found a fulfillment in the second temple destruction. There was no national repentance on the part of the nation of Israel. Nothing about the destruction of the city and the sanctuary was a blessing. There is no indication that the Jews expressed happy greetings at the Lord's coming in 3895. The horrible death and destruction can in no way be twisted to mean a happy and favorable time for the Jews. Yet, this is exactly what preterists do to find fulfillment of Matthew's Olivet Discourse.

This verse, in no uncertain terms, makes clear that Israel's repentance must precede the Lord's return. There is not a single solitary record of the nation of Israel experiencing repentance before or in connection with the destruction of Jerusalem. Not one! The Lord Jesus said Israel would not see Him until they repent. Preterists say Israel saw the Lord in the second temple destruction. Somebody is lying and it "ain't" the Lord!

Therefore, we conclude that that portion of Daniel's Seventieth Week that forms the basis of the Lord's instructions in Matthew 24:15–16 has yet to be fulfilled.

That said, we recognize that both Mark and Luke apply portions of the Lord's Olivet Discourse to the second temple destruction. Just so you, the reader, understand our position, we say that the Olivet Discourse as recorded in Matthew does not address the destruction of Jerusalem at all. Yet, the same Olivet Discourse as recorded in Mark and Luke addresses both the temporal destruction and final eschatological destruction of Jerusalem that will immediately precede the Lord's return.

We believe that Daniel 9:27 is a prophecy that has multiple fulfillments—fulfillment in the sense that the Old Testament pattern is the basis for the more than one expression of fulfillment. We define this relationship similarly to type and antitype. One author states:

> A type (τύπος) is a mold or a form for a product, and the antitype (ἀντίτυπος) is the reality. For example John the Baptist introduced Jesus as "the Lamb of God, who takes away the sin of the world!" (John 1:29). The lambs used in Old Testament sin offerings prefigured Jesus, the Lamb of God.[cclxviii]

All who study the Bible in depth come to recognize that God's programs and purposes foreshadowed in the Old Testament through events, persons, and institutions ultimately prefigured the person and work of Jesus Christ. The study of the prefigured event, person, or institution (Old Testament type) and the ultimate reality seen in the person or work of Jesus Christ (New Testament antitype) is called *typology.*

Recognizing what attribute of the type is the ultimate reality in the antitype is difficult without biblical notification. We know Jesus is the Lamb of God because scripture makes it explicit. Without explicit biblical notification, each is left to decide for him or herself. One area that requires examination with regards to this method is prophecy. Can a prophecy or some attribute of a prophecy form the basis of a type and have a New Testament antitype? We believe a prophecy can form a pattern that may repeat itself more than once.

This is called "pattern fulfillment" by some. It is our conviction that Daniel 9:27 fits this definition. The pattern of desecration of the Jewish worship site by an evil person repeats itself. Only this conclusion will maintain the integrity of Matthew, Mark, and Luke. Matthew's interest in the Danielic text at 24:15 is clearly limited to the appearance of the abomination of desolation. By definition, if Mark and Luke argue for events that are connected with the 3895 destruction of Jerusalem, while at the same time maintaining that a Danielic fulfillment of the abomination will occur, we must accept the notion that there will be at least two destructions of Jerusalem prior to the initiation of the eschatological temporal kingdom.[cclxix] Thus, the Olivet Discourse can have two major emphases: a temporal one (the second temple destruction) and an eschatological one (a third temple desecration immediately preceding our Lord's *parousia*).

The pattern of desecration of the Jewish worship site by an evil man has multiple fulfillments, which is evidenced by the 167 B.C. events of Antiochus Epiphanes. We define this type of fulfillment pattern as a special understanding necessary to interpret critical texts like Matthew 24:15 and Daniel 12:11. We recognize it to be the "already/not yet" fulfillment pattern. We echo Dr. Darrell L. Bock's understanding of the hermeneutical methodologies employed. Bock argues that

> Although typology is often retrospective, that is, often the pattern cannot be recognized until it is repeated, it is still prophetic because at its foundation is the idea that God works in certain patterns in working out his salvation. This pattern is fulfillable and is recognized as a fulfillment in

an event or person. Also many of the initial Old Testament texts found in the typological category are texts of promise tied to ideas of deliverance, kingship, or other key concepts that have eschatological overtones and suggest patterns of salvation in themselves. As a result of these factors, "typological prophetic" is an accurate description of this class of texts, although the nature of the prophetic connection often is different from purely prophetic texts. It would be accurate to say that typology is a way of thinking about God's work in history as it moves to consummation.[cclxx]

Therefore, we, as does Dr. Bock, believe we must allow

...for the possibility of a both/and fulfillment in light of the pattern of God's activity, where fulfillment can come in stages—*as in the case of texts about the coming of Christ.* The presence of both/and fulfillment does not mean that fulfillment in the church demands non-fulfillment in a future Israel or the other way around. With initial and future fulfillment, one can have some fulfillment in the church now and more fulfillment for Israel later. Such two-stage fulfillment is not a matter of *sensus plenior,* spiritualizing interpretation, or any other special appeal to a unique type of hermeneutic. It simply seeks to honor the progress of revelation within the canon. It recognizes the presence of "pattern" fulfillment (or typological-prophetic fulfillment) as that revelation progresses, a scriptural category of fulfillment that allows for fulfillment in stages with the possibility of incremental enhancements appearing as promise progresses. (italics added)[cclxxi]

This, we believe, is how Matthew 24:15 is correctly handled. The destruction of Jerusalem, which both Mark and Luke focused upon, did not see Daniel's Seventieth Week fulfilled. There was no abomination of desolation. However, there was the destruction of the temple and the city as Daniel 9:26 indicated.

Understanding Daniel 9 puts us in a position to fully appreciate Matthew 24 and the Lord's instruction that those living in Judea at the time must flee. It is little wonder that deception will be a major problem during this time. With the Lord's instructions so clear, without deception few would follow the plans of the evil one—one would think!

Conclusion
The Most Important Implication

We set out to demonstrate direct applicability of Matthew 24:1–31 and Daniel 9 to a future generation of the Church of Jesus Christ and to clear up issues and implications of interpretation. We proved the applicability of Matthew 24:1–31 by showing (1) that the initial interpretation by pretribulationists and preterists were founded on false premises; (2) that the term "elect" as used in Matthew 24:1–31 refers to members of the bride of Christ; (3) that Matthew's reformulation of the disciples' initial questions pushed our Lord's prophetic discourse's fulfillment to the eschatological end; and (4) applicability of Matthew 24:1-31 was assumed and taught by the church fathers.

If, as we have shown, the subject of Matthew 24 and Daniel 9 is the return of Christ and those events that surround it, then these passages do have direct applicability to the church and describe a period of unparalleled persecution the faithful of God will ever face, leading to the ultimate act of apostasy (as we defined it) by some. It behooves all of us to consider the critical implications of this for our lives. After all, this is more than an academic discussion. By implication, if Matthew 24 and Daniel 9 apply to the church, then a future generation of God's elect, the bride of Christ, will face the unparalleled persecution of Satan and his Antichrist drawn from Daniel 12:11 and re-emphasized by our Lord in Matthew 24:15. Naturally, if this is the case, the most pressing concern—humanly speaking—

is survivability. Regardless of one's view about the timing of the Lord's return to take away His bride, a future generation will face the consequences of Matthew 24 and Daniel 9. Even as the fictional series, *Left Behind* suggested, there will be people *left* behind.

If this group is correct that God will remove the first group of believers before the "great tribulation," and if a second group (some left behind and others who come to belief as a result of a period of unparalleled evangelism by a 144,000 Jews) will face Satan and his Antichrist's persecution, then most of those who die will be relatively new believers. Revelation 7:9 states, "After these things, I looked, and here was an enormous crowd that no one could count, made up of persons from every nation, tribe, people, and language, standing before the throne and before the Lamb dressed in long white robes, with palm branches in their hands."

As understood by that certain group referenced above, this passage depicts the number of individuals who suffer at the hands of Antichrist to be "a number which no man could number." Taken with Matthew 24:1–31, we must conclude that those who constitute this innumerable ethnic multitude will suffer through the beginning birth pains and then fall victim to the period of hard labor just prior to God's deliverance.

The question of survivability has that audience primarily in mind—those who will either be left behind or picked up after the intense persecution has resulted in the death of millions and millions. If certain groups are right, while God will remove the first wave of believers before the great tribulation, a second group depicted as "a number which no man could number," will suffer greatly at the hands of Antichrist. This innumerable ethnic multitude of relatively new believers will ultimately die at his hands and join the rest of the saints in heaven before the throne of God.

Let's think about that for a moment. "A number which no man could number" of peoples from every nation, tongue, and language will die at Antichrist's hands? By any measurement, that's a lot of people. Do these people have no remedy? Are their futures locked? Is physical survivability impossible for these relatively new believers? For those who believe that God will remove the church before the persecution of Satan and his Antichrist begins, at least they ought to be concerned for those who will be left behind.

The timing of the rapture and whether the Church will experience the "great tribulation" is a big deal! If it goes according to the way certain groups argue it will, the problem will be left for those left behind. If it goes against those who believed they would miss this terrible time of persecution, those who thought so will find little consolation in being right.

There has and will no doubt continue to be a great debate about just who will face this unparalleled time. Given the awful consequences of this period, which this book has sought to highlight, it is imperative that we not leave this matter to chance. Positive thinking is not enough. For the last several hundred years, men and women have argued their respective positions. Seen by many conservative evangelicals as the most important event yet to occur for believers alive on the earth, the timing of the rapture holds no small place in their thinking. Judging from the historic success of the *Left Behind* book series, the unprecedented Y2K fiasco, the terrorist attack on the World Trade Center in New York City, and the growing worldwide persecution of Christians many are crying, "Even so, come Lord Jesus!"

However, for the Lord to come, it is more than likely that millions and millions will die. Scripture promises that a final generation of believers will, one day, evacuate alive from the earth to heaven in the company of Jesus Christ. Yet, one day there will be a world full of people called upon to be that final generation of humanity to experience the climactic events of this present world order. The old adage that end time events "will all pan out in the end" will not be taken so lightly by that generation.

Again and finally, the question before us, if we have conclusively demonstrated beyond a shadow of a doubt that a generation of the church, the body of Christ, the bride of Christ, God's elect will face the great tribulation at the hands of Satan and his Antichrist, is this: What can God's elect do to survive? The options are few: *fight* or *take flight* or *stand in faith, trusting God's sovereign will*. Which one, we ask, is the right strategy for God's elect to survive the unparalleled persecution by Satan and his Antichrist?[cclxxii]

Endnotes

[i] David L. Turner, "The Structure and Sequence of Matthew 24:1–41," *GTJ* 10 (1989), pp. 3.

[ii] Ibid., p. 4.

[iii] Ibid. Turner writes, "The first of these mediating positions, which will be called the traditional preterist-futurist view, sees a portion of the passage (usually 24:4–14) as a general description of the course of the present age, and another portion as a 'double reference' prophecy of Jerusalem's destruction and the end of the age.... A second mediating position, which will be called the revised preterist-futurist view, sees alternating reference in these verses to the course of the age, the destruction of Jerusalem, and the coming of Christ." See Turner, "The Structure and Sequence of Matthew 24:1–s41," p. 4.

[iv] Ibid., p. 5.

[v] Ibid.

[vi] Book 1: Chapters 1–4 Narrative; Chapters 5–7 Discourse; Book 2: Chapters 8–9 Narrative, Chapter 10 Discourse; Book 3: Chapters 11–12 Narrative, Chapters 13 Discourse; Book 4: Chapters 14–17 Narrative, Chapter 18 Discourse; Book 5: Chapters 19–23 Narrative, Chapters 24–25 Discourse; The Passion – Chapters 26–28 Narrative.

[vii] John F. Walvoord, *The Rapture Question Answered* (Grand Rapids: Zondervan Publishing House, 1979), p. 43.

[viii] "This is that" is a well-known formula called a *peshar*, which was used by members of the Qumran community to alter passages of scripture they felt had a contemporary fulfillment for them. For a detailed discussion of the particular formula used, see Daniel J. Treier, "The Fulfillment of Joel 2:28–32: A Multiple-Lens Approach," *JETS* 40 (March 1997), pp. 13–26. Also, "The Reign of the Lord Christ," by Dr. Darrell L. Bock in *Dispensationalism, Israel and the Church*, p. 47.

[ix] John T. Carroll, *Response to the End of History: Eschatology and Situation in Luke–Acts* (Atlanta: Scholars Press, 1988), p. 129. Please notice end note 43 in that work.

[x] I. Howard Marshall, "The Significance of Pentecost," *SJT* 30 (1977) p. 358.

[xi] Ibid.

[xii] Prophetic activity in Acts is mentioned in 11:28, 13:1–3, 15:32, 21:9, and 21:10–11 involving both males and females. Dreams and visionary activity are listed in 12:6–7, 16:9, 18:9, 23:11, and 27:23. For more details, see B. J. Hubbard, "The Role of Commissioning Accounts in Acts," in *Perspectives on Luke–Acts*, ed. C. H. Talbert (Danville: Association of Baptist Professors of Religion, 1978), pp. 192–195.

[xiii] We are not able to be dogmatic concerning whether another period is or is not inserted between Pentecost and the day of the Lord from this passage alone. See "The Reign of the Lord Christ," by Dr. Darrell L. Bock in *Dispensationalism, Israel and the Church*, pp. 47–48.

[xiv] John F. Walvoord, *The Blessed Hope and The Tribulation* (Grand Rapids: Zondervan Publishing House, 1976), pp. 86–87.

[xv] We understand the debate regarding events and what days of the week they happened on during our Lord's final week on earth. Our point here is the space between the events.

[xvi] The term *elect* occurs in Matthew 24:22, 24, and 31.

[xvii] Johannes P. Louw and Eugene Albert Nida, *Greek–English Lexicon of the New Testament: Based on Semantic Domains*, electronic ed. of the 2nd edition, 1:361 (New York: United Bible Societies, 1996, c1989).

[xviii] Matthew 24:22, 24, and 31; Mark 13:20, 22, and 27; Luke 18:7; Romans 8:33; 1 Timothy 5:21; 2 Timothy 2:10; Titus 1:1; 1 Peter 1:1; and 2 John 1, 13. In Matthew 22:14; Romans 16:13; 1 Peter 2:4, 6, and 9; and Revelation 17:14, the translation is "chosen." At Luke 23:35 and Colossians 3:12, the translation is *Chosen One*.

[xix] One might question why most English translations alternate between "elect" and "chosen" as possible translations of *eklektos*. There is no theological or biblical reason. It is purely a matter of preference on the part of the translators. The terms are used interchangeably with no difference in meaning.

[xx] By this term, we refer to true humanity without sin.

[xxi] *The NET Bible First Edition (Noteless); Bible. English. NET Bible (Noteless)*, 2 Samuel 7:8–17 (Biblical Studies Press, 2005; 2005).

[xxii] Carl Friedrich Keil and Franz Delitzsch, *Commentary on the Old Testament*, 1:253 (Peabody, MA: Hendrickson, 2002).

[xxiii] The Hebrew word *šîlōh* should be rendered "whose it is," that is, *the scepter will not depart from Judah . . . until He comes* whose it [i.e., the scepter] *is* [or as the NIV puts it, *to whom it belongs*]. Similar words in Ezekiel 21:27, "until He comes to whom it [the crown, Ezek. 21:2] rightfully belongs" were addressed to the last king of Judah. (John F.

Walvoord, Roy B. Zuck, and Dallas Theological Seminary, *The Bible Knowledge Commentary: An Exposition of the Scriptures*, 1:98 [Wheaton, IL: Victor Books, 1983–c1985]).

[xxiv] Exodus 19:5, footnote 15 in the NET Bible at http://www.bible.org/netbible. Last accessed December 2007.

[xxv] F. F. Bruce, *The Epistle to the Galatians: A Commentary on the Greek Text*, includes indexes (Grand Rapids, Mich.: W. B. Eerdmans Pub. Co., 1982), p. 190.

[xxvi] Samuel P. Tregelles, *The Hope of Christ's Second Coming* (Chelmsford: Sovereign Grace Advent Testimony), p. 25. The most consistent exception is Matthew 24:36, which contradicts the basic tenet of pretribulationism that Matthew 24 does not apply to the church. This contradiction often escapes their notice.

[xxvii] A second class condition in the Greek, which means the author speaks from the position that the matter is not true.

[xxviii] This does not speak to the issue of eye transplants, a concept foreign to the mind of first-century humanity. This passage speaks to the capabilities of the people living in Galatia during the first century.

[xxix] It is a first class condition, which should be thought of in this sense, "if—and let us assume that this is true for the sake of argument—then...." See Daniel B. Wallace, *Greek Grammar Beyond the Basics* (Grand Rapids: Zondervan Publishing House, 1996), p. 690.

[xxx] James L. Boyer, "First Class Conditions: What Do They Mean?" *GTJ* 2 (Spr 81), p. 83. We assume Boyer would make this designation here, since this is his conclusion about the same occurrence in Mark 13:22.

[xxxi] We understand that a form of the verb "to be" is intended. But is it "is" or "were"? The difference is this: first class or second class condition. If it is a second class condition, the statement is patently false. A first class condition would offer more possibilities.

[xxxii] Johannes P. Louw and Eugene Albert Nida, *Greek–English Lexicon of the New Testament: Based on Semantic Domains*, electronic edition of the 2nd edition, 1:366 (New York: United Bible Societies, 1996, c1989).

[xxxiii] Horst Robert Balz and Gerhard Schneider, *Exegetical Dictionary of the New Testament*, translation of Exegetisches Wrterbuch zum Neuen Testament, 3:99 (Grand Rapids, Mich.: Eerdmans, 1990–c1993).

[xxxiv] An excellent defense of this position can be found at Bible.org: Studies by D. Ragan Ewing, "The Identification of Babylon the Harlot in the Book of Revelation." See http://www.bible.org/author.php?author_id=47&scid=0. Last accessed December, 2007.

[xxxv] Genesis 10:12 also uses the title in reference to either Nineveh or Calah. Scholars do not agree about the object of the referent in this passage.

[xxxvi] A. T. Robertson, *Word Pictures in the New Testament*, Vol. V c1932, Vol. VI c1933 by Sunday School Board of the Southern Baptist Convention, Re 11:8 (Oak Harbor: Logos Research Systems, 1997).

[xxxvii] G. K. Beale, *The Book of Revelation: A Commentary on the Greek Text* (Grand Rapids: W. B. Eerdmans; Paternoster Press, 1999), p. 592.

[xxxviii] David J. MacLeod, "The Judgment of Sodom," *Emmaus Journal* 2 (2002), p. 158, italics added in the original.

[xxxix] See Exodus 12:12; Jeremiah 43:12 and 44:8.

[xl] Timothy Friberg, Barbara Friberg, and Neva F. Miller, Vol. 4, *Analytical Lexicon of the Greek New Testament*, Baker's Greek New Testament Library (Grand Rapids, Mich.: Baker Books, 2000), p. 283 .

[xli] Horst Robert Balz and Gerhard Schneider, *Exegetical Dictionary of the New Testament*, translation of Exegetisches Wrterbuch zum Neuen Testament, 2:524 (Grand Rapids, Mich.: Eerdmans, 1990–c1993).

[xlii] The woman is said to flee to a "place" (τόπον). That place is τὴν ἔρημον (the desert or wilderness). Regarding this term, *The Exegetical Dictionary of the New Testament* states, "As a geographic term it refers either to the wilderness of Judea (Matt. 3:1; cf. John 11:54), i.e., the "stony, barren eastern declivity of the Judaean mountains toward the Dead Sea and lower Jordan Valley" (BAGD) and the "Araba" (= *steppe*, "desert") of the Jordan Valley itself (Mark 1:4 par.; cf. Funk 214), or to the Arabian desert, i.e., the Sinai Peninsula (Acts 7:30)." See s.v. ad loc.

[xliii] Ὅπου, with the present subjunctive and ἄν.

[xliv] Johannes P. Louw and Eugene Albert Nida, *Greek–English Lexicon of the New Testament: Based on Semantic Domains*, electronic ed. of the 2nd edition, 1:126 (New York: United Bible Societies, 1996, c1989).

[xlv] Spiros Zodhiates, *The Complete Word Study Dictionary: New Testament*, electronic ed., G1484 (Chattanooga, TN: AMG Publishers, 2000, c1992, c1993).

[xlvi] Eugene W. Pond, "Who Are the Sheep and Goats in Matthew 25:31–46?" *BSac* 159 (July 02), p. 294.

[xlvii] Those who argue that "the great city" is Rome have regularly argued that strong (if not conclusive) support for their interpretation can be found in Revelation 17:9, which describes the "seven hills/mountains" (eJpta o[rh) on which the woman sits. While this conclusion is supported by objective data, we reject it. If Rome is the seven hills/mountains and the woman = the great city = Rome, then Rome is seated on Rome. Rome cannot be the woman = the great city = Babylon the Great.

[xlviii] J. Massyngberde Ford adopts the position that the woman is Jerusalem in *Revelation*, The Anchor Bible Series (New York: Doubleday, 1975), pp. 284–293. Keith Krell at http://www.bible.org/page.php?page_id=3812, writes, "I have come to the conclusion there is only one city that can be called *'the great city,'* and that city is Jerusalem" (emphasis in original). At http://www.bible.org/page.php?page_id=54, one can find a detailed defense of our conclusion by D. Ragan Ewing, "The Evidence for Jerusalem as the Harlot." Last accessed December, 2007.

[xlix] Marvin Richardson Vincent, *Word Studies in the New Testament*, 1:78 (Bellingham, WA: Logos Research Systems, Inc., 2002).

[l] G. K. Beale, *The Book of Revelation: A Commentary on the Greek Text* (Grand Rapids, Mich.; Carlisle, Cumbria: W. B. Eerdmans; Paternoster Press, 1999), p. 216.

[li] Ibid., p. 221. Dr. Beale's work on the book of Revelation is helpful in many ways. However, his commitment to interpreting the entire book as spiritualized historical reenactment is most regrettable. He ignores John's repeated warnings that the book of Revelation is prophecy and should be interpreted as the book of Daniel is interpreted.

[lii] The gender of both ὄνομα (*onoma*, "name") and μυστήριον are neuter, while the gender of "Babylon" is feminine. This strongly suggests that μυστήριον should be understood as an appositive to ὄνομα ("a name, i.e., a mystery"). See note 15 of the NET Bible ad loc.

[liii] There is no explicit or implied basis for the conclusion that Peter wrote from the historical city of Babylon. The only support for this position is the notion that Peter does not use highly symbolic or cryptographic language in his epistle. Thus, this one example is highly suspect. However, the level of persecution the church experienced in Jerusalem prior to the destruction by the Romans required care when referring to believers living there. Acts 9:1–2 state, "Meanwhile Saul, still breathing out threats to murder the Lord's disciples, went to the high priest and requested letters from him to the synagogues in Damascus, so that if he found any who belonged to the Way, either men or women, he could bring them as prisoners to Jerusalem." Our interest in this passage is the fact that persecution and the use of a symbolic name appear together early on in the history of the church. The phrase Τῆς ὁδοῦ (the Way) reoccurs throughout the book of Acts and refers to those who follow Jesus Christ. That this name came from those on the outside looking in seems sure in light of the fact that it did not last. At least we can say that the believers did not label themselves as such.

[liv] Eusebius is commonly understood to claim for this view the authority of Papias and Clement of Alexandria.

[lv] Johannes P. Louw and Eugene Albert Nida, *Greek–English Lexicon of the New Testament: Based on Semantic Domains*, electronic ed. of the 2nd edition, 1:684 (New York: United Bible Societies, 1996, c1989).

[lvi] *Theological Dictionary of the New Testament*, Vols. 5–9, edited by Gerhard Friedrich. Vol. 10 compiled by Ronald Pitkin, ed. Gerhard Kittel, Geoffrey William Bromiley, and Gerhard Friedrich, electronic ed., 1:515 (Grand Rapids, MI: Eerdmans, 1964–c1976).

[lvii] Name (Berodach-Baladan in 2 Kings 20:12, KJV), meaning "Marduk has given a son!" Second Kings 20:12–19 and Isaiah 39 present a parallel account of Merodach-Baladan, son of Baladan, king of Babylon, sending envoys to King Hezekiah of Judah. Shalmaneser V, king of Assyria, captured Samaria in 722 B.C. and threatened King Hezekiah in Jerusalem, but died within a year's time. Sargon II succeeded him in 722. At that time, Merodach-Baladan, living south of Babylon in the land called Bit-iakin, formed an alliance with the Elamites and seized the throne of Babylon, referred to as the second jewel of the Assyrian crown. Sargon II immediately made efforts to regain Babylon as a province in the Assyrian Empire. Initially, he must not have been too successful, for Merodach-Baladan reigned over Babylon for ten years. In 710, Sargon succeeded in defeating him and captured the Babylonian fortresses. Merodach-Baladan escaped. After Sargon died in 705, Merodach-Baladan, in 703, was able to recapture and hold the throne of Babylon for a short period. It is considered most plausible that, during this short reign, Merodach-Baladan sent envoys to Hezekiah in Jerusalem, as he also is thought to have sent them to Edom, Moab, Ammon, and others, seeking to form an alliance against Assyria. The Arabian Desert between Babylon and Palestine made such an alliance ineffective, and the new king of Assyria, Sennacherib, thoroughly destroyed Merodach-Baladan and then turned to the nations on Palestinian soil. See Walter A. Elwell and Barry J. Beitzel, *Baker Encyclopedia of the Bible*, map on lining papers (Grand Rapids, Mich.: Baker Book House, 1988), p. 1442.

[lviii] It should not escape our attention that both powers derive from the same place: the wilderness (desert)—Isaiah 21:1 and Revelation 17:3. It is not clear whether Isaiah 21:1 should read, "wilderness of the sea," "wilderness by the sea," or "wilderness by way of the sea." However, the beast of Revelation comes from the sea by way of the wilderness.

[lix] Paul J. Achtemeier, Publishers Harper & Row and Society of Biblical Literature, *Harper's Bible Dictionary*, includes index, 1st ed. (San Francisco: Harper & Row, 1985), p. 374.

[lx] Walter A. Elwell and Barry J. Beitzel, *Baker Encyclopedia of the Bible*, map on lining papers (Grand Rapids, Mich.: Baker Book House, 1988), p. 928.

[lxi] Horst Robert Balz and Gerhard Schneider, *Exegetical Dictionary of the New Testament*, translation of: Exegetisches Wörterbuch zum Neuen Testament, 1:209 (Grand Rapids, Mich.: Eerdmans, 1990–c1993).

[lxii] 1 Kings 11:17; Deut. 7:26; 2 Kings 23:13.

[lxiii] A point labored in both Matthew and Luke. Their genealogical record establishes both Mary and Joseph to be fitting parents of Jesus.

[lxiv] The period of protective custody covers the second half of Daniel's Seventieth Week.

[lxv] A third possible use of *spermatos* in connection with a woman occurs in Hebrews 11:11. However, there is much debate about the correct translation of that verse. Some translations make Sarah the subject of the verse. Others make Abraham the subject, with Sarah as a parenthetical reference. The unusual use of *spermatos* with a woman argues against Sarah's identity as the subject.

[lxvi] The Greek translation of the Hebrew Old Testament utilized by many New Testament writers.

[lxvii] J. F. Walvoord, R. B. Zuck, & Dallas Theological Seminary. *The Bible Knowledge Commentary: An Exposition of the Scriptures* (1:33) (Wheaton, IL: Victor Books), 1983–c1985.

[lxviii] K. A. Mathews, *The New American Commentary*, electronic ed., Logos Library System, Vol. 1A: Genesis 1–11:26 (Nashville: Broadman & Holman Publishers, 2001, c1995), p. 247.

[lxix] By "nature," we naturally are referring to his humanity, since deity is not a product of birth.

[lxx] W. Radl, *Exegetical Dictionary of the New Testament*, electronic version, Libronix.

[lxxi] Ibid.

[lxxii] W. Harold Mare, "A Study of the New Testament Concept of the Parousia," in *Current Issues in Biblical and Patristic Interpretation: Studies in Honor of Merrill C. Tenney* (Grand Rapids: Eerdemans, 1975), p. 336.

[lxxiii] John F. Walvoord, "Eschatological Problems IV: New Testament Words for the Lord's Coming," *BSac* 101 (July 1944), p. 285.

[lxxiv] C. F. Hogg and W. E. Vine, *The Epistles to the Thessalonians* (Fincastle: Scripture Truth Book Co., 1959), p. 87.

[lxxv] Ibid., p. 88.

[lxxvi] Ibid. Hogg and Vine indicate that the beginning is prominent in 1 Thessalonians 4:15, 5:23; 2 Thessalonians 2:1; 1 Corinthians 15:23; James 5:7,8; and 2 Peter 3:4; the course in 1 Thessalonians 2:19, 3:13; Matthew 24:3,37,39; and 1 John 2:28; and the conclusion in 2 Thessalonians 2:8 and Matthew 24:27.

[lxxvii] I. Howard Marshall, "The Parousia in the New Testament—And Today," in *Worship, Theology and Ministry*, M. Wilkins, et al., eds., p. 194.

[lxxviii] Please see footnote 1 in I. Howard Marshall, "The Parousia in the New Testament—And Today," in *Worship, Theology and Ministry*, M. Wilkins, et al., eds., page 194. First Thessalonians 2:19, 3:13, 4:15, 5:23; 2 Thessalonians 2:1, 8; 1 Corinthians 15:23; James 5:7, 8; 2 Peter 1:16, 3:4, 12; 1 John 2:28; Matthew 24:3, 27, 37 and 39: Dr. John F. Walvoord indicates that all these verses refer to the rapture, with the exception of Matthew 24:3, 27, 37, 39; 1 Thessalonians 3:13; 2 Thessalonians 2:8 and 2 Peter 1:16, which refer to the second coming of Christ at the battle of Armageddon (Walvoord, "New Testament Words for the Lord's Coming," *BSac* 101 [July 1944], p. 285). This conclusion requires two separate *parousias*.

[lxxix] Scholars debate the priority of James to 1 Thessalonians. We shall follow the more conservative view of the dates of writing for the books of the New Testament. Therefore, we take James to be the first book written of the New Testament canon.

[lxxx] Patience is the major theme of vv. 7–11, expressed by μακροθυμεῖν/μακροθυμία (5:7 [twice], 8, 10) and ὑπομένειν/ὑπομονή ("stand firm," 5:11 [twice]). Although these words appear as synonyms in Colossians 1:11, the former group carries the added nuance of expectant waiting, while the latter suggests fortitude (Horst, *TDNT* 4:385–86). The idea of the former is stressed in vv. 7–8, set in the context of persecution (Strobel, *Untersuchungen*, 255–57). *Word Biblical Commentary*, Vol. 48, p. 190.

[lxxxi] Louw and Nida, 67.118.

[lxxxii] R. P. Martin, (200). Vol. 48: *Word Biblical Commentary: James*. *Word Biblical Commentary* (190). Dallas: Word, Incorporated.

[lxxxiii] Believers should expect to suffer unto the very revelation of Jesus Christ from heaven.

[lxxxiv] J. E. Frame, *The Epistles of St. Paul to the Thessalonians*, ICC (Edinburgh: T&T Clark, 1960), p. 4.

[lxxxv] BAGD, s.v., p. 260.

[lxxxvi] Daniel B. Wallace, *Greek Grammar Beyond the Basics* (Grand Rapids: Zondervan Publishing House, 1996) p. 156.

[lxxxvii] Charles A. Wanamaker, *The Epistles to the Thessalonians: A Commentary on the Greek Text*, spine title: *Commentary on 1 & 2 Thessalonians; includes indexes* (Grand Rapids, Mich.: W. B. Eerdmans, 1990), p. 230.

[lxxxviii] This view is shared by others. See Robert Jamison, A. R. Fausset and David Brown, *A Commentary, Critical and Explanatory, on the Old and New Testament* (On spine: *Critical and Explanatory Commentary*), Gen. 1:1 (Oak Harbor, WA: Logos Research Systems, Inc., 1997)

[lxxxix] Some might argue that the mark of the beast was something that was not revealed until the book of Revelation was written, so the lack of reference to it in 1 Thessalonians proves nothing. However, Paul's lack of reference does not prove lack of knowledge. If the lack of reference stood alone, we would not argue so strongly, but when taken with the other points, we see a strong case for our conclusion.

[xc] F. F. Bruce, *Word Biblical Commentary: 1 and 2 Thessalonians,* Vol. 45 (Dallas: Word, Incorporated, 2002), p. 130.

[xci] D. Edmond Hiebert, *The Thessalonian Epistles* (Chicago: Moody Press, 1971), p. 315.

[xcii] Morris, The First and Second Epistles to the Thessalonians, footnote 34.

[xciii] R. C. H. Lenski, *The Epistles of St. Peter, St. John and St. Jude* (Minneapolis: Augsburg Publishing House, 1945), p. 285. See also Mare, "A Study of the New Testament Concept of the Parousia," in *Current Issues in Biblical and Patristic Interpretation: Studies in Honor of Merrill C. Tenney,* (Grand Rapids: Eerdemans, 1975), p. 336.

[xciv] Scholars are not in agreement concerning the relationship between "the day of God" and "the day of the Lord." Are these synonymous expressions or do they represent two separate periods delineated? Richard J. Bauckham writes, "Whether 2 Peter intends a distinction between 'the Day of the Lord' (= Christ?) in v 10, and 'the Day of God' (= the Father) here, is very uncertain."[xciv] However, Kenneth O. Gangel would differ. Gangel writes, "Peter then repeated for emphasis the fact that at the commencement of eternity (here called *the Day of God*) *the heavens* will be destroyed *by fire and the elements will melt* [emphasis his]…That event concludes 'the Day of the Lord' (v. 10) and commences 'the Day of God.'" Gangel's argument is that "the day of the Lord" and "the day of God" are two separate periods. In essence, "the day of God" begins as "the day of the Lord" ends. In contradistinction, David H. Stern argues that *the day of God* is "the same as the 'day of the Lord'" (David H. Stern, *Jewish New Testament Commentary: A Companion Volume to the Jewish New Testament,* electronic ed., 2 Peter 3:12 [Clarksville: Jewish New Testament Publications, 1996, c1992]).

[xcv] See Revelation 16:17–21; 19:11–21; Matthew 25:31–47; and Zechariah 13–14.

[xcvi] See a discussion of the dating of Matthew's gospel in Donald A. Hagner, *Matthew 1–13, WBC* (Dallas: Word Books, 1993), pp. lxxiii – lxxiv.

[xcvii] D. A. Carson and D. J. Moo, *An Introduction to the New Testament* (Grand Rapids: Zondervan Publishing House, 2005).
[xcviii] Daniel B. Wallace, "Matthew: Introduction, Argument, and Outline," http://www.bible.org.
[xcix] Mark Allen Powell, "The Plot and Subplots of Matthew's Gospel," *NTS* 38 (1992), p. 199.
[c] Ibid.
[ci] Allen Ross, *The Triumphal Entry*, http://www.bible.org/page.asp?page_id=3945. Last accessed December, 2007.
[cii] Ben Witherington III concludes, "It is unlikely that Jesus ever used the term *parousia* to refer to some future eschatological event." Therefore, Matthew inserted the term to flavor his use of the Olivet Discourse material.
For Witherington convincing argument see *Paul and the End of the World: A Comparative Study in New Testament Eschatology* (Downers Grove: InterVarsity Press, 1992), p. 171.
[ciii] See Mark 13:3.
[civ] Douglas Hare, *The Son of Man Tradition*, p. 168.
[cv] Larry V. Crutchfield, "Rudiments of Dispensationalism in the Ante-Nicene Period—Part 1: Israel and the Church in the Ante-Nicene Fathers," *BSac* 144 (July 87). See footnote 7, p. 256.
[cvi] http://conservativeonline.org/journals/2_4_journal/church%20_fathers_foundations_dispensationalism_frm.htm. Last accessed 2001.
[cvii] Crutchfield, "The Blessed Hope and the Tribulation in the Apostolic Fathers," pp. 101–102.
[cviii] Crutchfield's assessment fails to explain the scriptural basis for this belief. Matthew 24 places the Lord's return in the context of persecution. Daniel 7 places the Lord's return in the context of a Roman persecution at the hands of a ruler who will rise out of Roman ancestry. The ten horns develop from a Romantic basis. These factors provide an excellent basis for the belief of the fathers.
[cix] *Matthew and the Didache*, Huub van de Sandt, ed. (Minneapolis: Fortress Press, 2005), p. 193.
[cx] B. M. Metzger, *The Canon of the New Testament* (Oxford: Clarendon Press, 1987), pp. 49–50.
[cxi] Kurt Niederwimmer, *The Didache: A Commentary*, tr. L. M. Maloney, ed. H. W. Attridge (Minneapolis: Fortress Press, 1998), p. 1.
[cxii] J. A. Kleist, *The Didache*, et al. (Maryland: The Newman Press, 1948), p. 3.
[cxiii] This would explain the textual differences between Mark and Matthew and Luke's gospels.

[cxiv] The information that follows was taken from the website of Glenn Davis; see http://www.ntcanon.org/Eusebius.shtml. Last accessed December, 2007.

[cxv] The majority of writings in this category did not have apostolic authority as far as believers were able to determine. Thus, lacking a direct relationship to an apostle, these works could not be equated with Paul's writings, for example, but they did have value.

[cxvi] Eusebius, *Ecclesiastical History* 3.25.7.

[cxvii] Niederwimmer, *The Didache*, p. 4.

[cxviii] Translated by J .B. Lightfoot. Adapt. and mod. ©1990. Athena Data Products.

[cxix] There is debate about the ending of the Didache. It is possible that some verses were lost. Various suggestions have been put forward regarding what those verses were, but no one can be sure.

[cxx] To see a similar chart and related matters, see Niederwimmer, *The Didache*, p. 209. J.M. Court, "The Didache and St. Matthew's Gospel," *SJT* 34 (1981?), pp. 111–112.

[cxxi] *Matthew and the Didache*, van de Sandt, p. 193.

[cxxii] Ibid., p. 215.

[cxxiii] Alan J. P. Garrow, *The Gospel of Matthew's Dependence on the Didache*, (London: T & T Clark International, 2004) p. 215, footnote 14.

[cxxiv] Ibid., 213.

[cxxv] For a defense of this position, see chapter thirteen in Garrow, *The Gospel of Matthew's Dependence on the Didache*, pp. 190–215.

[cxxvi] Justin Martyr *Dialogue* VII.

[cxxvii] Ibid., Chap. CX. cf. chaps. XXXII, XLIX, and CXXI; *First Apology* LII.

[cxxviii] Justin Martyr *First Apology* LII. Cf. *Dialogue* XXXII, XLV, XLIX, LII, CX, and CXXI.

[cxxix] Justin Martyr *Dialogue* CX.

[cxxx] Ibid., Chap. XXXII.

[cxxxi] Larry V. Crutchfield, "The Early Church Fathers and the Foundations of Dispensationalism," *CTJ,* 2 (December 1998) p. 398.

[cxxxii] Larry V. Crutchfield, "The Early Church Fathers and the Foundations of Dispensationalism," *CTJ,* 3 (April 1999) p. 26.

[cxxxiii] Philip Schaff, *History of the Christian Church*, 8 vols. (Grand Rapids: Wm. B. Eerdmans Publishing Co., 1960), 2:750.

[cxxxiv] Larry V. Crutchfield, "The Early Church Fathers and the Foundations of Dispensationalism," *CTJ,* 3 (April 1999) p. 48.

[cxxxv] Irenaeus, *Against Heresies* V, XXVI, 1.

[cxxxvi] Irenaeus, *Adversus Haereses V*, Chapter XXV, 2. See http://www.newadvent.org/fathers/0103525.htm. Last accessed December, 2007.

[cxxxvii] Irenaeus, *Adversus Haereses V*, Chapter XXV, 5. See http://www.newadvent.org/fathers/0103525.htm. Last accessed December, 2007.

[cxxxviii] Irenaeus, *Adversus Haereses* V, Chapter XXIX, 1. See http://www.newadvent.org/fathers/0103529.htm. Last accessed December, 2007.

[cxxxix] Irenaeus, *Adversus Haereses III*, Chapter VII, 2. See http://www.newadvent.org/fathers/0103307.htm. Last accessed December, 2007.

[cxl] Irenaeus, *Adversus Haereses V*, Chapter XXV, 1. See http://www.newadvent.org/fathers/0103525.htm. Last accessed December, 2007.

[cxli] D. G. Dunbar, "Hippolytus of Rome and the Eschatological Exegesis of the Early Church," *WTJ* 45 (Fall, 1983), pp. 338–339.

[cxlii] Hippolytus, *Treatise on Christ and Antichrist*, sec. 60, located at http://www.earlychristianwritings.com/text/hippolytus-christ.html. Last accessed December, 2007.

[cxliii] Ibid, paragraph 61. This is clear evidence that the church fathers saw a connection between the Seventieth Week of Daniel and the Lord's return.

[cxliv] Hippolytus of Rome, *Treatise on Christ and Antichrist*, sections 60–67. See at http://www.earlychristianwritings.com/text/hippolytus-christ.html. Last accessed December, 2007.

[cxlv] Douglas R.A. Hare, *The Son of Man Tradition* (New York: Fortress Press, 1990) p. 168.

[cxlvi] Barbara Aland, Kurt Aland, Matthew Black et al., *The Greek New Testament*, fourth ed. (Federal Republic of Germany: United Bible Societies, 1993, c1979), p. 68.

[cxlvii] Daniel B. Wallace, "The Article with Multiple Substantives Connected by Kai in the New Testament: Semantics and Significance" (Ph.D. dissertation, Dallas Theological Seminary, 1995), pp. 195–196.

[cxlviii] *The NET Bible First Edition (Noteless); Bible. English. NET Bible (Noteless).*, Matt. 13:24–30 (Biblical Studies Press, 2005; 2005).

[cxlix] *The NET Bible First Edition (Noteless); Bible. English. NET Bible (Noteless).*, Matt. 13:36–43 (Biblical Studies Press, 2005; 2005).

[cl] The Greek preposition ἐν (in) indicates that an object is within the sphere of reference. If one can imagine a circle with a dot in the very middle of it, he has the basic sense of this preposition. Thus, the great

separation takes place within the timeframe known as "the end of the age." The same usage occurs in Matthew 13:49.

[cli] Barbara Aland, Kurt Aland, Matthew Black et al., *The Greek New Testament*, fourth ed., 87 (Federal Republic of Germany: United Bible Societies, 1993, ©1979).

[clii] Horst Robert Balz and Gerhard Schneider, *Exegetical Dictionary of the New Testament*, translation of Exegetisches Wröterbuch zum Neuen Testament, 2:97 (Grand Rapids, Mich.: Eerdmans, 1990–c1993).

[cliii] Grace Seminary, *Grace Theological Journal Volume 11*, 11:90 (Grace Seminary, 1990; 2002).

[cliv] "To have birth pains, to suffer pain in connection with giving birth, birth pains." Johannes P. Louw and Eugene Albert Nida, *Greek–English Lexicon of the New Testament: Based on Semantic Domains*, electronic ed. of the 2nd edition. 1:256 (New York: United Bible societies, 1996, c1989).

[clv]Horst Robert Balz and Gerhard Schneider, *Exegetical Dictionary of the New Testament*, translation of Exegetisches Wr☐terbuch zum Neuen Testament, 2:152 (Grand Rapids, Mich.: Eerdmans, 1990–c1993).

[clvi]Johannes P. Louw and Eugene Albert Nida, *Greek–English Lexicon of the New Testament: Based on Semantic Domains*, electronic ed. of the 2nd edition, 1:242 (New York: United Bible Societies, 1996, c1989).

[clvii]John F. Walvoord, Roy B. Zuck and Dallas Theological Seminary, *The Bible Knowledge Commentary: An Exposition of the Scriptures*, 1:1072 (Wheaton, IL: Victor Books, 1983–c1985).

[clviii]Carl Friedrich Keil and Franz Delitzsch, *Commentary on the Old Testament*, 7:275 (Peabody, MA: Hendrickson, 2002).

[clix] D. A. Carson, *New Bible Commentary: 21st Century Edition*, rev. ed. of *The New Bible Commentary*, 3rd ed. / edited by D. Guthrie, J.A. Motyer, 1970, 4th ed., Is 23:15 (Leicester, England; Downers Grove, Ill., USA: Inter-Varsity Press, 1994).

[clx] The Evangelical Theological Society, *Journal of the Evangelical Theological Society Volume 36*, 36:168 (The Evangelical Theological Society, 1993; 2002).

[clxi] *The NET Bible First Edition (Noteless); Bible. English. NET Bible (Noteless)*, Deut. 4:29–30 (Biblical Studies Press, 2005; 2005).

[clxii] The eschatological day of the Lord is not to be confused with the great tribulation. The great tribulation is the wrath of Satan and his Antichrist against God's elect (Rev. 12:7) and the day of the Lord is God's wrath against all wickedness from the heavens to the earth (Isa. 27 and Rev. 6:12–17).

[clxiii]James Swanson, *Dictionary of Biblical Languages With Semantic Domains: Greek (New Testament)*, electronic ed., GGK5392 (Oak Harbor: Logos Research Systems, Inc., 1997).

[clxiv] P.D. Miller, *The Divine Warrior in Early Israel*, (Cambridge: Harvard University Press, 1973) pp. 172–174.

[clxv] For a defense of this conclusion, see Tremper Longman, III, "The Divine Warrior: The New Testament Use of An Old Testament Motif," *WTJ* 44(1982) pp. 290–307.

[clxvi] Barry C. Davis, "Is Psalm 110 a Messianic Psalm," *BSac* 157 (Apr 00) p. 160. See footnote 1.

[clxvii] Herbert W. Bateman, IV, "Psalm 110:1 and the New Testament," *BSac* 149 (Oct 92) p. 438.

[clxviii] Ibid., p. 453.

[clxix] Joseph Addison Alexander, *The Psalms Translated and Explained* (Edinburgh: Andrew Elliot and James Thin, 1864; reprint, Grand Rapids: Zondervan, nd), p. 456.

[clxx] John Aloisi, "Who is David's Lord? Another Look at Psalm 110:1," *DBSJ* 10 (2005) p. 108.

[clxxi] Ibid.

[clxxii] *Theodotion Version* of the Greek translation of the book of Daniel is closer to Matthew's Greek than the Septuagint.

[clxxiii] Ronald B. Allen, "The Pillar of Cloud," *BSac* 153 (Oct 96) p. 393.

[clxxiv]Horst Robert Balz and Gerhard Schneider, *Exegetical Dictionary of the New Testament*, translation of Exegetisches Wörterbuch zum Neuen Testament, 3:367 (Grand Rapids, Mich.: Eerdmans, 1990–c1993).

[clxxv] ἐπισυναγωγῆς, which means "gather."

[clxxvi] The Greek says: ὑπὲρ τῆς παρουσίας τοῦ κυρίου ἡμῶν Ἰησοῦ Χριστοῦ καὶ ἡμῶν ἐπισυναγωγῆς ἐπ᾽ αὐτόν, which literally means, "concerning the coming the Lord our and our assembling to him."

[clxxvii] Wallace, The Article with Multiple Substantives, p. 201.

[clxxviii] Wallace rejects option 1 because "the identical category is unattested for *concrete* impersonals in the NT." See Wallace, *Greek Grammar: Beyond the Basics*, p. 290. We might add here that for Paul to refer to the same event by two entirely different titles joined by "and" would appear highly unusual and suspect. We agree with Wallace at this point.

[clxxix] Wallace rejects this option summarily stating "to my knowledge, no eschatological scheme sees the *parousia* as a part of the rapture." See Wallace, *The Article with Multiple Substantives*, p. 201.

[clxxx] Scholars, for the most part, accept a connection between 2 Thessalonians 2:1 and 1 Thessalonians 4:13–18, which is the *Locus Classicus* regarding the heavenly evacuation.

clxxxi See Revelation 7:1; Jeremiah 49:36; and particularly Daniel 11:4.

clxxxii Gerhard Kittel, Gerhard Friedrich, and Geoffrey William Bromiley, *Theological Dictionary of the New Testament*, translation of Theologisches Wörterbuch zum Neuen Testament (Grand Rapids, Mich.: W.B. Eerdmans, 1995, c1985), p. 1161.

clxxxiiiSpiros Zodhiates, *The Complete Word Study Dictionary: New Testament*, electronic ed., G5056 (Chattanooga, TN: AMG Publishers, 2000, c1992, c1993).

clxxxivJohannes P. Louw and Eugene Albert Nida, *Greek–English Lexicon of the New Testament: Based on Semantic Domains*, electronic ed. of the 2nd edition, 1:611 (New York: United Bible societies, 1996, c1989).

clxxxv Wallace, Greek Grammar: Beyond the Basics, p. 359.

clxxxvi These are the predominate nuances of ὑπομένω. See BADG s.v. 2.

clxxxviiJohannes P. Louw and Eugene Albert Nida, *Greek–English Lexicon of the New Testament: Based on Semantic Domains*, electronic ed. of the 2nd edition, 1:332 (New York: United Bible societies, 1996, c1989).

clxxxviiiHorst Robert Balz and Gerhard Schneider, *Exegetical Dictionary of the New Testament*, translation of Exegetisches Wör□terbuch zum Neuen Testament, 2:22 (Grand Rapids, Mich.: Eerdmans, 1990–c1993).

clxxxix Ibid.

cxc Ibid.

cxci Johannes P. Louw and Eugene Albert Nida, *Greek–English Lexicon of the New Testament: Based on Semantic Domains*, electronic ed. of the 2nd edition, 1:316 (New York: United Bible societies, 1996, c1989).

cxciiHorst Robert Balz and Gerhard Schneider, *Exegetical Dictionary of the New Testament*, translation of Exegetisches Wörterbuch zum Neuen Testament, 1:279 (Grand Rapids, Mich.: Eerdmans, 1990–c1993).

cxciiiHorst Robert Balz and Gerhard Schneider, *Exegetical Dictionary of the New Testament*, translation of Exegetisches Wörterbuch zum Neuen Testament, 3:18 (Grand Rapids, Mich.: Eerdmans, 1990–c1993).

cxcivJohannes P. Louw and Eugene Albert Nida, *Greek–English Lexicon of the New Testament: Based on Semantic Domains*, electronic ed. of the 2nd edition, 1:234 (New York: United Bible societies, 1996, c1989).

cxcvHorst Robert Balz and Gerhard Schneider, *Exegetical Dictionary of the New Testament*, translation of Exegetisches Wörterbuch zum Neuen Testament, 3:248 (Grand Rapids, Mich.: Eerdmans, 1990–c1993).

cxcviDallas Theological Seminary, *Bibliotheca Sacra Volume 121*, 121:46 (Dallas Theological Seminary, 1964; 2002).

cxcviiJohannes P. Louw and Eugene Albert Nida, *Greek–English Lexicon of the New Testament: Based on Semantic Domains*, electronic ed. of the 2nd edition, 1:484 (New York: United Bible societies, 1996, c1989).

[cxcviii]Johannes P. Louw and Eugene Albert Nida, *Greek–English Lexicon of the New Testament: Based on Semantic Domains*, electronic ed. of the 2nd edition, 1:757 (New York: United Bible societies, 1996, c1989).
[cxcix] H. Strathmann, 'mavrtu", ktl.', *TDNT*, IV, p. 502.
[cc] I. H. Marshall, *Commentary on Luke, NIGTC*, (Grand Rapids: Eerdmans Publishing Co., 1983) p. 768.
[cci] This word does not come first in a Greek sentence grammatically, but it is the first word logically.
[ccii]Timothy Friberg, Barbara Friberg and Neva F. Miller, vol. 4, *Analytical Lexicon of the Greek New Testament*, Baker's Greek New Testament library (Grand Rapids, Mich.: Baker Books, 2000), p, 288.
[cciii] ESV; ISV; KJV; NET; NIV; and NRSV.
[cciv] The same phrase occurs in Daniel 11:31 with the exception of the article (βδέλυγμα ἐρημώσεως).
[ccv]Flavius Josephus and William Whiston, *The Works of Josephus: Complete and Unabridged*, includes index, Wars 5.526–532 (Peabody: Hendrickson, 1996, c1987).
[ccvi]Flavius Josephus and William Whiston, *The Works of Josephus: Complete and Unabridged*, includes index, Wars 5.547–558 (Peabody: Hendrickson, 1996, c1987).
[ccvii]Flavius Josephus and William Whiston, *The Works of Josephus: Complete and Unabridged*, includes index, Wars 5.566–569 (Peabody: Hendrickson, 1996, c1987).
[ccviii]Flavius Josephus and William Whiston, *The Works of Josephus: Complete and Unabridged*, includes index, Wars 6-.3 (Peabody: Hendrickson, 1996, c1987).
[ccix]John F. Walvoord, Roy B. Zuck, and Dallas Theological Seminary, *The Bible Knowledge Commentary: An Exposition of the Scriptures*, 2:77 (Wheaton, IL: Victor Books, 1983–c1985).
[ccx]John F. Walvoord, Roy B. Zuck and Dallas Theological Seminary, *The Bible Knowledge Commentary: An Exposition of the Scriptures*, 2:79 (Wheaton, IL: Victor Books, 1983–c1985).
[ccxi]Timothy Friberg, Barbara Friberg and Neva F. Miller, vol. 4, *Analytical Lexicon of the Greek New Testament*, Baker's Greek New Testament Library, 416 (Grand Rapids, Mich.: Baker Books, 2000).
[ccxii] NET Bible.
[ccxiii] Contra G. Mussies, "The Morphology of Koine Greek as Used in the Apocalypse of St. John: A Study in Bilingualism" (Leidon: E.J. Brill, 1971) p. 96.
[ccxiv] Romans 1:18ff is one example.
[ccxv] Matthew 27:64 ("deception"); Romans 1:27 ("error"); Ephesians 4:14 ("deceitful"); 1 Thessalonians 2:3 ("deceit"); 2 Thessalonians 2:10

("deception"); 1 John 4:6 ("error"); James 5:20 ("error"), 2 Peter 2:18 ("error"); 2 Peter 3:17 ("error"); and Jude 11 ("error").

[ccxvi] The term Matthew uses for the Lord's quote from Daniel is τὸ βδέλυγμα τῆς ἐρημώσεως, which matches the wording in the Septuagint (LXX), with which Theodotion agrees at Daniel 12:11. However, instead of the genitive singular, Daniel 9:27 has the same phrase, but as a genitive plural. This may prove important in that the Lord quotes Daniel 12:11 and not Daniel 9:27.

[ccxvii] *The NET Bible First Edition*; Bible. English. NET Bible; *The NET Bible*, Dan. 11:31 (Biblical Studies Press, 2006; 2006).

[ccxviii] Leon Wood, *A Commentary on Daniel* (Grand Rapids: Zondervan Publishing House, 1973), p. 294.

[ccxix] http://reformed-theology.org/ice/newslet/bc/bc.98.10.htm

[ccxx] The Septuagint, Theodotion, the Peshitta, and the Vulgate.

[ccxxi] Of interest to the reader might be this: the Greek historian upon whom the history of the Persian Empire is based did not know of Belshazzar.

[ccxxii] E.R. Thiele, *The Mysterious Numbers of the Hebrew Kings*, (Grand Rapids: Kregel Publications, 1994) pp. 71–72.

[ccxxiii] Gerhard Larsson was a professor at the Royal Institute of Technology in Stockholm, Sweden. Larsson's specialty was mathematics. He spent a number of years testing Knut Stenring's hypothesis mathematically to determine the accuracy and probability of Stenring's suggestions that the Old Testament chronological references are based on a three-calendar system.

[ccxxiv] Larsson's system initially was advanced by Knut Stenring and detailed in his book *The Enclosed Garden*. As a conservative who believes in the Bible as the inspired Word of God, we reject Stenring's basic assumptions. His hypothesis about how the Old Testament came to have the unique chronology found in its pages has no basis whatsoever. *As is so often the case, unbelievers can discover truth, but not appreciate its significance.* It is clear that Stenring's involvement and belief in kabbalistic teachings clouds his judgment about the inerrancy of scripture. Stenring and others believe the Bible to be a coded document in which the true underpinnings of the universe lie hidden. Thus, his interest in biblical chronology is misguided. However, we understand that Stenring did not create the chronology in the Bible. He merely attempts to explain it. He lays out the chronology in a reasoned way. His error is the suggestion that one person edited the Old Testament and put the chronology in it. This is patently false.

[ccxxv] G. Larsson, The Secret System: A Study in the Chronology of the Old Testament (Leiden: E.J. Brill, 1973) p. 3.

ccxxvi Ibid., p. 8. While Stenring and Larsson both recognize the chronological facts present in the text of the Old Testament, we reject their explanation for how the text came to exist. We believe God superintended the process of the human writers to ensure an accurate record. Since Moses, the author of the Penteteuch, was educated in Egypt, we are not surprised that he would have familiarity with the Egyptian solar calendar. However, it is clear that due to the nature of what is written in much of Genesis; Moses must have gotten that information directly from God. Since the content of Genesis is not during Israel's history when sacrifices and feasts were a required part of their daily life, there is no need for the people to have used a calendar to keep up with the seasons. Not until the Exodus did the people have a need to have a very accurate calendar so as to obey God's instructions concerning the yearly feasts.

Our point is this: God must have given Moses the specific dates that appear in the book of Genesis. Moses wrote down what God told him. Therefore, the chronological sequences came from God. They are as trustworthy as God is trustworthy.

ccxxvii G. Larsson, "A System of Biblical Dates," *SJOT* 16 no. 2 (2002), pp. 4–5.

ccxxviii Ibid., 5.

ccxxix Ibid., p. 7.

ccxxx Ibid., p. 8.

ccxxxi G. Larsson, *The Secret System*, (Leiden: E.J. Brill, 1973), pp. 21–22.

ccxxxii This is the outcome of the NASB; the ESV has either *anointed one* or *anointed* for all thirty-nine occurrences.

ccxxxiii The NASB translators' decision to capitalize *Anointed* in Psalm 2:2 is a theological decision in light of the use of this psalm in the New Testament to refer to the Lord Jesus. However, there is no grammatical basis for this in the Massoretic text.

ccxxxiv Thomas E. McComiskey, "The Seventy 'Weeks' of Daniel against the Background of Ancient Near Eastern Literature," *WTJ* 47 (Spr 1985) p. 25.

ccxxxv *The NET Bible First Edition*; Bible. English. *NET Bible*; *The NET Bible* (Biblical Studies Press, 2006; 2006).

ccxxxvi Neither Theodotion nor the Septuagint suggests anything other than simple copulative or continuation as the connection between these two verses.

ccxxxvii 2 Chronicles 30:5 and Esther 1:19 are two possible exceptions. However, closer examination reveals a distinction between the decree and the content.

ccxxxviiiH.W. Hoehner, "Chronological Aspects of the Life of Christ—Part VI: Daniel's Seventy Weeks and New Testament Chronology," *BSAC* 132, (Jan 75) pp. 56–57.

ccxxxix Peter D. Miscall, *Isaiah* (Sheffield: Sheffield Academic Press, 1993), p. 110.

ccxl John Goldingay, *Isaiah* NIBC, (Peabody: Hendrickson Publishers, Inc., 2001), p. 261.

ccxli Klaus Baltzer, *Deutero-Isaiah: A Commentary on Isaiah 40–55*, trans. Margaret Kohl, ed. Peter Machinist, (Minneapolis: Fortress Press, 2001), p. 220.

ccxlii A date of 25.1.3233 on the Egyptian solar calendar.

ccxliiiRobert Laird Harris, Gleason Leonard Archer and Bruce K. Waltke, *Theological Wordbook of the Old Testament*, electronic ed. (Chicago: Moody Press, 1999, c1980), p. 550.

ccxliv http://www.roman-emperors.org/titus.htm (Last accessed December, 2007)

ccxlv F. F. Bruce, *New Testament History*, (Garden City: Doubleday & Company, Inc., 1980), pp. 380–382.

ccxlviGerhard Kittel, Gerhard Friedrich, and Geoffrey William Bromiley, *Theological Dictionary of the New Testament*, Translation of *Theologisches Wörterbuch zum Neuen Testament* (Grand Rapids, Mich.: W.B. Eerdmans, 1995, c1985), p. 1324.

ccxlvii Kenneth S. Wuest, *Wuest's Word Studies from the Greek New Testament: For the English Reader*, 1 Jn 2:20 (Grand Rapids: Eerdmans, 1997, c1984).

ccxlviii M. De Jonge, "The Use of the Word 'Anointed' in the Time of Jesus," *Novum Testamentum*, Vol. 8, Fasc. 2/4 (Apr. – Oct., 1966), p. 142.

ccxlix We are mindful of Tim Meadowcroft's conclusions regarding the possibility that the usage of *mashiyach* in Daniel 9:26 may intend something other than a literal person. However, we are not able to appreciate his conclusions because he rejects the fact that the book of Daniel was written long before the second century. By relocating the writing of the book of Daniel in the second century before Christ, Meadowcroft abandons the divine inspiration of the book. Therefore, his conclusions are suspect in this author's opinion. See Tim Meadowcroft, "Exploring the Dismal Swamp: The Identity of the Anointed One in Daniel 9:24–27," *JBL* Vol. 120 (Autumn, 2001), pp. 429–449.

ccl James Swanson, *Dictionary of Biblical Languages With Semantic Domains: Hebrew (Old Testament)*, electronic ed., DBLH 4162, No. 3 (Oak Harbor: Logos Research Systems, Inc., 1997).

[ccli] The word is often used in the LXX in statements that intimate God's will to root out men for their sins or to cast off the chosen people for their disobedience. See *Theological Dictionary of the New Testament*, Vols. 5–9, edited by Gerhard Friedrich; Vol. 10, compiled by Ronald Pitkin., ed. Gerhard Kittel, Geoffrey William Bromiley and Gerhard Friedrich, electronic ed., 5:170 (Grand Rapids, MI: Eerdmans, 1964–c1976).
[cclii] This Greek verb is often used as a translation of the Hebrew verb *yiccarat*.
[ccliii] J. L. Burns, "The Future of Ethnic Israel in Romans 11," in *Dispensationalism, Israel and the Church*, eds. Craig A. Blaising and Darrell L. Bock (Grand Rapids: Zondervan Publishing House, 1992), p. 206.
[ccliv] I. Howard Marshall, *The Gospel of Luke: A Commentary on the Greek Text*, includes indexes, *The New International Greek Testament Commentary* (Exeter [Eng].: Paternoster Press, 1978), p. 116.
[cclv] Ibid.
[cclvi] See Hastings, 103–106 for a defense of this conclusion.
[cclvii] L. R. Fisher, "The Temple Quarter," *JSS* 8 (1963), pp. 34–41.
[cclviii] D. L. Bock, Proclamation from Prophecy and Pattern: Lucan Old Testament Christology, (Sheffield: JSOT Press, 1987), p. 119.
[cclix]I. Howard Marshall, *The Gospel of Luke: A Commentary on the Greek Text*, includes indexes. *The New International Greek Testament Commentary* (Exeter [Eng.: Paternoster Press, 1978), p. 576.
[cclx] Klaus Baltzer, "The Meaning of the Temple in Lukan Writings," *HTR* 58 (Jul., 1965), p. 273.
[cclxi]Robert Jamieson, A. R. Fausset, et al., *A Commentary, Critical and Explanatory, on the Old and New Testaments*, On spine: *Critical and Explanatory Commentary*, Dan. 7:22 (Oak Harbor, WA: Logos Research Systems, Inc., 1997).
[cclxii]Horst Robert Balz and Gerhard Schneider, *Exegetical Dictionary of the New Testament*, translation of Exegetisches Wörterbuch zum Neuen Testament, 2:318 (Grand Rapids, Mich.: Eerdmans, 1990–c1993).
[cclxiii]R. Laird Harris, Gleason Leonard Archer and Bruce K. Waltke, *Theological Wordbook of the Old Testament*, electronic ed. (Chicago: Moody Press, 1999, c1980), p. 531.
[cclxiv] Suetonius, *Lives of the Caesars: Titus*. See at http://www.fordham.edu/halsall/ancient/suet-titus-rolfe.html.
[cclxv] Craig A. Evans, *Mark 8:27–16:20*, *WBC* Vol. 34b (Nashville: Thomas Nelson Publishers, 2001) pp. 318–319.
[cclxvi] Ἀπ' ἄρτι, on the other hand, speaks of the present in contrast to the future: *from now on*. It is, therefore, used in sayings concerning the

eschatological future (Matt. 23:39; 26:29, 64) or oriented to the future (John 13:19).

^{cclxvii} See D.C. Allison, Jr., "Matt. 23:39 = Luke 13:35b as a Conditional Prophecy," *JSNT* 18 (1983) 77, for defense of this conclusion. See more details at Horst Robert Balz and Gerhard Schneider, *Exegetical Dictionary of the New Testament*, translation of Exegetisches Wörterbuch zum Neuen Testament, 1:159 (Grand Rapids, Mich.: Eerdmans, 1990–c1993).

^{cclxviii} Dallas Theological Seminary, *Bibliotheca Sacra Volume 161*, vnp.161.641.12 (Dallas Theological Seminary, 2004; 2005).

^{cclxix} Clearly, there are elements of Mark/Luke's accounts that require fulfillment connected with the A.D. 70 destruction. However, it does not require that every element of the Olivet Discourse was fulfilled.

^{cclxx} D.L. Bock, *Proclamation from Prophecy and Pattern* (Sheffield: JSOT Press, 1987), pp. 291–292.

^{cclxxi} D.L. Bock, "Current Messianic Activity and OT Davidic Promise: Dispensationalism, Hermeneutics, and NT Fulfillment," *TrinJ* 15:1 (Spr 1994), p. 70.

^{cclxxii} We recognize that there are those who believe Daniel's final week is past, yet would maintain a future rapture as we define it. Partial preterists, among whom R.C. Sproul is counted, would argue this position (See *The Last Days According to Jesus*, R.C. Sproul for a defense of this position). Our decision to limit this discussion to those who would describe themselves as rapturists in relationship to a yet future fulfillment of Daniel's final week is biased. We see the question of Daniel's final week's applicability to New Testament theology as fact. Therefore, those who reject a possible future application of the final week are in error. That said, we do allow for the possibility that the final week's fulfillment may not look exactly as we presently understand it. There may be facts we are yet to understand that will add to our understanding and color our present interpretation of this critical text.

Printed in the United States
106917LV00003B/5/A